SHAPING AMERICAN
HIGHER EDUCATION

LOGAN WILSON

Shaping
American Higher Education

AMERICAN COUNCIL ON EDUCATION

WASHINGTON, D.C.

© 1972 by American Council on Education
One Dupont Circle
Washington, D.C. 20036

Library of Congress Catalog Card No. 79-182304
ISBN 0-8268-1379-8
Printed in the United States of America

Preface

M‌Y EARLY YEARS were spent near a campus, and much of my time since has had to do with the concerns of colleges and universities. It was therefore with some misgivings in 1961 that I detached myself from a campus and moved to Washington to become president of the American Council on Education. One attraction of the new post was that it afforded a central vantage point for involvement in many of the basic issues and problems relating to all of the nation's campuses. The present volume highlights certain aspects of that involvement over a ten-year period, and the twenty-six papers chosen for publication here reflect my own observations and opinions, without necessarily reflecting views of the Council.

As almost everybody knows, the 1961–71 decade in higher education was one of spectacular growth and change. Toward the end of the decade, change was often marked by turbulence that has left an aftermath of uncertainty and confusion. Certainty prevails only regarding the increased importance of higher education to our society and the complexity of issues yet to be resolved. Now, as in the past, many forces are at work to shape educational outcomes that will bear heavily on our destiny as individuals and as a nation.

Although the Council's influence in shaping educational out-comes during the past ten years would be difficult to specify precisely, working with its large and varied membership has broadened my own perspectives of the academic community's diverse interests. The Council's role as an intermediary with the federal government and other agencies has expanded my awareness of extramural influences in educational evaluation, decision making, and action. The complexities of the Council's duty to represent fairly its diverse constituents and the difficulties inherent in its coordination function have continuously reminded me that there are no simplistic or universally accepted answers to many of the questions at hand and to the challenges ahead.

Since its establishment in 1918, the American Council on Education has tried consistently to improve our system of higher education and move it in directions that would be of maximum usefulness to the nation and to mankind. My association with that effort since 1961 has brought me into contact with a wide variety of persons and groups, including some of the best minds in the higher education community and elsewhere, and the experience has been an exciting one. Many of the topics I deal with in this volume stem from interactions I have had with individuals sharing common concerns but holding diverse viewpoints. My own viewpoints over the years have been set forth in many different places, and thus it seemed to me and some of my associates that it would be worthwhile to bring a cross section of them together between the covers of a single book.

Although I am not under the illusion that the significance of the topics automatically gives importance to my statements about them, I hope to convey to the reader something of the impressive sweep of concerns coming within the Council's purview from 1961 to 1971. The substantive matters included are by no means the only ones the Council dealt with during this period, and, indeed, some of the topics that interested me personally were never on our formal agenda. As I point out, many of the papers were composed for particular occasions, but my intent was always to focus attention on the necessity for a realistic approach to problems and issues of general import in higher education.

Some of the major concerns of the last ten years, incidentally, were with us long before 1961 and others appear to be perennial. Educational problems, unlike mathematical problems, often do not lend themselves to permanent solutions. Drastic social change sometimes resurfaces old issues, and proposed resolutions are not invariably as innovative as their proponents would have us believe. Even so, I like to think that real progress is not a delusion. Despite current difficulties, I believe that, in the main, higher education has been steadily shaped into better forms and more useful functions. With proper respect for the indispensability of continuity and full realization of the need for change, I am convinced that we can look forward with confidence to ever widening horizons.

Acknowledgments

A T THE BEGINNING of each chapter of this volume, I mention the place and time of the original address or the book or journal for which the article was first prepared. Here I want to make acknowledgment to publishers of books and journals, indicating titles initially used, for all papers that have previously appeared in print, whether in quite similar or somewhat different form.

"Perspectives for the American Council on Education," *Educational Record*, January 1962.

"A Better Partnership for the Federal Government and Higher Education," *Educational Record*, April 1963; *Emerging Patterns in American Higher Education*, ed. Logan Wilson (American Council on Education, 1965). Present title, "A Better Partnership with the Federal Government."

"Form and Function in American Higher Education," *Emerging Patterns in American Higher Education*, ed. Logan Wilson (American Council on Education, 1965).

"Higher Education and 1984," *School and Society*, October 2, 1965; CASC Newsletter, No. 9, 1965; *Airforce and Space Digest*, 1965.

"Higher Education and the National Interest," *Campus 1980*, ed. Alvin Eurich (Delacorte Press, 1968). Present title, "The National Interest."

"State Coordination of Higher Education," *Washington Education*, January 1967.

"Is the Student Becoming the Forgotten Man in Higher Education?" *School and Society*, February 6, 1965; *College and University Business*, March 1965; *Phi Gamma Delta Journal*, April 1965; *College Store Journal*, April-May 1965; *The College and the Student*, ed. Lawrence E. Dennis and Joseph F. Kauffman (American Council on Education, 1966). Present title, "The Forgotten Student."

"The Professor and His Roles," *Graduate Comment*, April 1966; *Improving College Teaching*, ed. Calvin B. T. Lee (American Council on Education, 1967).

"A Few Kind Words for Academic Administrators," *Education Digest*, May 1969; *Educational Record*, Winter 1969; *AGB Reports*, April 1970.

"The Concerns of Trustees," *Campus Tensions: Report of the Special Committee on Campus Tensions* (American Council on Education, 1970).

"Carrots and Sticks in the Higher Learning," *Texas Quarterly*, Summer 1967.

"Merit and Equality in American Higher Education," *Educational Record*, Winter 1970; *The Campus and the Racial Crisis*, ed. David C. Nichols and Olive Mills (American Council on Education, 1970). Present title, "Merit and Equality."

"Alternatives to College for Everybody," *Higher Education for Everybody? Issues and Implications*, ed. W. Todd Furniss (American Council on Education, 1971).

"Analyzing and Evaluating Costs in Higher Education," *Educational Record*, April 1961; *Vision and Purpose in Higher Education*, ed. Raymond F. Howes (American Council on Education, 1962); *College Student Personnel Readings and Bibliographies* (Houghton-Mifflin, 1970). Present title, "Analyzing and Evaluating Costs."

"Setting Institutional Priorities," *Current Issues in Higher Education*, ed. Kerry Smith (Association for Higher Education, 1965); *College and University Business*, January 1965; *Whose Goals for American Higher Education?* ed. Charles G. Dobbins and Calvin B. T. Lee (American Council on Education, 1968); *Learning and the Professors*, ed. O. Milton and Joseph Shoben (Ohio University Press, 1968); *Twenty-five Years: 1945–1970*, ed. Kerry Smith (Jossey-Bass, Inc., 1970).

"Myths and Realities of Institutional Independence," *Graduate Comment*, 1964; *Proceedings of Illinois Conference on Higher Education*, 1967. Present title, "Institutional Autonomy."

"Whose Universities?" *The College and the Student*, ed. Lawrence E. Dennis and Joseph F. Kauffman (American Council on Education, 1966).

Abuses of the University (Michigan State University, 1968); *Paradox, Process and Programs*, ed. Ronald W. Roskinds and Robert I. White (Kent State University Press, 1968).

"Changing University Governance," *Educational Record*, Fall 1969.

"Defending the Universities," *Educational Record*, Fall 1970. Present title, "Upholding the Integrity of the University."

On a more personal level, my thanks are owed to several Council associates—Charles G. Dobbins, Louis Hausman, and Olive Mills—and to Fred C. Cole, president of the Council on Library Resources, Inc., for helping to select the twenty-six papers reproduced here from among the many I have written during the past decade. I am additionally grateful to Miss Mills for her editorial aid. The introductory commentary has been prepared by David D. Henry, president emeritus of the University of Illinois. This contribution gives me especial pleasure for, quite aside from his chairmanship of the American Council on Education in 1961 when I assumed office as president, I regard him as one of the ablest educators of this era.

Contents

Introduction

THOSE WHO have followed Logan Wilson's writing and speaking over the years of his prominence in higher education have come to expect thoughtful and insightful commentary, expressed with succinctness and force. Also characteristic is tightly reasoned inquiry. The present volume fits that pattern.

Dr. Wilson writes about higher education from a unique vantage point. He came to the presidency of the American Council on Education in 1961 with experience gained from diverse assignments and responsibilities—as teacher, counselor, author, researcher, dean, university president, state system chancellor, planner, consultant, and acknowledged professional leader. Each role added breadth to his views and understanding to the history, development, and structure of higher education. As Council president, he was called upon to meld his varied professional experiences into a philosophical context that, for many, provides a sound setting for the future of higher education in the United States. *Shaping American Higher Education* reflects ideas, attitudes, and convictions that have undergirded this remarkable professional career.

The book does more than note, describe, and project. It presents discriminating analysis, the more persuasive for being rooted in reality. It reveals an academic man thinking as well as observing, a scholar as well as an interpreter.

The chapters, adapted from published articles and addresses, were almost all prepared between 1961 and 1971. The backdrop is the decade of the 1960s, one of the most significant periods in the history of higher education in this country. Phenomenal growth and tumultuous change were chief characteristics, and the 1970s open with an array of left-over problems, conflicts, tensions, and demands whose sound resolution will require a clear understanding of the years preceding. *Shaping American Higher Education*—both the discussions and their implications—will contribute to that understanding and to the continuing dialogue on specific issues that will help mold form and function in our colleges and universities.

The first of the five parts is given the theme title, "Shaping Higher Education." Its seven chapters examine higher education as a "system" or nonsystem, whichever is the perspective of the topic discussed. The relationships of the federal government and higher education have a prominent place, as does the role of the American Council on Education. In scope, rather than being a "rehash" of recommendations for federal assistance, this section deals broadly with the national interest.

Our resolution of these public policy issues will be heavily influenced, of course, by the relative values we attach to freedom and order, to equality and excellence, to the particular and the universal, to present satisfaction and future benefit. To make the Great Society a reality, it is manifest that wise discernment and resolute action are called for if higher education is to be a main instrument for its achievement.

Here, in essence, is the central issue of the future support of higher education. Our values, not our resources, will determine whether higher education will fulfill its potential for serving American society.

The sweep of history is conveyed in this section. The relationship of higher education to national goals is clearly stated and with the sense that the future of higher education is indeed being shaped now, both by inaction and by what is done at the federal level, at the state level, and in the private sector. The author skillfully draws upon statements of national commissions and spokesmen to give those recommendations new relevance. Particularly is this true as he traces the effects of social forces on today's issues of public policy.

One point should be made about Part Two and the succeeding sections. Contrary to assertions in some recent reports and in other superficially informed commentaries, "the establishment in higher education has not been complacent about the status quo." Many educators, among them Logan Wilson, were trying to get at the heart of institutional weaknesses long before "the carpers and the revolutionaries had even thought much about them." Further, something was done about them in many places. Those who pronounced this weakness, that shortcoming as new discoveries in 1970, with a demand for "radical reform," merely show their naïveté and ignorance. The inventory of changes for improvement, already a part of the record of the sixties, is a solid base for the continuing changes that must take place.

Mr. Wilson's analyses go far beyond generalizations, however. He has obviously kept thoroughly informed about campus life and speaks with the authority of one familiar with problems and achievements from the institutional point of view. Hence, an important feature of the book is the combination of national perspective and institutional reality.

Part Two itself deals with how higher education is shaped by students, professors, administrators, and trustees. "The *Forgotten* Student" is hardly a suitable description in 1971—as Mr. Wilson points out—and although what happened in student relations after 1964 is not pursued in this section, the subject returns for some attention in later chapters. Nonetheless, the discussion throughout reminds readers that the leaders in higher education were concerned about the faults in institutional practices long before there were headlines about "student unrest."

"Some sidelights on the college experience" is an apt description of Part Three, which is titled "Higher Education's Varied Objectives." The later phrase may be somewhat misleading, for the treatment is more indicative than comprehensive, and not all the outcomes identified are necessarily to be regarded as objectives. More to the point is the excellence of what is here (some of the best writing in the book). The treatment of the work ethic, of the need for "adequacy" as well as "excellence" of education for the marketplace which does not exclude stress on personal values—all this is stimulating and charts new ways and new paths.

After the practical commentary of "Costs and Priorities" in Part Four, the book concludes with six forward-looking statements on "The University—Its Nature and Nurture." They have as their backdrop the forces and ideas at work for change on the campus. In the searching analysis of the conflict and competition inherent in the university as a social organization are serious and continuing implications for administration. The limits and conditions on institutional autonomy, the benefits and abuses of "faculty control"—both highly affective in institutional health—are accorded thoughtful and sensitive exploration. In logical sequence comes "Changing University Governance," and "Upholding Institutional Integrity" is an appropriate summary view.

Certain main themes run throughout the book, as they do over the long course of institutional life. Examples are the repeated stress on the relationship of higher education to national purpose; the need for change; the planning essential for orderly change; and the necessity that institutional goals and practices, as well as national expectations, be related to a concern for quality and for the essentially intellectual and cultural character of the university enterprise.

In 1961, anticipating the main debate of the decade, Dr. Wilson wrote: "Increasingly we sense that it is not enough to be the most affluent society in a competitive and troubled world. . . . a strong nation requires a set of unified purposes transcending any mere summation of private and selfish ends. . . . a value system which allocates resources primarily to the satisfaction of present consumer demands is not necessarily the one best suited to meet future needs. . . . an enduring society must have basic institutions that are both vigorous and viable."

From this definition of the national purpose stems the argument for change. Believing in a "pluralistic society" and wanting "to uphold the many worthwhile aspects of diversification in educational support and control," he repeatedly advances the thesis that "we must move with resolution to modify and strengthen this system."

Change without planning, however, is an invitation to chaos. "To those of you who are disaffected or alienated, I suggest that before you reject existing practices or attempt to change them, you begin by making an honest effort to understand why things are the way they are." However, "we no longer have any option between disjointed laissez faire enterprise on the one hand and planned, integrated activity on the other. The only real choice remaining for educational institutions and associations is whether we shall get together and do the job ourselves, or wait for other agencies of public policy to regiment it for us."

Such a view of planning led Dr. Wilson in 1966 to endorse formalized devices at the state level for "coordination." The rapid rise of such agencies in recent years supports the strength of his position. The theoretical concept is sound, but most commentators overlook the bureaucracy, sometimes created within coordinating agencies, whose purpose is to limit or control rather than to co-ordinate. Dr. Wilson worries about this development—and with good cause in a number of states. "I am concerned about any move which in effect displaces the more experienced institutional leaders ... and makes them into sideline witnesses of public policy forma-tion. ... I believe that the public interest requires the active participa-tion of professional educators rather than their complete displace-ment by politically constituted committees, commissions, and other agencies remote from the real scenes of action." He further warns against "developing central bureaucracies ... that would be prone to claim superior wisdom about what ought to be done to and for our colleges and universities."

Another element in planning to which increasing emphasis must be given is institutional research. Such research, however, must go beyond the customary gathering of statistical data required for budgetary purposes. Evaluation of educational methods, procedures, and organization must become part of the process.

Institutional mission is probably the most critical of the themes, for here we have the core of the concern for the future. The bridge between the national interest and the planning for change either at the institutional or statewide level is the setting of institutional goals. Logan Wilson believes that what is retained in institutional life and what is added should reflect the intellectual and cultural mission of the university. He admits to tertiary education other concerns for other institutions, but he would hold to the historic boundaries for colleges and universities. Dr. Wilson's distinction could clarify some of the current debate on "educational opportunity."

The current and wide interest in and advocacy of enlarging educational opportunity at the post-high-school level as a means of providing every individual a chance to develop to his fullest potential must be carefully examined. The postulate of increased opportunity does not carry with it the corollary that study at a college or university is for all the appropriate method. Persons who are not motivated to be members of an academic community, those whose needs cannot be appropriately filled by a college or university, and those who do not have the capability to succeed in an academic undertaking should not be encouraged or expected to pursue study in our institutions of higher education.

As Dr. Wilson and others have emphasized, not every college or university should undertake to do everything for all who seek admission. Untenable expectations created, unsuitable roles assigned or assumed inevitably produce a distortion and weakening of the positive function that can be effectively performed. Option and opportunity to attend must be available, but it does not follow that the experience of higher education should be forced on or expected of those for whom it is unattractive or uninteresting. Nor should the university—especially—be called on to change its basic structure to accommodate those who are not motivated toward its specific objectives and who are not intellectually oriented and culturally curious. Much of the current discussion about restructuring the university misses this simple but fundamental point.

It is characteristic of Dr. Wilson that his view of the future is optimistic. His criticisms are not diluted and his probing spares no tradition. He ignores no problem and he appreciates that the system is buffeted by "the winds of change." But he regards the foundation as sturdy. "More successfully than any other nation, we have indeed reconciled the demands for quantity and quality in higher education."

Whatever we choose to do about shaping the future of American higher education, our contemporary colleges and universities and those yet to come are committed by their missions to the development of a broader understanding of mankind and to the furtherance of a civilization whose benefits can be shared by all men. Nobody can foresee just what our nation and the world will be like in 1984, but, as someone has aptly said, civilization is what happens when men have intelligent desires and, within limits, history can be what we want it to be.

Dr. Wilson believes that our colleges and universities will have important roles in shaping such a future. The way will not be easy, and we are being tested from within and from without. But he does not doubt that the system, modified and improved, will survive the turbulence of the times to render indispensable services to the nation and to all mankind.

DAVID D. HENRY

President Emeritus,
Distinguished Professor of Higher Education,
University of Illinois

Part One

SHAPING HIGHER EDUCATION

In this address, given at the Council's Forty-fourth An-
nual Meeting in October 1961, just three months after I
became president, my purpose was to review the main
strengths and weaknesses of the American system of
higher education and to set forth my views about ap-
propriate roles for the Council as a coordinating agency.

Perspectives for
the American Council on Education

A GENERAL UNEASINESS and an aroused public spirit among the American people are being manifested of late in an intense concern with the national purpose. Increasingly we sense that it is not enough to be the most affluent society in a competitive and troubled world. Our changed attitudes derive from several realizations. The first is that a strong nation requires a set of unified purposes transcending any mere summation of private and selfish ends. Second, a value system which allocates resources primarily to the satisfaction of present consumer demands is not necessarily the one best suited to meet future needs. And third, an enduring society must have basic institutions that are both vigorous and viable.

Implicit, if not explicit, in each of these realizations is the pivotal position of education. The President's Commission on National Goals was headed by an educator, and the chapter on education in its 1960 report is a telling one. If we are to survive and prosper as a nation, we indeed must know what our goals are and believe in them firmly. They are necessarily the main reasons for the existence of the varied institutions and associations with which we are connected.

3

On this occasion, however, I shall not talk about either national goals or educational objectives. Rather the burden of what I have to say pertains to means rather than ends. To an audience composed largely of administrators, I hardly need stress that unactivated thoughts and sentiments about goals can lead only to frustration and failure.

It is timely for us, in these sessions, to consider a desirable future pattern of higher education. Although some may face the prospect reluctantly, everybody knows that our institutions must undergo changes. Existing physical facilities must be vastly expanded, and new facilities created. More teachers and better teaching will be required to enlarge and improve educational opportunity for augmented numbers. Research, public service, and the concern with international affairs inevitably will be intensified and extended. As we educators keep saying, these things call for an accelerated investment of time, energy, and money.

Although my remarks here do not imply that the more obvious steps are not also the most important, my main thesis is that the less obvious changes needed are not the least important. My contention is that an enlarged investment in American education as it is now structured will not assure the attainment of either our educational or our national goals. In fact, I believe the contemporary pattern is not well adjusted to present needs, much less those of the future.

The American System of Higher Education

In this country, we really have no formalized system of education. On the primary and secondary levels, there are approximately forty-eight thousand basic administrative units, each with a large measure of independent control of schools. When it comes to higher education, the autonomy of units on the same campus is suggested in a description of the large American university as an agglomeration of entities connected only by a common plumbing system. Moreover, not even this connection exists among the separate campuses of the two thousand or so colleges and universities that make up higher education in this country.

If educational adequacy is to be judged solely by the number and variety of institutions, then perhaps we have no cause for worry. Counting only institutions listed in the U.S. Office of Education directory, there are 585 of the junior college type, 718 four-year institutions, 462 which offer work through the master's level, 205 which grant the doctorate, and 41 unclassified. Of all these, there are 12 under federal control, 375 under state control, 311 under local government units, 520 private and nondenominational, 494 Protestant, 294 Roman Catholic, and five Jewish.

No other nation even approaches ours in the number and diversity of institutions of higher education. They range in size from those including mere dozens of students to those enrolling more than forty-five thousand. Some admit only the few of top ability and clearly defined interests, whereas others accept any high school graduate and offer credit courses in everything from needlecraft to nuclear physics. The kinds of student cultures found on American campuses vary from the so-called collegiate, or "rah rah," to the predominantly vocational, academic, and nonconformist. Among these institutions, one sees the whole spectrum between the extremes of a community of individuals and a bureaucratic collectivity of trainees.

In general, our colleges and universities are more affected by outside social forces than they once were. Some are autonomously apart from their immediate environment, but most are caught up by it and cannot escape popular conceptions about what they ought to be. Their curricula are heavily influenced by changing occupational requirements; their size is affected by the rise of large-scale enterprise; their structure, by the growth of bureaucracy; their expansion, by the sharp population rise; and even their aims, by requirements that the larger society imposes. To be sure, in few places have we gone as far as the Russians in merely professing broad aims while actually training specialists to meet political and economic requirements. Regardless of trends toward uniformity, nonetheless, the varied totality represented by our system of higher education still comes close to that supposedly impossible ideal of being all things to all men.

American colleges and universities continue to be characterized by localized independence in decision making. Their institutional freedom is related to their never having been subjected to the control of any political, religious, or other centralized national agency. We take justifiable pride in a system that is characterized by diversification, decentralization, local autonomy, and free competition.

The strengths of such a system, however, should not blind us to its weaknesses. That it has been on the whole well adapted to the demands of the past is no evidence for its being equally well adapted to the needs of the foreseeable future. I am not suggesting that we suppress the real values of academic freedom or that we abandon the utility of institutional diversity. Higher education's dispersed support and control, its free interplay of competition and cooperation have in general served us well. Even our disagreements about the means and ends of education are often the manifestations of a healthy condition. Unplanned diversification, nonetheless, is not to be equated with the best interest of any particular college or university, much less that of our entire educational structure. As it is, we have in this country a congeries of institutions, varying greatly in governance, size, atmosphere, programs, faculty quality, student characteristics, and intellectual standards.

In some states regulations are so lax that diploma mills are allowed to get away with open fraud. Certain regions have altogether too many indiscriminately established and inadequately maintained institutions. In other sections, there is a dearth of colleges and universities. Almost everywhere there is little evidence of a logical and carefully evolved division of labor. Candor should impel us to acknowledge, therefore, that the "rich diversity" of our educational ideal can become in reality little more than a poor divisiveness. The virtues of decentralization likewise carry their attendant defects. Mere arithmetic addition of disparate educational enterprises may not produce a total endeavor sufficient for our national needs. Warranted fear of any arrangement resembling a procrustean bed seems to be accompanied by an unwarranted disregard for the actuality that decentralization per se affords no built-in protections against outside imposition.

Furthermore, in an era of increased interdependence, decentralization leads to an unevenness of educational opportunity which limits the entire nation's manpower potential. Although no sensible person would advocate having our military manpower needs handled separately by private and public agencies in the fifty states of the union, this is, in effect, what some believe to be the only proper educational approach to broader and more complicated manpower requirements.

Like diversification and decentralization, local autonomy is a widely cherished aspect of the American system of higher education. Its usefulness to the advancement of learning should not be underestimated, and even the provincial standards it has sometimes fostered have not been entirely lacking in utility. Yet the important denominators of intellectual achievement are universal and long since ceased to be matters for local determination.

The Costs of Unilateral Action

As it has become more important to the general welfare, higher education has also become more complicated, expensive, and interrelated. Entrenched views of institutional autonomy not only increase unnecessarily the price we must pay for an adequate educational system but also decrease both its efficiency and effectiveness as a coordinated instrumentality serving the best interests of the nation as a whole.

My remarks do not imply that education at any level should be subservient to political needs, and I wish to stress my view that the body politic, like the institutions it contains, should be regarded as a service agency to individuals. But in a free society important forms of competition must be regulated if chaos is to be avoided. Is there a valid reason for exempting educational institutions from this common requirement?

Although we like to think of educational changes as reflecting an orderly growth, the actual process has often been quite different. For all the instances where interinstitutional competition has strengthened the rivals involved, there are at least as many where wasteful duplication and the proliferation of mediocrity have ensued. Attitudes of educators as well as laymen, various critics have observed, impede a sensible division of responsibilities and an appropriate set of relations within and between institutions. Much lip service is given to the concept of diversity, but in practice there is an indiscriminate tendency to imitate the prestigious model of the university. Popular pressures build up to convert junior col-

leges into senior colleges, to have four-year institutions add graduate level work, and to expand universities endlessly in horizontal
directions. In the scramble, of course, unit costs rise unnecessarily,
quality gets diluted, and shared objectives are forgotten.

Not only do state and regional needs tend to be neglected amid
narrowly partisan efforts, but also national objectives often never
even enter into consideration. Piecemeal incentives have been
devised on the federal level to offset the fortuitous circumstance
that most of our institutions were not established and are not maintained primarily to serve national objectives. As these financial
measures become more conspicuous, they do produce a changing
pattern, but responses to them are sometimes slow and reluctant.
Some federal measures are indeed ill-conceived, and, as can be
expected, their institutional implementation is not always enthusi-
astic. In view of centralized coordination and planning under voluntary and strictly educational auspices, however, the legislative and
executive branches of the federal government can hardly be blamed
for moving into a vacuum which must be filled.

Paradoxes
of Organization

Up to this point I may have given the impression that little
coordination exists among our educational institutions. Actually, of
course, American higher education does have a complex scheme of
overall organization. Numerous associations, mostly voluntary in
membership, have evolved to promote varied but common ends.
Perhaps because it is loosely rather than tightly articulated, higher
education in the United States has spawned a large number and
almost bewildering variety of groupings.

There are those consisting of individual members drawn from
a wide range of scholarly, scientific, and professional fields. They
congregate periodically by localities, states, regions, and on a nationwide basis. Even more encompassing alignments of allied disciplines
are to be seen in the National Research Council, the American
Council of Learned Societies, and the Social Science Research
Council. These in turn, along with the American Council on Education, have formed a "holding company" known as the Conference Board of Associated Research Councils. There are likewise

such comprehensive organizations of academicians as the Association for Higher Education and the American Association of University Professors.

Administrative and staff employees—presidents, deans, directors, athletic coaches, and others—also have their consortia. To complete the picture, there is a national association of governing boards. It is no wonder therefore that some members of the academic community feel overorganized as well as underpaid. The contemporary American educator frequently spends a lot of time away from his campus in workshops, seminars, conferences, conventions, meetings, and other extramural activities. Thus, unpaid and intermittent participation in a voluntary, collective enterprise brings about such coherence and unity as the structure of higher learning manifests.

In addition to these associations of individuals as such, there are other organizations where participation is largely representational of the various segments or divisions of a college or university. Even more inclusive are the groupings of entire institutions. We are familiar with such organizations as the American Association of Junior Colleges, the American Association of Land-Grant Colleges and State Universities, the Association of Urban Universities, the various regional accrediting associations, the Association of American Universities, the Association of American Colleges, as well as the American Council on Education. These associations are well known to everybody in this room. I doubt, however, that anybody here could name more than a fraction of the 512 regional and national educational associations, or the 141 college professional, honor, and recognition societies, or the 413 state education associations, the 50 religious education associations, or the 15 international education associations which total more than eleven hundred organizations—nearly all voluntary in nature—having to do in one way or another with American education.

Beyond the associations consisting mainly of educators, still other individuals and groups are involved in the total organization of American higher education. For instance, there are lay boards of trustees and visitors, legislatures, governors, state budget officers, statewide commissions and superboards, semipolitical regional agencies and compacts, cooperative interinstitutional arrangements for mutual developments, more than forty executive agencies of the federal government, the Congress itself, and so on. For institutions as well as individuals these frequently impose mandatory rather than merely permissive relationships.

In brief, although the two thousand and more American colleges and universities may be inclined to go their separate ways, there is certainly no lack of agencies and associations intended to promote many kinds of unified effort. The sheer number and multifarious functions of these aggregations create further problems in themselves, however, so that paradoxically the whole of American higher education is both underorganized and overorganized.

As Council Chairman David Henry has recently pointed out, it is still difficult for many persons to think of education in national terms. Even educational leaders are prone to behave as if the most pressing problems were confined to their particular specialties, campuses, or constituencies. This attitude persists despite the increased mutuality of disciplines, the expanded interconnections of institutions, and the growing interdependence of nations. Instead of a united effort to resolve the basic educational issues confronting the nation, accordingly, our collective endeavor is being confused and weakened by vested-interest group pressures, splinter movements, and fragmented approaches.

Whether voluntary enterprise is capable of achieving the long-range as well as the immediate objectives required of American higher education, if our nation is to survive and flourish, remains to be seen. In any event, more concerted effort is necessary, and we no longer have any option between disjointed laissez faire enterprise on the one hand and planned, integrated activity on the other. The only real choice remaining for educational institutions and associations is whether we shall get together and do the job ourselves, or wait for other agencies of public policy to regiment it for us.

Roles for
the Council

The American Council on Education's main reason for being stems from these and other fundamental problems. If the Council did not exist, as many have observed, it certainly would have to be created. Fortunately, it is already a going concern in which most of the decision-makers of higher education participate. Now serving more than a thousand institutions and almost a hundred educational associations, not to mention other organizations, the Council has proved to be a useful instrumentality in the past, and it can become an even more useful one in the future.

To measure up to the difficult tasks ahead, however, the Council must be modified and strengthened. Purposes and programs should be reconsidered in the light of changing circumstances. The fact that our obligations are to serve the broad interests of education and the nation rather than the narrow interests of a limited membership should not, in my opinion, be interpreted as a mandate to undertake any and all educational assignments. The confused division of labor in American higher education ought to be simplified rather than complicated further by what the Council itself does. Our activities should complement rather than duplicate those of other organizations; further, our own diffused aims and programs need to be consolidated and brought into sharper focus.

Although the Council ought not to abandon its involvement in substantive concerns, the greatest unmet need for service from our kind of organization appears to concern educational processes and relationships. A serious shortcoming of our educational system is that separated problems are not brought into a total perspective. Conversely, unified planning is not formulated and communicated throughout the nation. Strategically situated to bridge gaps found in the interstices of our system—gaps between disciplines, institutions, and associations—the Council can and should be a major agency in developing a more coherent and meaningful pattern of education for the future.

A recent opinion survey made by an outside agency for the Council revealed within educational and other circles a favorable but rather fuzzy image of what the Council is and what it does. We certainly want to keep that image favorable, and I hope that we can make it distinct and strong. With increased financial support from our membership, from foundations, and from others who are in a position to appreciate the essential values of the Council to the welfare of education, we will sharpen our objectives, strengthen our staff, and improve our services to education and to the nation. I would remind you, however, that the Council must continue to depend mainly upon the good will, the brains, and the dedication of its member representatives to carry forward our common endeavor.

Because we have the most heterogeneous membership of any educational association, identity of interest regarding critical issues will at times be lacking. It is therefore unrealistic to expect the Council or any other agency always to be able to speak "with one voice" for higher education. But by serving as a forum and clearinghouse, the Council can continue to grow in usefulness not only to its own members but also to government and the public at large by giving effective expression to the "voice" or "voices" of education, as the case may be. As a democratic organization, the Council necessarily must derive many of its perspectives from the prevailing views of its members. Even so, I trust that all of you concur with the principle of continuing to assure our various committees, commissions, and the staff itself the detachment required for nonpartisan inquiry, analysis, and recommendation. Much of the prestige the Council has long enjoyed results directly from the objectivity of its deliberations and actions.

Most of us agree that the basic structure of the Council is sound. A number of our members have suggested, however, and I agree, that the Council's leadership role would be enhanced by the creation of a fairly sizable central board in which the authority and responsibility of several present groups would be unified. Such a body, adding a new dimension of strength and wisdom to our deliberations and actions, would merit very high respect and confidence among the public as well as educators, and thus would be able to speak and act with even greater authority for all higher education.

One of our major tasks is to increase the impact of the Council. Although I agree with our Executive Committee that it would be a mistake for the Council to become an action or lobbying organization as distinguished from one engaged in broader pursuits, we do have an obligation to influence educational developments in the right direction. Whether we like it or not, this involves a closer and more effective liaison between educational leaders and key figures in the legislative and executive branches of government.

Neither higher education nor the government is well served when the representations being made come mainly from special interest groups which often are either ignorant of or indifferent to total needs and the priorities implicit in them. If we educators wish to avoid a negative role of mere *reaction* to proposed legislation that is frequently inadequate and unwise, then our only alternative is to assume a positive role of *action* for better legislation.

This past year the Council demonstrated the possibility of getting a consensus among educational institutions and associations on proposed legislation of significance. The Council statement *A Proposed Program of Federal Action to Strengthen Higher Education* proved that, with adequate communication and consultation, we are capable of unity on a wide range of issues. We can concert our aims by extending and improving this procedure and by implementing it through individual efforts throughout the fifty states, as well as in Washington.

During my first four months in Washington, I have found the members of Congress receptive to and grateful for the information and aid given by the American Council and other educational groups. But also representatives and senators have said repeatedly that what they most need is what they seldom get—expressions of interest, concern, and judgment from educators known to them in their own districts and states. No matter what steps may be taken to strengthen the Council and other national organizations, no really effective representation for higher education can be achieved in Washington without active involvement by the individual colleges and universities. Thus our task is joint and inseparable.

To conclude, I have intended neither to minimize the assets nor to maximize the liabilities of our present system of higher education. I like to live in a pluralistic society and I want to uphold the many worthwhile aspects of diversification in educational support and control. My thesis is that we must move with resolution to modify and strengthen this system. Further, I have tried to demonstrate that the problems confronting us are solvable, and that in my judgment the American Council on Education has an important, in fact, a vital role to play in their solution. By joining efforts, I am convinced that we can keep our institutions free and make them ever more useful to mankind.

This paper was presented during February 1963 at a Harvard University Seminar on Education and Public Policy. The seminar, one in a series arranged by Professor Seymour E. Harris, included among its main discussants President Nathan Pusey and several other academic presidents in that region. In my remarks, I outlined six principles that should underlie the developing partnership between the federal government and higher education.

A Better Partnership
with the Federal Government

MORE THAN FIVE GENERATIONS have passed since the federal government first concerned itself with education, and to many of us it seems absurd that we should still argue whether there should be such a concern. There is nothing absurd, however, about the continuing need to consider the nature and extent of the involvement. In my view, the rapidly growing interdependence of the government and higher education calls for an unending assessment of the partnership.

In the year 1776 there were only nine institutions of higher learning in this country; today there are more than two thousand. Our history attests the critical role colleges and universities have had in this nation's security and progress, and our present circumstances magnify rather than diminish this role. Inasmuch as the final responsibility for our collective security and welfare can reside only in the federal government, a close partnership between government and education in our kind of society is unavoidable. Our present task is to make this partnership as effective as possible.

Noting one aspect of the relationship, President Eisenhower's Science Advisory Committee stated in 1960: "The partnership is a

14

fact. It has done much more good than harm. It seems certain to grow in importance unless the American people decide to accept a second-rate standing in terms of power, of comfort, of knowledge." The committee's report sets forth some guidelines for the advancement of science. It lists broad principles, such as giving federal support for excellence, increasing the number of first-rate teaching and research centers, attracting more talented students into science, encouraging new fields of knowledge, and so on. It makes pointed recommendations for the nation's further progress in science. Fortunately, many of these guidelines for the development of science are now being used extensively.

Unfortunately, the need for comparable guiding principles for federal participation in the development of higher education as a whole has not been widely recognized. In some quarters there is still a strong sentiment that the functioning of our colleges and universities should be strictly a local, state, or private concern. This attitude often reflects ignorance of the heavy commitment the federal government already has in certain sectors of higher education. A review of the piecemeal, ad hoc pattern of federal programs in turn suggests that even in Washington there is reluctance to face up to the implications of what is unquestionably a permanent and growing partnership. To be sure, Congress has evidenced many specific concerns. The keen legislative interest in what medical school research can do for the bodies of the elderly is obvious, even though there is apparently less interest in what liberal arts colleges can do for the minds of the young. Various federal agencies have been explicit about the missions or tasks they have wanted colleges and universities to perform for them. Similarly, diverse segments of education have been active in trying to promote federal aid for their particular objectives.

The fragmented nature of the federal participation in higher education does not mean that a unified approach to a comprehensive problem has never been put forward. This year, and for several recent years, the American Council on Education—to mention but one agency—has set forth such a program. President Kennedy himself recently made a broad proposal that aims toward expanding individual opportunities, improving quality on all levels, and strengthening vocational, special, and continuing education. The proposal does not advocate having the federal government take over local responsibilities, but contends that, in the present era, state, local, and private efforts are not enough. The main principle specified regarding federal participation is that, in President Kennedy's words, it "should be selective, stimulative and, where possible, transitional."

Although the current political expediency of an omnibus bill for all levels and kinds of education may seem dubious, there can be no question about the wisdom of viewing comprehensively the needs of our entire educational system. Before we decide how the federal government can most appropriately and effectively aid in meeting these needs, we must come to agreement on basic principles and establish guidelines for future action. The President's January 29 message can be used as a starting point.

Acknowledging my temerity for getting into what should be the task of a high-level committee or commission for leading educators and others, I shall venture my own tentative views. They stem in the main from my recent experiences with the American Council on Education, where we are frequently in a mediating role between the federal government and higher education, and I want to emphasize that the observations are mine and do not necessarily represent the Council's position. The six principles offered for your consideration are set forth—not in the expectation that anybody will now endorse my bill of particulars—but in the hope that the educational community will soon reach its own consensus.

However this may be, our future is being shaped *now*. Certainly, it is high time we reach a better understanding within our own community and in the nation at large about the ongoing partnership between the federal government and higher education.

1. *The national interest principle.* In assisting higher education, the federal government should make national interests, rather than local or special needs, paramount. Most of us would probably agree that the federal government must concern itself with extending educational opportunity, promoting economic growth, upgrading manpower, undergirding our security, and advancing our collective well-being. Colleges and universities are essential to the achievement of these objectives, in addition to pursuing their own

special and distinctive ends. Likewise, individuals must be educated for useful citizenship as well as for the furtherance of their private purposes.

It is a mistake to assume that all institutional and personal educational objectives are equally important to the national welfare and hence equally deserving of federal support. Although I favor a concerted effort to increase the number and geographic spread of first-rate teaching and research centers, I doubt that any sensible person would favor taking federal research and development funds away from such institutions as Harvard, M.I.T., Chicago, Michigan, and California and spreading them thinly among a large number of institutions where aspirations often exceed capabilities.

Aside from the wastage entailed in an indiscriminate, across-the-board doling out of federal money, even our greatest institutions, which are truly national and even international in their service, render services to special constituencies which seem to me to be inappropriate for federal support. The Harvard Houses, for example, are a fine environment for undergraduate learning, but the expense entailed is certainly beyond what the federal government should be expected to underwrite. Or, to consider the curriculum itself, there may be many subjects in addition to theology for which we should not expect financial support from Washington. Of course, I have been in the nation's capital long enough to know that it has no monopoly of wisdom regarding education's best interests, but I have also been on enough campuses to know that provincial judgments sometimes put stadium enlargement ahead of library improvement, and find more pride in a resplendent marching band than in a roster of Woodrow Wilson fellows.

We should remember that few, if any, of the two thousand or more colleges and universities in this country were founded by communities, states, churches, or private groups with the national interest primarily in view. (In fact, the military academies at West Point and Annapolis are the only long-standing institutions having this original purpose.) In a society as mobile and interdependent as ours is today, however, the federal government must promote the national interest by assisting important educational endeavors for which local, state, or private support is either lacking or insufficient.

This aid may mean placing an expensive scientific installation, such as a particle accelerator, on the campus of a single university already possessing great human and material resources. It also may mean special assistance to poor states that pull down the level of our manpower by lagging badly to the rear of the academic procession.

In brief, federal aid should not be ladled out to any segment of the population merely to ease the burden of carrying local or special obligations. When the national interest is not being adequately served, however, I believe there is no substitute for federal concern and support.

2. *The resource development principle.*   Federal assistance should be conceived, not as a form of benevolence to institutions and individuals, but as an investment in a national resource. Neither colleges and universities nor students should be aided merely because they are needy, but because of their potential contribution to our collective achievement as a people. Although I doubt that many members of Congress think of appropriations for education as being in the same category as veterans' pensions and old age relief, there manifestly is not a full appreciation of education's importance as an indispensable element in the nation's security and well-being.

As the President's January message mentioned, some 40 percent of the nation's economic growth and productivity in recent years has been attributed to education. You may recall his dramatizing the cost of inadequate education by stating that the loss of only one year's income as a result of unemployment is more than the total cost of twelve years of education through high school. For this audience, no reminder is necessary concerning the greater earning power and productivity of the college-trained. A 1963 American Council on Education brochure, *Higher Education as a National Resource*, puts it this way in stating the case for federal concern.

American higher education is a priceless asset fundamental to the national purpose. It cannot be spoken of simply in terms of the value of buildings and equipment, the total number of persons served, the teachers involved, or the research performed. The nation's colleges and junior colleges, universities, research institutes, and professional schools are all of these things, but something more. Broadly conceived, higher educa-

tion constitutes a precious national resource essential to the achievement
of great national goals and to the achievement of worthy aspirations of
individual citizens. It is a resource also in the sense that, given favorable
conditions, it is as capable of self-renewal as is a properly conserved
forest.

This same statement goes on to point out the growing pressures on higher education—the pressures of enrollment increases
and of new knowledge. The potential human resources in all regions
of the country are of similar capability, but the means to finance
higher education are very unevenly distributed. This latter circumstance makes it especially difficult in some states and regions
for institutions to give adequate support to graduate and professional education, and the problem is complicated even further by
the siphoning-off of talent to more prosperous sections. In view of
the tax revenue limitations of localities and states, together with
the declining proportion of total support from private sources, how
can one escape the conclusion that our federal government must
assume a larger role in the conservation and improvement of higher
education?

In summary, the expansion and improvement of higher education are too vital to our future to be left entirely in the hands of
local and private enterprise. Adequate financial support for the
nation's colleges and universities must be regarded as a funding
operation rather than a relief measure, and the cost must be treated
as an investment in human capital rather than an ordinary expenditure. The investment required is indeed a heavy one, but not nearly
so heavy as the penalties we and oncoming generations will have
to pay for failure to conserve and strengthen a critical national
resource.

3. *The selective principle.* If the federal government is not
to assume the whole burden of support for higher education, its
decisions of necessity imply priorities. Colleges and universities are
quite accustomed to getting their moneys with strings attached,
but custom does not lessen the desire of some to have substantial
federal grants to spend as they please. To spread decision making,
there are also those who would prefer to have Congress dole out

funds to the fifty states for internal allocations, or else resort to simple formulas for spreading them everywhere.

Since it is neither possible nor desirable for the federal government to take over the entire support of higher education, some selectivity by levels, institutions, programs, and projects must be exercised. This being so, almost certainly a more suitable pattern can be found than the one now resulting from our piecemeal approach. To move more systematically, however, there should be a meeting of minds between government and education about priorities of importance and urgency. For example, a better case can be made for federal aid on higher than on lower levels. I am not arguing that higher education is more directly related to the national interest or that its needs are more urgent. Admittedly, more dollars are needed to bolster primary and secondary education, but these are the levels where local concern, understanding, and support are strongest. We pride ourselves on the fact that our common schools are community-centered enterprises. Our colleges and universities, on the other hand, have always had a different structure of support and control. Their constituencies are more widely dispersed; political and geographic boundary lines are less relevant to the services they perform; their policies are much less susceptible to uniformization.

In principle I advocate appropriate federal aid for all levels of education and see no necessity for an *either-or* alternative. Further, the private-public schism is far less serious on the higher level, and lesser sums of money are required to produce stimulative or multiplier effects in response to changing national needs. Even in higher education, as I said earlier, I do not believe in federal assistance to disciplines across-the-board. From the point of view of liberal education, art and philosophy may be more essential than astronomy and engineering, but is this a valid reason for expecting the Department of Defense or any other federal agency to give support to all aspects of the curriculum? In my opinion it is the responsibility of individual institutions rather than of the central government to maintain balance in education, and to resist or countervail influences to the contrary.

The other side of the coin, however, is that institutions can maintain balance successfully only if the government underwrites fully the costs of federal projects undertaken by colleges and universities. Not only is the government falling short of meeting institutional indirect costs on research projects, but also it is not reimbursing out-of-pocket local costs for ROTC, international education programs, and various other services institutions perform for federal agencies.

Working through the American Council on Education and other voluntary associations, colleges and universities are getting together about their own priorities of importance and urgency. There is still a need, nonetheless, for more agreement on all sides about the ordering of events. More persons must become aware that the expansion and improvement of faculties and facilities should precede any massive program of scholarships and other student aids. Or, to give another example, the development of graduate and professional education is perhaps a less popular objective, but its continued encouragement is hardly less urgent than the multiplication of junior colleges and other undergraduate institutions. In summary, I believe our only real choice is to encourage a step-up of federal assistance to education. As we implement this decision, I hope that we shall choose to do those things which will be of maximum benefit to both government and education.

4. *The complementary principle.* Federal aid should strengthen rather than weaken diversity of support and control, and should complement rather than supplant local effort. Alongside its shortcomings in an era of rapid social change, the American system of higher education has some great strengths which should be maintained. The dualism of public and private institutions, for instance, upholds the pluralism of our culture, and varied sources of financial support keep higher education as a whole from being subservient to extraneous influences. Likewise, the tradition of autonomous governance and the wide variation in aim and scope foster a free competition in the advancement of knowledge which is of inestimable value to a dynamic society.

Despite the protests of those who oppose federal aid on the grounds that it weakens the diversity of support and control, I contend that it has had and can continue to have an opposite result. Wisely and fairly distributed, government funds further a mixed pattern of support which is beneficial to all institutions, both public and private. Although I favor outright grants for certain kinds of aid and am cognizant of the difficulties inherent in matching requirements, I also feel that in most situations federal aid should be linked to incentives for increased local and private support.

Paradoxical as it may seem, I believe that many institutions could safeguard their autonomy and freedom more effectively by tightening their internal organization. Often without either faculty or administrative authorization from their own campuses, too many different voices speak in Washington for their segmented interests and even, in some cases, for education as a whole. This disjunctivity not only confuses Congress and the federal agencies but also tends to block a unified approach to interrelated problems.

Over and beyond the need for more internal cohesion, colleges and universities will stand a better chance of upholding their integrity through voluntary joint agreements among themselves than by going their separate ways. Collectively they can resist distorting influences that only the strongest of them can resist individually. Of course, unified action implies a common code of ethics in some new areas of relationships where no such code now exists, and perhaps even the necessity for self-policing. To borrow a phrase from a recent Carnegie Corporation *Quarterly*, there is a growing "inseparability of politics and education," and it is for us to make the most of this fact of modern life. Past experience alone should remove the fear many persons still have that federal support necessarily carries with it federal control. Speaking as one who has dealt with state legislatures, private donors, and the federal government, I agree with McGeorge Bundy that support from Washington has been and can continue to be "a reinforcement of the freedom of the higher learning." Our common task is to see that federal aid offsets the shortcomings and builds on the strengths of the American system of higher education.

5. *The merit principle.* Although federal assistance will be needed to increase the availability of higher education, it will be needed even more to improve quality. Quantity and quality are not conflicting objectives, but expansion and improvement are sure to compete with each other for whatever funds are available. The

heaviest local pressures will probably be for throwing all possible resources into expansion, and hence I want to stress the critical need for federal funds to keep qualitative improvement moving forward. I am apprehensive about the neglect of quality in higher education because of the great magnitude of the funding operation that will be necessary to underwrite expansion between now and 1980. Everybody knows about the "tidal wave" of students, but few persons are vividly aware of just what it signifies. The problem is more readily grasped when we realize that, to cope with it, we hypothetically would have to double the size of all existing colleges and universities, *and* establish a thousand more institutions with an average enrollment of twenty-five hundred. The pressures for expansion are my main argument for the merit principle as a guideline for allocating a considerable proportion of moneys from Washington.

Since egalitarian sentiments will probably be on the side of expansion at the expense of improvement, I favor a discriminating use of federal allocations to make certain that standards are maintained and strengthened. To this end, government money will produce the best results if it is distributed according to the merit principle instead of being scattered everywhere with a dead-leveling effect.

Despite occasional charges of bias and favoritism against government agencies and the panels of experts used by them to determine which individuals, projects, programs, and institutions are worthy of assistance, the procedures they usually employ seem to me to be the only appropriate ones for many kinds of undertakings. The National Science Foundation, for example, in utilizing advisory panels drawn from the academic community itself, much more closely approximates procedures used on most college and university campuses to allocate funds than do across-the-board schemes.

Conversely, I think that federal funds should not be given as subsidies for budget-balancing purposes to institutions perennially on the verge of bankruptcy nor to institutions with overly ambitious ventures. In addition, title IV of the present National Defense Education Act seems to me to be misconceived in its support only for new and expanded graduate programs. In effect, it encourages vertical and horizontal expansion without regard to strengthening existing programs.

In altogether too many states we can already observe the unfortunate consequences of what someone has aptly called the "university syndrome"—the overweening desires of large numbers of junior colleges to become senior colleges, and of four-year institutions to become universities. There is nothing wrong per se with such aspirations, but in the process of change, unfortunately, some of them are transmogrified rather than transmuted. The nation has no need for more second- and third-rate institutions at any level, but it does have a desperate need for more first-rate centers on all levels. In short, we cannot afford to lose sight of the importance of quality in higher education.

6. *The coordinated plan principle.* Federal assistance should be guided by a long-range plan for the most logical development of the American system of higher education as an entity. As I have said elsewhere, there is now too much unplanned diversification among our colleges and universities. We really have no tightly definable "system" of higher education, but rather a congeries of institutions. Some regions have too many indiscriminately established and inadequately maintained institutions, and elsewhere there is a dearth of colleges and universities. Decentralization has its virtues, but these often have their own reverse defects, so that unregulated diversity can result in divisiveness. Disparate educational endeavors, for instance, do not always produce the total endeavor required to meet our national needs, and the unevenness of educational opportunity limits the entire nation's manpower potential.

Just as we can no longer afford to behave as a mere federation of states in international affairs, so can we ill afford to continue educational policies and practices which do not make sense in an era of increased interdependence within the nation. The costs of unilateral action have become too high, and the penalties of wasteful competition too great. In the past it may have mattered little that we were relatively oblivious to national objectives in higher education, but the time has arrived when all of our colleges and universities must participate in those purposes essential to our common survival and well-being.

In view of the changed circumstances, we in higher education should not expect the federal government merely to underwrite the status quo. Both our institutions and our government must aim for higher and better things. There simply must be more institutional cooperation and unity of effort, and these must be guided by a sense of common purpose. Other than meeting the need to expand our system of higher education, what other objectives do we have in view for 1980? In my view, we are fortunate in being one of the few modern nations not having a ministry of education which supports and controls the educational establishment. Lacking this central direction of enterprise, however, we are under the necessity of demonstrating that cooperation, no less than coercion, can bring us together and accomplish national objectives. Patterns of state, regional, and national cooperation have already emerged. Some of our states and regions now have long-range plans. It remains for us to develop some plan for the nation as a whole.

The American Council on Education is moving in this direction. Our Commission on Federal Relations and our Commission on Plans and Objectives for Higher Education are addressing themselves to the kinds of questions that must be answered. We are calling upon the most knowledgeable persons we can bring together, for example, to promote a better partnership between the federal government and higher education. Since the Council is the major organization of colleges, universities, and associations in the field of higher education, we are making every effort to formulate proper guidelines and get widespread acceptance of them.

We are moving ahead as promptly as we can in the full knowledge that the actions of the Congress and the more than forty federal executive agencies are already making policies and setting directions which affect the future of American higher education. There is no longer any option in educational circles between institutional laissez faire and coordinated enterprise. Each institution should have its own sense of public mission, of course, but my own conviction is that the educational community has a right and a responsibility to participate with the government in determining the policies and directions that will, as much as any other factors, shape our whole future. I hope that by now you share this conviction with me and will lend your support to its reinforcement.

The O. Max Gardner Award Dinner is held annually on one of the campuses of the University of North Carolina to give special recognition to selected faculty members. As their main speaker in Raleigh on March 22, 1964, I tried to focus attention on some major problems embedded in the relations of structure and function in educational organization.

Form and Function

NOWADAYS THERE IS a steady stream of foreign observers of higher education in this country, and in my Washington job I meet some of them. Whether at the start or the finish of their campus junkets, they are frequently bewildered by the structural and functional ramifications to be found within and among our colleges and universities. The visitors are usually impressed by the magnitude of what we have been able to achieve in higher education, but they sometimes wonder whether it is because of or in spite of existing arrangements.

Since they often come from countries where organized higher learning is centrally directed, they are likely to ask such questions as these: How are your American institutions supported and controlled? What is the division of labor among them? Who decides how many junior colleges, technical institutes, liberal arts colleges, and universities are needed, and where? What means do you use to get cooperation and coordination? Why do you have so few national standards? Is your fragmented scheme of things an economical and effective way of meeting national needs? My opening parry is that nobody has ever fully described, much less thoroughly analyzed that complex entity called "the American system of higher education." Many of our arrangements have resulted more from historic accident than from conscious design, and most of our twenty-one hundred or so colleges and universities have been left relatively alone to develop in their separate ways. As a consequence, our countryside is dotted with a large number and great variety of institutions, ranging from those of dubious quality to some of the world's most distinguished colleges and universities.

Visitors from abroad may have the mistaken notion that our lay trustees control everything, and must have explained to them that governing boards seldom really govern. In most situations boards function through their executive officer, the president. He, in turn, delegates much of his authority to other administrative officers. The faculty likewise is involved in the decision-making process, and in some institutions even the students share in academic governance.

Contrary to what those neatly arrayed organization charts might lead us to believe, lines of real authority and responsibility are often difficult to trace. This sometimes confused state of affairs is often rationalized as academic freedom, however, and because many members of the academic community place a high premium on being able to pursue their own interests with as little restraint as possible, the disarray is widely accepted.

The Prevalent
Laissez Faire

Outside observers are aware that we pride ourselves on the broad diffusion of power within our institutions and on dispersed, rather than centralized, support and control from without. Beginning on the departmental level in colleges and universities, we have made a watchword of "independence." Proceeding upward to the national level, where the authority of the U.S. Office of Education is markedly less than that of any foreign ministry of education, the spirit of laissez faire abounds.

Within recent years we have come to acknowledge the growing interdependence of departments, divisions, schools, colleges, and universities, and their relations to society at large. It is witnessed in many places by the creation of interdisciplinary fields, bureaus, institutes, and other structural devices intended to bridge the gaps caused by increased differentiation and specialization. To bridge campuses, we have of necessity begun to develop statewide planning, state and regional coordinating agencies, and consortia and other voluntary groupings, and are attempting to think more systematically about the mounting federal involvements in higher education. We have long recognized an intricate network of relations among individual scholars and scientists, administrative officers and others, as well as among institutions and the various interest groups within them. Today the unifying influences of state, regional, and national agencies and associations are not to be minimized.

Even so, the time is now at hand in educational ranks when we must admit that many of our structural arrangements are very loose-jointed and perhaps ill adapted to rapidly changing circumstances. By 1980 we shall need to enlarge many existing institutions and establish hundreds of new ones just to accommodate sheer numbers. Not only must vastly more students be taught, but also they must be taught more and in less time. Research and public service demands will press ever more heavily upon us.

In the light of these enlarged and more complicated functions, what structural changes should we now have under consideration? How should we proceed on local, state, regional, and national levels? Will the initiative come from educators, or will changes be thrust upon us?

In his history, *The American College and University*, Frederick Rudolph has recently said, "Resistance to fundamental reform was ingrained in the American collegiate and university tradition, as over three hundred years of history demonstrated. . . . Except on rare occasions, the historic policy of the American college and university [was]: drift, reluctant accommodation, belated recognition that while no one was looking, change had in fact taken place."[1] I would note that resistance to articulation and to change is no longer a tenable position for us and our institutions. Too much insistence on outmoded forms of sovereignty can lead only to chaos. In our technological age, the knowledge industry has become one of our most important industries, and higher education is in a pivotal

1. New York: Alfred Knopf, 1962. P. 491.

rather than a peripheral position in the swift pace of events. We have no option, therefore, but to adapt ourselves and our organizations to changing circumstances.

The Need
for Institutional Appraisal

To begin on the unit level, every college and university must continuously examine its reasons for being, assess its current strengths and weaknesses, and envisage what it hopes to be and can expect to become in the decades ahead. We have assumed too often that anything done in the name of higher education necessarily must be worthwhile. In part because our institutions do have high purposes and yield many intangible benefits to society, we have disliked using anything resembling the balance sheets of business enterprise to appraise our efforts.

Many of our institutions are trying to do too many different things. In manifesting the "university syndrome," they spread their material and human resources thinly and as a result do nothing really well. Even in single-purpose, liberal arts colleges, where the emphasis is almost entirely on teaching, there are often no applied criteria for judging teaching performance. Almost everywhere, the curriculum, or what is taught, is more the product of historic accretion than contemporary design. New courses are added helter-skelter, and virtually nothing is discarded. The rigidity of departmental structures is such that new fields like biophysics, genetics, and linguistics cannot be readily fitted into the traditional scheme. The growth of semiautonomous institutes, centers, and laboratories poses still other structural problems. (One university had eighty such institutes at last count, and another had twenty-five in the international area alone.)

Despite years of debate and inquiry within academic circles, there is still no consensus about such basic matters as the effects of class size on different kinds of learning, the valid uses of television and programed instruction, or what constitutes a balance between teaching and research. The academic sense of dignity of some would be offended by the thought of anything akin to unit costing or to the economic input-output analysis used to gauge productivity in other types of carefully reasoned endeavor. Of course, there has been experimentation with the relations between form and function in the higher learning. We have found out a lot about the learning process, and unquestionably most of our colleges and universities are better environments for teaching, research, and public service than they once were. Still, higher education as a whole has lagged in the development and application of systematic knowledge about its own processes.

Although bureaus or offices of institutional research are already in being on a number of campuses, organized inquiry of this kind is still generally the exception rather than the rule. It is indeed ironic that academicians, who have become indispensable to the advancement of the larger technology, should have done comparatively little to develop a technology of education. The economists, for example, have developed extensive bodies of knowledge in such fields as agricultural economics and labor economics, but until quite recently have paid very little attention to the economics of education. Or, to generalize about our whole profession, it is interesting, in view of the broad range of intellectual inquiry to be found in colleges and universities, that we do not know more conceptually about the activities common to our immediate enterprise.

Our lack of expertise about structure and function in higher education in our own country is often revealed when members of the American academic community are called upon to advise about educational matters in developing nations. Perspectives may be demanded to which we have thus far given little thought. Relations between means and ends which have merely been taken for granted must be assessed and priorities evaluated. The time dimension must be taken into account. Careful consideration has to be given to alternative arrangements, with an eye to their efficiency and effectiveness. Where material and human resources are severely limited, any investment in education must be weighed alongside other investments.

Although we Americans already have three centuries of experience behind us in the evolution of higher education and have more resources than any other nation for its further development, we too must proceed less haphazardly in the future than we have in the past. Our resources for education are not unlimited, and we must use them to the best possible advantage. A logical place to start implementing this resolve is within our colleges and universities.

The Need for State
and Regional Coordination

Turning now from problems of form and function on the local level, let us look at similar concerns on state and regional levels. Those of you who have noted the 1963 Robbins report on higher education in Great Britain have doubtless been impressed by the kindred nature of some of our problems. This report mentions that it would be a misnomer to speak of a system of higher education in England today if by "system" one means a consciously coordinated organization. There, as here, institutions have grown up separately, and what system there is has come into being as the result of a series of particular initiatives, concerned with particular needs, and providing no way of dealing conveniently with all of the problems of higher education as a whole. Despite the existence of a University Grants Committee and increasing reliance upon financing from the central government, surprisingly little planning and coordination has resulted. The report goes on to point out important changes now occurring, and to face up to the urgency of still more changes.

Although we are further along than the British in certain respects, virtually all of our states and regions now confront problems that cannot be solved by leaving institutions completely to their own devices. The Robbins study points out weaknesses that derive from a continuing absence of coordinating principles and generalized objectives. This criticism does not mean that all activities must be planned and controlled from one place, but it does suggest more attention to interdependence and less insistence upon independence. As someone has said, unlimited freedom of action must give way to the right to choose within a structure that limits but sustains choice.

One evidence of political limitations on institutional autonomy is an increase in the number of boards having responsibility for the supervision of more than one institution. Although nobody has yet assembled complete and reliable information about coordinating agencies, one source lists nine states as having single boards responsible for governing all public higher education. Twelve other states are reported as having boards with more limited authority over institutions which, in turn, have their individual boards.

Most of these "master" or "advisory" boards exclude professional educators from membership and are comprised of politically appointed laymen with a legislative mandate to establish and maintain coordination. Their most common function pertains to budgetary concerns, and the next most common is some form of program planning. Studies of future needs in higher education, standards, admissions, degree-granting qualifications, forms of accreditation, uniform reporting practices, and related matters are also typical concerns. In addition, many of these boards define institutional objectives, and establish the role and scope of institutions under their jurisdiction.

No other state, so far as I know, has gone as far as California in developing a fully integrated master plan. Its legislatively authorized Coordinating Council for Higher Education has prepared and begun implementing a plan for the "development, expansion, and integration of the facilities, curriculum, and standards of higher education, in junior colleges, state colleges, the University of California, and other institutions of the state, to meet the needs of the state during the next ten years and thereafter."

Even though educational leaders have played active roles in the California council, and have been used in advisory capacities everywhere, the initiative behind mandatory coordination in most states comes from outside, rather than inside, academic circles. In view of the entrenched tradition of institutional sovereignty, the extramural stimulus is understandable, but has the unfortunate aspect that resistance to change often places educators in the role of passive observers rather than active participants in shaping the larger destinies of their institutions.

Moreover, we ought jointly to be making systematic studies of these various schemes, assessing their uses and abuses, and displaying more initiative ourselves in trying to improve the efficiency and effectiveness of our common endeavor. In only a small handful of states have the presidents of both private and public institutions voluntarily come together to form coordinating councils that make decisions and take actions of real import.

Institutions have shown they can function jointly for some common purposes without outside mandate to do so as evidenced by the existence of six regional accrediting associations. Further instances of autonomous institutions working in harness without any compulsion to coordinate their activities are to be seen in the numerous consortium arrangements created in recent decades. Virtually every region and state now has groupings of this kind. They may involve the pairing of a small college and a large university, a newly established institution with an old one, a number of highly developed universities with a plan for sharing very expensive facilities, and what not. They range from simple, bilateral arrangements for the free exchange of student credits to elaborate, multilateral arrangements for joint faculty appointments, coordination of adult education and extension programs, pooling of library resources, cooperative use of radio and television facilities, and other mechanisms. The most comprehensive and formally organized interinstitutional as well as interstate forms of joint planning and activity are exemplified in the three regional compacts, but the sanction behind the Southern Regional Education Board, the Western Interstate Commission for Higher Education, and the New England Board of Higher Education is legislative rather than institutional.

It is no news that these trends are not always welcomed in academic circles. Some hold that most of the politically motivated schemes aim primarily at the reduction of expenditures rather than the promotion of expansion and improvement in higher education. Others may approve the ends in view but deplore the bureaucratic proliferations which seem to accompany these structural changes. Still others in educational ranks go along willingly only with *voluntary* coordination and planning which stem from the institutions themselves. Those who are dubious about the effectiveness of voluntary arrangements, however, argue that they tend merely to preserve the status quo of individual institutions and often ignore the larger public interest.

Meantime, the movements toward more cooperation and coordination proceed mostly without benefit of careful analysis of the forms and processes entailed. Some advocates of particular institutions or particular kinds of institutions continue to display a reluctance to look realistically at what the division of labor ought to be within a given state or region for dealing with teaching, research, and public service functions. Conversely, indiscriminate zeal for cooperation and coordination can lead into hastily considered arrangements that do violence to the integrity of the institutions involved.

With the tremendous costs immediately ahead in the rapid expansion and improvement of higher education, we can no longer afford blunders in the location of institutions, wasteful duplication of programs, unplanned and piecemeal local responses to wider needs, and the general lack of unity which have characterized too many of our collective endeavors in the past. To plan wisely and act decisively, however, we must be guided by judgments based on objective knowledge of the relations between form and function in higher education.

Growing Interdependence

Although decentralization of support and control has long been a dominant motif in American higher education, the growing interdependence of our whole society has produced countervailing influences. These influences are centripetal in nature. Their operation takes place on all levels but comes into focus on the national level. Even the most provincial institutions are necessarily involved in them, and together they form an intricate communications network extending all across the nation. With nerve centers mainly in Washington and New York, numerous educational agencies and organizations, mostly voluntary in their membership, help to give coherence to the American system of higher education.

To begin with, there are dozens of national organizations of individual teachers, scholars, and scientists, ranging from the Ceramics Educational Council with about one hundred twenty-five members to the American Chemical Society with almost a hundred thousand. Even more comprehensive alignments of persons in allied disciplines are to be noted in such organizations as the American Association for the Advancement of Science and the American Council of Learned Societies. Administrative and staff officers also have their national associations. Another basis of national organization is exemplified by segmental parts of institutions and of specialized types of institutions. Representatives of law schools, extension divisions, junior colleges, Protestant colleges, Catholic colleges, urban universities, unaccredited colleges, proprietary schools, and what not are banded together. In the field of student personnel work alone, there are at least thirty different associations and there are more than fifty organizations of whole institutions and segmental parts of them.

In addition, there are several "umbrella" associations, such as the American Council on Education, which include not only institutions but also other associations.

At the national level there are other membership organizations and agencies which perform specialized services. Some examples are the Institute of International Education, the National Merit Scholarship Corporation, the Educational Records Bureau, the College Entrance Examination Board, and the Educational Testing Service. Many special-purpose agencies have been established to handle common problems and cope with issues which cannot be dealt with unilaterally by the nation's twenty-one hundred colleges and universities. The large philanthropic foundations also need to be taken into account as influences on the development of higher education, for they also concern themselves with a large range of college and university matters.

Finally, at the national level there is the federal government itself, with dozens of its agencies involved in higher education. Every college in the country is now affected by federal programs, and many leading universities receive the bulk of their research funds from these sources. Until now a relatively minor factor in American education, the U.S. Office of Education now has a projected budget of $2.15 billion. These and other circumstances reveal that important decisions are no longer being made exclusively at local and state levels, but increasingly are being made at the national level. Even at the national level, unfortunately, many associations and agencies are acting unilaterally. Vested interests are sometimes pushed without regard for the common good, and the agencies representing divergent points of view are so numerous that communication among them is in itself a problem. When the Congress addresses itself to nationwide concerns in higher education, it sometimes hears a babel rather than a chorus of voices speaking from the academic sector.

The need for more cooperation and coordination is thus as obvious on the national level as on each of the other levels. At every juncture we must cope more effectively with issues that ultimately center on flexibility, autonomy, resources, priorities, planning, and the public interest. Local demands must be balanced against wider needs, and short-range pressures against long-range objectives.

The necessity for more and better education no longer has to be argued, nor does the urgency for making a greater investment in it. To move ahead expeditiously, however, we must change some of our ways of thinking about education in general and about higher education in particular. On every campus, more of our best academic minds ought to concern themselves with basic questions of form and function in higher education. Moreover, at the highest policy level, our system of education, hardly less than our postal system, merits cabinet recognition.

In conclusion, I acknowledge that I have no definitive answers to many of the questions raised, but neither does anybody else at the present. Fortunately, we live in a democratic and not an authoritarian society, and I trust that you share my confidence in our ability and willingness to arrive at collective solutions to our common problems. With the proper determination, I am sure that we can maintain and strengthen the American system of higher education to meet our nation's changing needs.

Speaking to the Association of Urban Universities at their meeting in Pittsburgh during the fall of 1964, I discussed the major social changes influencing American higher education and delineated some of the options ahead which would determine outcomes in 1984.

Higher Education and 1984

M Y TEXT is not taken from George Orwell's depressing view of the future. I suggest a look ahead to 1984 in American higher education because two decades is about the time required from kindergarten through a Ph.D. In 1984, some of this year's first-graders will be working on their dissertations.

There was some crystal ball gazing recently on the elementary and secondary educational levels in a booklet published by the World's Fair Hall of Education. It summarizes the forward look of a few schoolmen to the year 2000. They see the child of tomorrow as being able to learn at home by secluding himself in an egg-shaped, plastic "study-sphere" equipped with film screen, television, microphones, tape recorders, and a "complete retrieval system for information from any part of the world." For those youngsters whose parents might prefer not to have them under foot—or under plastic—there would be the option of attending the School of Tomorrow. It is described as a huge, windowless structure covering fifty city blocks, enrolling sixty thousand students, and providing a completely controlled environment.

What a "space age" college or university campus of tomorrow may be like, I have no idea, and I cannot imagine how the student of the future may "plug in" on higher education. But before we begin to visualize strange, egg-shaped structures in which the collegians of 1984 painlessly may acquire knowledge, we might remind ourselves that a good deal of teaching still goes on in buildings erected before 1894. Moreover, I know professors and their students well enough to doubt that anybody ever will be able to design a "completely controlled environment" for them, much less get them to accept it willingly.

Despite the essential conservatism of academic institutions, however, the winds of social change already are being felt. Still to be seen is whether their force will be used to improve as well as expand our educational system and whether that system will be used to the fullest so that we and our children may lead happier and more useful lives.

Social Changes
Affecting Higher Education

Meanwhile, we must look realistically at the social changes affecting higher education and decide what to do about them. The main factors of change which will bring modifications in our educational system are: population growth, technological advance, urbanization, equalitarianism, and internationalism.

The term "population explosion" is familiar to the point of being hackneyed. Everyone knows that we hardly can build new schools fast enough and that many colleges are turning away prospective students. "The tidal wave of students," another cliché, carries the mistaken connotation that it is a temporary phenomenon. Although population growth necessarily must taper off in the future, it looks now as if enrollment in colleges and universities will rise to eleven and a half million by 1984—a figure almost triple the current four million. The certain prospect of more college-age youth, and more wanting to attend college, implies an institutional expansion far beyond anything we have yet seen. We could effect this expansion by tripling the size of existing institutions or by increasing their number from the present two thousand to six thousand. My guess is that we shall compromise between these two extreme courses of action.

As we confront the tremendous task of expanding and improving our whole system of higher education, we ought to be guided wherever possible by what can be learned from research and development focused on education itself. At present, for example, we are relatively uninformed about what makes a good regional balance among junior colleges, four-year colleges, technical institutes, and comprehensive universities. Nobody seems to know much about such a basic consideration as the optimum size for a particular kind of institution. Few persons seem to be giving much serious study to the individual and social implications of the great increase recently in student borrowing as a means of financing education. Meantime, by our actions we are triggering sequences of events which may reach far into the future, and whether we plan ahead or improvise, it can be foreseen that our colleges and universities will have to accommodate vastly increased numbers.

It is unlikely that the educational programs of tomorrow will be simply those of today on a larger scale. Student populations not only will be larger, but also more heterogeneous. Older persons needing to update or extend their knowledge and skills, married women wishing to reenter the labor market, retired persons bored with their enforced leisure, and hosts of others will be looking to our colleges and universities. As the pace of change accelerates, the rate of obsolescence in previously learned patterns also will rise, and formal education for some may well become a lifelong process. Urban colleges and universities may be expected to play especially important roles in the fields of adult and continuing education.

Few of our campuses will survive as neat and tidy little communities apart from the world around them. Already the quiet groves of academe are disappearing in many places as trees and grass give way to high-rise buildings and asphalt parking lots. Nearly everywhere there is heavy two-way traffic between the campus and the community.

In terms of the organization of learning, it seems certain that we shall have more evening and part-time programs, fewer lock-step course and credit requirements, easier student transfer, fewer parochial standards and more national norms of achievement, and fewer disciplinary rigidities and more flexibility. As change takes place, however, we shall need to remind ourselves constantly that doing things differently does not necessarily mean doing them better. I doubt that ten-story dormitories are superior to two-story buildings as environments for student living, and quite a few of us are dubious about the magnitude of campus parking areas as a measure of educational progress. Laxity of standards easily can be mistaken for flexibility of standards, and, hence, those of us who really care about education must do all we can to see that expansion is not attended by dilution in the quality of what will become an increasingly important enterprise.

Turning now from demographic to technological change, one encounters another familiar term, "the explosion of knowledge." I shall not comment here on the involved problems of information storage and data retrieval, curriculum modernization, and improvement in instructional methods. Although it never has been necessary for everyone to know everything, our institutions confront the unavoidable task of having to teach more as knowledge itself multiplies.

We have read and heard much about closed-circuit television, teaching machines, language laboratories, and the various electronic devices expected to revolutionize many kinds of learning. Much less has been said, however, about any drastic efforts to improve the teacher himself. On most campuses he still is left entirely alone in the sanctity of his classroom and laboratory. To be sure, his colleagues criticize and evaluate his research, but few of them pay any attention to his teaching. One of my predictions for the years ahead is that we shall remedy this neglect and thereby greatly improve classroom and laboratory instruction.

The rapid growth of knowledge also will require more general attention to its organization, synthesis, and dissemination. To cope with the continuing expansion of knowledge in virtually all fields and to counter its further fragmentation, we must develop "systems concepts" to educate the kind of human beings who can function in a knowledge-oriented society. In the physical and biological sciences, unifying conceptions already are pulling related disciplines closer together. The practically trained engineering graduate today is the broad generalist rather than the narrow specialist. While it is regarded as heretical in some academic circles to think that the humanities need anything except more financial support, in my opinion they, too, are in need of internal reform. In general, the prospects for revitalizing liberal education never were better, but it will have to be a forward- rather than a backward-looking kind of liberal education.

Another trend of our era which is affecting all levels of education is urbanization. More than 84 percent of the American people now live in 212 metropolitan areas, and these same areas encompass 80 percent of our productive industry. These facts mean that the main burden of the educational job ahead will be upon large urban institutions. Our educational programs, in the main, have to be conducted where the people are, because most students get their advanced training near their homes. About 75 percent of all college students attend less than 25 percent of the existing colleges and universities, with the majority of them in cities of one hundred thousand or more.

It is no wonder that every town of any size wants a college and that every large city wants at least one comprehensive university. Higher education itself has become big business and now is recognized as a growth industry. During the past decade, public expenditures for higher education have gone up from $1 billion to $5 billion, and the next two decades doubtless will witness an even heavier investment. Impressed by the Boston and California education-industry complexes, other metropolitan areas are becoming aware of the need for closer and more effective alliances between the campus and the community.

With a more complex social order accompanying the growth of technology and urbanization, the market for abilities of the uneducated declines as that for the highly educated rises. Trained manpower and science-based industry emerge as determining factors in our economic growth and become no less important than markets, natural resources, and transportation in the continuing prosperity of communities and regions.

Decisions
about Alternatives

In short, it seems that we have moved from a stage in which too little was expected of higher education to one in which we may be expecting too much. None can foresee clearly the implications of new scientific and technological requirements for the labor force, and it would be an error to treat education merely as a dependent variable whose direction is determined solely by forecasts of manpower needs. We must remember that education not only responds to but also helps produce technological advance and economic growth. Moreover, the complex interrelations between educational attainments and the labor force, scientific advance, occupational requirements, and educational planning cannot be reduced to simple formulas.

There is a danger that our colleges and universities may lose their integrity by becoming mere educational service stations or supermarkets. The campus must not be isolated from the world around it, but it must be insulated against pressures that in effect would displace the freedom of teaching and inquiry with a subservience to utilitarian needs of the moment. I would agree that our institutions should be seed beds of ideas for social action programs, but I doubt the wisdom of involving them directly in the operation of such programs. Although urban institutions have as their mission public service no less than teaching and research, we need to guard against overemphasizing the service function at the expense of everything else.

Further, I believe that in our urban institutions and large universities special efforts should be made to offset the growing depersonalization of higher education. As the university becomes involved in more outside concerns, it would be unfortunate if the sense of community among teachers and learners were lost. Many of the best values of higher education are bypassed when students are on the campus merely to attend classes and professors see them only in aggregations. Still another aspect of depersonalization is the tendency to regard the college population as manpower digits and to value the ends of education largely in terms of an increase in the gross national product. I hope that we shall continue to hold to our faith in the improvement of human beings as an end in itself.

And speaking of human beings, despite our national accomplishments in mass education, the movement toward more equalitarianism in American society implies new obligations for many of our colleges and universities. We are all aware that the people at large now sense as never before the crucial role played by our educational system as a determiner of individual life chances. This is why our schools and colleges have been objects of litigation and arenas of conflict in recent years in the struggle for equality of opportunity. As I have said elsewhere, the formal or legalistic resolutions of issues should not lull us into the mistaken notion that the struggle is over. The mere removal of procedural obstacles to equality of educational opportunity gives no assurance that it will become a reality. It is beyond the power of the law to grant educated competence to any individual or category of individuals, and the less dramatic but more involved problems still lie ahead.

In a democratic society, not only do we have an obligation to eliminate discriminations against Negroes and other minorities, but we also have a collective need to do something more positive educationally for all of the culturally deprived. Aside from a moral responsibility, we must make more effective use of education as a means of turning these people into more productive citizens to strengthen our total economy and stabilize our society. We can ill afford to ignore that their needs are, indeed, our needs if this nation is to grow in strength.

We have learned by now that no merely political scheme to redistribute wealth will eliminate the problem of poverty. To level up the bottom groups without also leveling down the top, more effective use must be made of education as a social and economic instrument. Our really basic problem is to make the underprivileged into useful individuals.

Although more of our people must be brought to higher educational levels, with opportunities open to all who have the capability and ambition regardless of their financial means, let us not foster the growing delusion that everybody should go to college or that some kind of academic degree is required as a ticket of entry for every occupation of any respectability. We need to bear in mind also that native differences in ability tend to become more rather than less conspicuous as a result of education.

Moreover, education alone should not be expected to carry the whole burden of furthering equalitarianism and transforming our society. Other social institutions must share in the responsibility for combating ignorance, incompetence, prejudice, delinquency, disorder, and immorality. The products of higher education have enabled us to transform nature, however, and I hope that during the next twenty years we can learn more about how to transform ourselves.

Finally, I come to internationalism as a trend of the times which must receive greater recognition in our system of higher education. The contemporary world is, indeed, growing smaller and educated intelligence no longer can be provincial or parochial. A basic understanding of other cultures and other peoples is increasingly needed by every citizen of our nation, and thus a new dimension must be added to the education of our youth. Most American colleges and universities have foreign students in residence and some of their own abroad, and nearly everywhere a few internationally flavored courses have been added. Notwithstanding these efforts, something more basic than grafting on specialized courses needs to be done to infuse new perspectives into the arts, humanities, and social studies. Perhaps we could borrow some of the conceptual thinking of mathematics and the physical sciences, where fundamental ideas disregard national boundary lines and universal thought modes prevail.

Whatever we choose to do about shaping the future of American higher education, our contemporary colleges and universities and those yet to come are committed by their missions to the development of a broader understanding of mankind and to the furtherance of a civilization whose benefits can be shared by all men. Nobody can foresee just what our nation and the world will be like in 1984, but, as someone has aptly said, civilization is what happens when men have intelligent desires and, within limits, history can be what we want it to be. I hope that our colleges and universities will have important roles in shaping this future.

In these remarks made at a regional meeting of the Association for Higher Education in Seattle, Washington, on December 2, 1966, I singled out for comment some of the main problems and issues in the movement toward the statewide coordination of public colleges and universities and gave a preview of a Council-sponsored inquiry then getting under way.

Statewide Coordination

ALTHOUGH it would be comforting to attribute the independence enjoyed historically by most American colleges and universities to a popular appreciation of the virtues of institutional autonomy, we may as well acknowledge that this independence has been in part a reflection of public indifference to higher education. At the turn of the century, few persons went to college (about 4 percent of the college-age group), and until the last decade or so many campuses were proudly aloof from the communities around them. Wide latitude was permitted in the establishment, support, and control of institutions; local independence in decision making was the rule. Academic matters seldom became political issues, and usually institutions were left relatively free to determine their own role and scope.

The average college or university changed very slowly, and nobody thought much about coordinating the efforts of different institutions. The diversification, decentralization, and institutional autonomy achieved under these circumstances are now widely held to be unique strengths of American higher education.

Recently we have become more aware of the weaknesses that

exist alongside the strengths; unplanned diversification is being called into question as a model for further developments. As higher education becomes more complicated and expensive, pressures for expansion and improvement are often attended by demands for improved efficiency and effectiveness. Although we still pride ourselves on the cultural pluralism of our free society and on the autonomy of our intellectual institutions, the growing importance, cost, and interdependence of educational agencies are forces that compel changes in the tradition.

Higher education, in brief, has become too crucial to the general welfare for its development to be left entirely in local hands. Many of the urgent issues and problems cannot be dealt with adequately by individual institutions acting unilaterally, and piecemeal approaches do not yield satisfactory patterns. With the growing collectivism of modern life, more and more decisions and actions affecting the present and future of higher education are being transferred from the private to the public arena, and from the local to the state or national level.

One evidence of this trend has been the widespread formation in recent years of statewide boards, commissions, or councils designed to give policy direction to public higher education. In our kind of society, the emergence of such agencies has been inevitable and in many respects desirable, but we should not blink the fact that such agencies often reduce the authority of the boards, administrators, and faculties of individual institutions. Considering the tendency of many academics to resist the centralization of educational authority and to scrutinize relentlessly the actions of institutional trustees and administrators, it is indeed astonishing how quiet they have been about the drastic reorganization that has taken place in the governance of public higher education since World War II.

The trend toward statewide coordination has been gaining momentum since the early 1950s, but when the American Council on Education chose "Autonomy and Interdependence: Emerging Systems in Higher Education" as the theme of its 1964 annual meeting, we were hard put to identify more than a handful of individuals who had systematically examined this important subject. As some of you know, Malcolm Moos, Francis Rourke, Lyman Glenny, A. J. Brumbaugh, M. M. Chambers, T. R. McConnell, and a few other writers were the only commentators who had paid much attention to the movement. One outcome of the Council's 1964 meeting, I might add, was the book I edited, *Emerging Patterns in American Higher Education.*

Although the drive for coordination has only recently become widespread, a framework for the statewide regulation of higher education was established by New York State in 1784; moreover, consolidated *governing* boards have long been in existence: Nevada, Montana, and South Dakota each had a state governing board before the turn of the century. Similarly eleven states established the single governing board arrangement between 1900 and 1945. Since 1951, however, the trend has been entirely toward unified *coordination* rather than unified direct governance.

The flux of change, confusions of definition, and other factors prevent giving precise descriptions of the present status of coordination in American higher education. It is hazardous to be categorical, but, according to the best information available, the following statements appear to be correct. Wyoming, Alaska, and Hawaii each have only a single senior-grade public institution within their borders; therefore, they presumably have no problem of coordination. States which are reported to have no single agency for coordinating or directing higher education are Alabama, Delaware, Louisiana, Maine, Nebraska, New Jersey, Tennessee, and Vermont, but I know that in several of these states the matter is under consideration.

Studies
of Coordination

Although state coordination of higher education had not been the subject of much inquiry prior to 1964, the deficiency is being remedied. The Public Affairs Research Council of Louisiana recently published a comprehensive survey, *Coordination and Planning*, that is mostly descriptive in nature. The American Council on Education is currently making a study that has analytical and evaluative emphasis, under the direction of a California political scientist, Robert Berdahl.[1] Our inquiry employs a fivefold classi-

1. *Statewide Coordination of Higher Education* (Washington: The Council, 1971).

fication of existing arrangements. It categorizes the New York scheme, which is unique, as a governing-coordinating board. According to Berdahl's findings, the second category—the single governing board—exists in the following states: Arizona, Florida, Georgia, Idaho, Iowa, Kansas, Mississippi, Montana, Nevada, New Hampshire, North Dakota, Oregon, Rhode Island, and South Dakota. A division within the state board of education has some responsibilities for higher education in Michigan and in Pennsylvania. There is now some form of coordinating council, board, or commission (as they are variously designated) in effect in Arkansas, California, Colorado, Connecticut, Illinois, Kentucky, Maryland, Massachusetts, Minnesota, Missouri, Ohio, Oklahoma, New Mexico, North Carolina, South Carolina, Texas, Utah, Virginia, and Wisconsin. Only three states now have voluntary associations performing coordinating functions: Indiana, West Virginia, and Washington.

In another survey of the subject, J. G. Paltridge, of the Berkeley Center for Research and Development in Higher Education, has noted three main trends in recent years. First, voluntary coordination is giving way to legally established agencies, as exemplified in Colorado, Ohio, and Michigan. Second, coordinating agencies that had only limited regulatory powers are being given broader authority, as in New Mexico and Texas; those groups which hitherto were largely advisory, as in Wisconsin, are becoming more regulatory. Third, organizations whose controlling boards have been composed of institutional representatives are being transformed (for example, in Kentucky and Maryland) into boards composed of lay members representing the general public; a variation of this trend consists of adding more noninstitutional representatives and placing institutional members in nonvoting roles.

From what I have read and heard about the Council of Presidents in the state of Washington, I judge that it has performed the coordinating function well enough to forestall pressures to establish a more formal mechanism with legislatively specified authority, but the trend throughout most of the nation is clearly in another direction. Moreover, to quote from a brochure which the council issued in 1964, "The State of Washington, in terms of the present distribution of types of public institutions for post-high school education, has a happier inheritance than many states." President

Odegaard's recent annual report also notes that considerable agreement exists about the need to establish a fourth state college and to have "a separate system of community colleges organized within 20 districts so defined geographically as to bring community college educational opportunities within a convenient distance of the population in all parts of the state." In passing, I will comment that Washingtonians seem to be able to achieve through cooperation and voluntary association what is accomplished only under political mandate in many other states.

As the Pliner survey for the Public Affairs Research Council of Louisiana points out, most states with coordinating agencies have aegis over all public colleges and universities, though some have separate jurisdictions for junior colleges, and a few draw private institutions into planning and other special activities. A number of states are still undecided about how to draw community colleges and private institutions into unified planning and coordination. It should be noted, however, that the Federal Higher Education Facilities Act of 1963 requires every state to have a single agency to determine building construction priorities among all eligible institutions, private as well as public.

In most states, the coordinating boards for public higher education are appointed by the governor, with the consent of the senate, and are intended to represent the general public rather than individual institutions. Such boards range in size from seven to eighteen members, who serve staggered terms of office varying from four to fifteen years, and who typically meet once a month. They usually elect their own officers, name their committees, and employ their own professional staffs. These staffs range in size from one to twenty.

Functions
of Coordinating Agencies

In the study which the American Council on Education has under way, we shall inquire into the qualifications of board members, their power and prestige in comparison with those of board members for individual institutions, the problems they encounter in staff recruitment, the professional backgrounds of staff members, and many other matters relating to the functioning of these agencies.

The functions of commissions or coordinating boards characteristically involve analysis of institutional budgets for construction, operational cost studies, the development of accounting codes and of uniform policies and procedures, and similar matters. In recent years, these agencies have engaged more intensively in master planning. Such planning entails giving attention to the role and scope of existing institutions, developing criteria for the establishment of new branches and new institutions, and furthering the more efficient use of staff and facilities. Many of the boards not only set priorities for new buildings but also must approve all construction plans. In addition, they review budget requests and make recommendations to the governor and the legislature. Some have devised formula approaches to which all institutions must adhere in their presentations to the legislature.

As to programs, virtually all of the boards have authority to approve requests for new programs and to recommend elimination in cases of unnecessary duplications among existing programs. In fact, in one state, the commission even has the authority to veto individual course offerings. In most places, however, the programmatic focus is not on the details of a particular curriculum, but on high-cost areas such as graduate and professional work where an undue proliferation of programs leads to both waste and mediocrity. Some of the commissions or boards also make recommendations about policies regarding faculty and students.

These coordinating agencies have negative as well as positive reasons for being. Some years ago I was a university president in a large state which had eighteen or twenty degree-granting public colleges and universities. The programmatic duplication among them and the competition for increased funds had become so acute that the legislature placed a ban on all new academic programs. True, there had been a Council of State College Presidents for some years, but their main purpose was to uphold a tacit agreement not to undermine one another in institutional hearings before legislative appropriations committees. Seldom, if ever, did they discuss a voluntary approach to a more sensible division of academic labor among their institutions. To make a long story short, the legislature established a Commission on Higher Education to do for the institutions what they were either unable or unwilling to do for themselves.

This episode, I suspect, illustrates the negative side of the story in a number of other states. Prior to the development of systematic coordination, most states simply had congeries of institutions, some of which were indiscriminately established, inadequately maintained, and poorly directed insofar as serving the best public interest was concerned. With institutional rivalry rather than careful attention to real needs behind some of the seemingly endless vertical and horizontal expansion of local endeavors, it is no wonder that the rich diversity of the education enterprise was at times wastefully competitive. Institutional autonomy run rampant not only increased unnecessarily the price of public higher education but also reduced its overall effectiveness. When rapid population growth and other factors added to the spiral of rising costs, it became obvious in many states that a coordinating mechanism had to be developed. Moreover, governors and legislatures increasingly felt the need for a buffer between themselves and the pressures generated by junior colleges wanting to become four-year institutions, of senior colleges wanting to change into universities, and of universities wanting to expand ad infinitum.

But this recital is by no means the whole story; fortunately, there are many positive reasons for the growth of coordinating agencies. On all sides there has been increased awareness of the need to distribute funds equitably among existing institutions, and to have an orderly plan for their expansion and for the establishment of new institutions. An agency that reviews programs and budgets can be viewed constructively as a means for implementing goals rather than as a device for keeping costs down. The less affluent as well as the more affluent states are now sold on the importance of education as an investment and on the advantages of central planning. Boards or councils specifically charged with responsibility for public higher education can usually do a better job of dealing with complex problems than can governors and legislatures, who must cope with the whole spectrum of public problems.

There is no single type of agency, of course, which is equally well suited to the needs of all fifty states. The scheme that works effectively in a state with only a few public colleges and universities might be inappropriate, even harmful to a state with dozens of institutions. Traditions as well as present circumstances must be considered. Although T. R. McConnell has concluded that the voluntary or informal arrangement has lost its viability almost everywhere, it still seems to function successfully in Washington State. Certain states, as I have mentioned, have successively tried different arrangements, and as yet are not satisfied. The California scheme, widely regarded as a carefully worked-out prototype, is now under fire within the state itself.

In the Fall 1966 issue of the Council's journal, the *Educational Record*, Algo D. Henderson, in a critique of state planning and coordination, points out that central coordination is one thing and central operation another. The real test of coordination, he contends, is effectiveness in achieving goals rather than economy in using funds. Conformity and mediocrity often go hand in hand, and the first public concern should be not with distributing limited funds but with assuring that there be adequate funds to achieve those goals on which high values are placed.

Moos and Rourke, in their book *The Campus and the State*, pointed out in 1959 that colleges and universities are not analogous in most respects to other state agencies. There is an efficiency in allowing freedom to professional workers and others engaged in the higher learning, and permissiveness rather than authoritarianism is the appropriate scheme of governance. It should be remembered, furthermore, that educators themselves have developed regulatory mechanisms and coordinating devices through voluntary associations of individuals and institutions, accrediting agencies, consortia, and various other means.

We need look only at the rebuffs encountered occasionally by the organized medical profession as well as by trade unions to realize, however, that our society's tolerance for syndicalism is limited. In a political democracy it is inevitable that basic problems having to do with the support and control of public higher education—and, increasingly, of private also—should become political issues. Overall state needs necessarily must have priority over the needs and desires of individual institutions. Some of the most critical problems today are interinstitutional rather than intrainstitutional, and politically appointed or elected officials need objective as well as expert advice in the search for solutions. The periodic budgetary requests from individual institutions no longer constitute adequate guidelines for higher education to expand and improve over the next year or two, much less the next decade or two. The long view must be substituted for the annual and the biennial view.

Issues to
Be Resolved

For these and other reasons it is clear why the power structure of higher education has been changing rapidly in most states. A unified view of statewide needs and plans to meet these needs is essential. With greatly increased funding demands, it is unrealistic to maintain that institutions of higher education should somehow be exempt from the tests of efficiency and effectiveness applied to other human enterprises. It is unrealistic also for professional educators to expect that intensified public interest in higher education will not be accompanied by a desire to participate at least indirectly in the critical decisions about its present and future. This groping for new forms of public agencies reflects a healthy awareness of what is at stake. Before we rigidify existing arrangements or too hastily create new ones, however, we educators and the general public need to ask and answer some basic questions. I shall mention a few here:

First, within a state, a region, or the nation, what kinds of decisions are best made by local authority and what kinds by central authority? What are the gains and losses each way? How much of our traditional autonomy must we discard to become more efficient and effective?

Second, to what extent does enlarged public control of higher education inevitably entail more political and less academic participation in planning and conducting the total enterprise?

Third, will the increased use of statewide governing and coordinating bodies result in a more rational approach to the growing problems of support and control? What are the undesirable effects on individual institutions? How can they be minimized? What are the desirable effects? Are trends tending to politicize decisions which ought to be made by professionals? Should the executive officers of these statewide agencies function as chancellors of systems or as secretaries of the agencies appointing them? What role should private colleges and universities play in developing state-wide plans and policies and in achieving common educational goals? What role should community colleges play?

Fourth, what can be done to strengthen the leadership of professional educators? Granting that fundamental questions of educational policy are now being answered with little objective information, what kinds of objective knowledge do we need to correct this deficiency?

Nobody has the answers to all these questions, but we cannot delay further action until we know precisely where we want to go and how to get there in American higher education. Even so, I wish to emphasize that we should not plunge heedlessly into the frenetic activity of developing statewide systems and state schemes to allocate federal funds, implementing the recommendations of anonymous task forces, or bolstering interstate compacts and a multitude of other arrangements which, superimposed on those we already have, may confuse rather than clarify the decision-making process in higher education. I firmly believe that institutional independence must necessarily give way to new forms of interdependence, but as we devise these new forms I think it is a serious mistake to bypass and undermine the recognized leadership of American higher education.

I am concerned about any move which in effect displaces the most experienced institutional leaders (including those on the faculty) and makes them into sideline witnesses of public policy formation. Basic issues in higher education are indeed matters to be determined by the public, but I believe that the public interest requires the active participation of professional educators rather than their complete displacement by politically constituted committees, commissions, and other agencies remote from the real scenes of action. Moreover, I think we need to be cautious about the possibilities of developing central bureaucracies—in either our state capitals or the national capital—that would be prone to claim superior wisdom about what ought to be done to and for our colleges and universities.

With regard to these concerns, I refer again to the study of statewide systems which the American Council on Education is now undertaking. In our inquiry we expect to go into a selected group of states, and we hope to gather firsthand evidence on such matters as: the adequacy of enabling legislation; the quality of planning; the quality and adequacy of agency staff; the ability of states to increase their support for higher education; institutions' flexibility and openness to experimentation; the reactions of administrators, faculties, and students; the degree of insulation from political intervention; effectiveness in increasing accessibility and improving quality of programs. We are giving the researcher and those working with him complete freedom to get at the facts, analyze them objectively, and evaluate them candidly. We are well aware in advance that, since one man's meat may be another man's poison, the reactions we shall encounter will be diverse. We hope, however, that our findings will provide guidelines to a broader consensus.

One of the few items in this book that were originally written to be read rather than heard, this paper appeared in a somewhat different form in a 1968 symposium entitled Campus 1980, *edited by Alvin C. Eurich.*

The National Interest

IN THE PAST, campuses were often merely enclaves in the surrounding society. What happened in higher education was of no great import for most of the adult population, and comparatively few of their sons and daughters went to college. Various levels of government helped support academic institutions, but higher education itself was seldom a political issue. Even when publicly supported, most institutions were left relatively alone to determine their own role and scope. They changed slowly, grew mainly by gradual accretion, and rarely gave much thought to long-range planning.

The persistence of collegiate Gothic or Georgian architecture on the campus, however, belies the fact that, underneath the brick and ivy surface, striking transformation has taken place in American higher education: virtually all colleges and universities are now caught up in the vital concerns of a rapidly changing society. Their former independence or autonomy is being displaced by interdependence with other institutions and agencies. In particular, there is a growing mutuality of relations between institutions of higher education and government.

In recent years certain trends in higher education have been markedly influenced by actions of Congress—in particular, by their indirect support of advanced learning by contracts for goods and services, and by categorical rather than general aid. From some quarters the complaint has been heard that federal funds for research in the physical sciences and engineering have forced the humanities into the background. There is also the familiar criticism that the emphasis on research has resulted in a corresponding neglect of teaching, particularly in the major universities. The liberal arts colleges, in turn, are alleged to have become the neglected members of the whole academic community.

Colleges and universities are much more affected by outside social forces than they once were. To remain viable, they can hardly escape taking into account popular conceptions about what they ought to be. Their curricula are heavily influenced by changing social and vocational requirements; their size, by the rise of large-scale enterprise; their structure, by the growth of collectivism and bureaucracy; their expansion, by population increases; and even their aims, by the requirements which the larger society imposes. And in a democracy, the larger society makes its basic needs and wishes felt through political mechanisms.

Perhaps, then, it is inevitable that higher education should become more politicized, and in many respects this development may be desirable. Although academicians are not as conservative as physicians about the social organization of their enterprise, historians have demonstrated that few of the important innovations in colleges and universities have originated within professorial ranks. Moreover, if institutions were left entirely alone and merely given financial support with no strings attached, wasteful duplication of effort would soon become insupportable. The interrelations of campuses with one another and with other sectors of society as well as the common problems of higher education which necessitate a united approach call for an emphasis on interdependence rather than independence.

But to expect that a united front can be achieved through existing governmental structures is an unwarranted assumption; before it can be accepted, some imperative questions must be answered. Although we appear to be moving toward a national society and a

corresponding nationalization of public policy, the states still contribute more toward the support of basic higher education than
does the federal government. They do so despite inherent limitations in their tax structures and despite the irrationality of using
state boundary lines as bases of compartmentalization in planning
to meet the nation's future educational needs. Moreover, existing
confusions about the spheres of responsibility and authority in relations between the states and the federal government obscure still
further the feasibility of using present political approaches to solve
nationwide educational problems.

Although this country has no National University, most of
our leading colleges and universities are indeed national in the
scope of their service. How can the sights of other institutions be
raised without discouraging local initiative? How can a national
effort be made to improve higher education in some states and
regions without indirectly forcing others down to a common level?
These are merely some of the questions now up for discussion and
action in the political arena.

Since the answers to them affect the life chances of millions of
Americans and bear directly on the future of the nation, it is inevitable that educational issues become political issues. The politicalization of higher education is in effect a public tribute to its greatly
enhanced importance. The challenge to all who really care about
colleges and universities is, not to try to turn back the clock of
history, but to make the most of the reality we now confront.

The Federal
Involvement

Sentiments favoring decentralization, the nature of federalism,
and constitutional problems of separation of church and state—these
and other factors have caused the historical pattern of federal
involvement in higher education to be primarily indirect, project-
oriented, diverse, and sometimes contradictory. Three kinds of federal involvement were established as early as one hundred years
ago: (a) direct establishment and operation of institutions; (b)
direct endowments of land and funds to aid state or local establishments and operations; and (c) indirect support of the advancement of knowledge by contracts for goods and services. These

historical approaches are being supplemented by loans and grant-in-aid programs for educational facilities and students. All of these approaches have been aimed primarily at meeting specific government needs; only indirectly or secondarily have they been intended to fulfill national educational purposes. Thus, federal involvement in higher education is, at the same time, both productive and erosive; a more coherent approach is called for.

While the federal government has been as sensitive as the institutions themselves about centralized control and domination, a growing recognition that the output of higher education—manpower, goods, and services—is essential and integral to the social welfare of the people and the national interest has furthered federal involvement. Serious national concern about education was manifested in the past several decades by the Hoover National Advisory Committee on Education Report in 1931 and the Truman Commission Report in 1948; but the passage of the National Defense Education Act in 1958 finally gave legislative recognition to the nexus between the needs of the nation and higher learning. In addition, the growing use of government funds to procure services from institutions has taken on a new political interest not only because of its increased volume but also because of its direct relationship to the needs of the government.

The complexity and indirectness of federal aid has created between government and higher education a relationship which defies simple categorization. It can be called a buyer-seller affiliation, in the sense that the university sells goods and services. It can be called a doctor-patient relationship, in the sense that the university diagnoses and treats the ills of society. It can be called a lawyer-client association when the university gives advice to various branches of government; and certainly it can be called a mortgagor-mortgagee relationship when the government assumes the role of banker in lending money to institutions for educational facilities. Because the relationships are so diverse and so encompassing, the output of the university so essential to the government, and the funds of the government so necessary if the purposes of education are to be fulfilled, the university has evolved into what might be called a quasi-governmental institution.

Although a basic mutuality of interest prevails, the form and manner in which federal funds flow into the educational sector often produce tensions. The policy of categorical grants and contracts, for instance, may distort institutional objectives and deplete institutional resources. The government requirement that institutions share the cost of research projects—some of which are not related to institutional purposes—may be disadvantageous to the institution, which must then spend its own funds on projects external to its basic interests. The fierce competition for federal funds which pits school against school, department against department, and scholar against scholar, results in disunity and a weakening of loyalty to the institution.

The machinery of "advice"—task forces and advisory panels to the federal government—has also become a subject of controversy. To the arguments of the "insiders" that laissez faire, based on the merit principle, is the best way to run science, the "outsiders" have responded that, under this system, much merit goes undetected and that in any case one government mission must be to build excellence wherever the potential exists. The government's reliance on the project system and its understandable concentration of research in institutions of demonstrated excellence (to the extent that twenty-five universities get 60 percent of the federal research grants) may perpetuate an imbalance in the quality of institutions.

Although few would argue that project support should be reduced or that funds should be diverted from the great centers of learning, it is contended that ways must be found to produce a wider geographic spread of participation and to permit more institutional determination of what research and which researchers are to be supported. Recognizing these problems, a recent presidential statement on research contracts emphasized: (a) that funds should be distributed so as to improve quality where it is not at present high, and (b) that quality where it already exists must be supported. For these aims to be realized, of course, there must be sufficient funds for both.

Thus, indirect approaches for supporting higher education as a means of broad development are being questioned. Should cost sharing in government-supported research continue to be the norm? Or, should funds be provided over and above the full cost of such research as means of strengthening total institutional programs? Should all research-supporting agencies develop programs of institutional grants as supplements to project grants for the support of basic research? Can ways be found to involve more institutions in the government research effort without sacrificing quality and without weakening leading institutions?

Other indirect approaches for supporting higher education— such as tax laws and various federal policies which would encourage the states and private philanthropy to make more funds available for institutional budgets—are being explored. Directly and indirectly, the federal government is being asked to offset the increasing budget deficits and higher charges levied on students.

The cost of education is such today that a dualistic system, one which balances the public with the private sector, cannot be maintained without governmental aid to private education. Those who plan for higher education's future are confronted by such critical problems as how public funds can be acceptably channeled to support private institutions, which institutions should receive this assistance, and under what circumstances, and whether it is constitutional to underwrite church-related colleges and universities.

Because of its expanded needs, the nation can make full use of the facilities afforded by virtually all private institutions. Economically, it makes no sense to establish new institutions while staff and space in existing colleges and universities go underutilized. More important, in the minds of many, is the desirability of maintaining a pluralistic system of higher education and avoiding a monolithic scheme of support and control. A strong independent sector, it is argued, not only has its intrinsic values in a democratic society, but also is a useful competitive element and counterbalance to the public sector. Forcing private institutions to become just like their public counterparts to become eligible for tax support would indeed diminish their values for preserving a dualistic system.

Although educators do not object to governmental regulation and surveillance in the transportation industry, in the food and drug industry, and in other areas, most of them are strongly opposed to similar controls over the quality and quantity of education. Taxpayers, on the other hand, are understandably reluctant to exempt institutions of higher education from accountability for the expenditure of public funds, and to leave the purposes of academic enterprise to institutional determination. The growing interrelations of government and higher education therefore give rise to new challenges in the present and future.

Basic Policy Issues and Higher Education

Some of the circumstances affecting the present and future of American higher education are matters of fact rather than of opinion or preference. Population growth and increased student demand, the needs of a complex economy for more highly trained manpower, an egalitarian push for equality of advanced educational opportunity, spectacular and unanticipated gains in knowledge—these and other circumstances are not debatable. But about the kind of educational system our society ought to have in response to changing needs, there are diverse opinions and preferences. And there is also a growing recognition that today's basic policy decisions *shape* as well as *anticipate* tomorrow's world.

In a rapidly changing society, tradition as a guideline for long-range development is necessarily weakened. Old ways of thinking and doing in higher education lose their viability. Moreover, the pressures to expand and improve the educational system cannot be met by gradual, unplanned growth. The establishment of a new medical school, for example, requires years of planning and the advance commitment of at least $30 million to $40 million. The output of scientists and engineers, unlike the output of automobiles, cannot be stepped up overnight simply by overtime on assembly lines already in existence. The growing sentiment to universalize fourteen rather than twelve years of formal education and the need to revolutionize technical education pose public policy questions which call for decision and action now.

One set of issues centers on the broad question, Who should go to college? Even though some institutions are becoming more selective, the system as a whole is becoming less so, as is evidenced in the constantly increasing proportion of the college-age group enrolled in college. In plans for the future, places will have to be provided somewhere for all high school graduates who wish to continue their formal education. This broader clientele implies, of course, that in the future educational purposes and standards will be even more widely diverse than they have been. It also implies that the public must assume more responsibility for financing both institutions and individuals.

The public junior or community college is one answer to the problem of providing relatively low-cost higher education on a massive scale. These institutions already represent a fast-growing sector in American higher education, and their proponents champion them as the best way of handling the problem of sheer numbers. Others, however, believe that the junior college is in actuality little more than a two-year extension of high school, lacking in many of the opportunities to be found in senior colleges and universities. They would argue that comparable educational programs are no less costly in one type of institution than in another.

For the young person of considerable talent and affluence, whether he will go to college is seldom a real question, and where he will go is largely a matter of personal choice. But for the individual of average ability and very limited financial means, whether he will go to college and where depends largely on the opportunities that society provides for him and his kind. Mass education, in contrast to elite education, is therefore intricately bound up with public policy issues. An interesting example of a publicly determined approach to the "institutional mix" of educational opportunities is illustrated by the state of California. At present, California maintains seventy-four (a total of more than one hundred is projected by 1980) publicly supported junior colleges which admit all high school graduates, eighteen state colleges which have four-year curricula and some graduate offerings for students who finish in the top third of their high school graduating classes, and the University of California, with its nine campuses which are open only to those high school graduates who finish in the top eighth of their classes. The California system thus represents not only a carefully planned and controlled division of labor among institutions, but also a deliberate stratification of educational opportunity.

The state of New York, where private higher education has historically been the dominant pattern, has approached the "who shall go to college and where" question differently: their system of state scholarships gives the holders more individual choice, and in effect has subsidized persons rather than institutions. It should be noted, of course, that New York is beginning an intensive development of public institutions and that California, by means of low student charges in public institutions, has indirectly subsidized individuals as well as the colleges and universities under state control.

Issues having to do with expanding and improving educational opportunity must be looked at in relation to issues of support and control. Some states are already committed to providing further opportunity for all high school graduates who want it; but others have made no public decisions so far about how far down the talent ladder the "equal access" principle is to extend. In some states, public assistance goes only to public institutions and to the students enrolled in them; in others, state assistance is provided to private institutions as well as to individuals, who may attend any accredited college or university where they can gain admission.

A current difficulty in choosing sensibly among the alternatives available for the expansion and improvement of educational opportunity is our lack of objective knowledge to use as a guideline in anticipating the varied consequences of such matters as public assistance to institutions (including private) versus public assistance to students; massive scholarship versus massive student loan programs; the most appropriate governmental level—local, state, federal—for determining various needs and priorities.

As has been noted, the federal government has in recent years concerned itself increasingly with all of these public policy questions. In the past, our long-established tradition of decentralization and the existence of federalism in matters of education has tended to relegate central government to the role of giving grants-in-aid to states and to other agencies of education. But of late the federal government has more and more become the prime mover. The heavy commitment of local and state revenues to established programs and the availability of more discretionary funds on the federal level has, of course, made Washington's innovative role more feasible.

In any event, it is clear that vastly more financial support will be required to underwrite the necessary changes in American higher education. This enlarged investment is likely to be accompanied by alterations in traditional forms of support and control. But how? Can existing institutions be utilized more effectively and expansion accomplished more economically by increased public aid to private institutions? Is it fair to this generation of college students and to future generations to force them to carry a heavier part of the financial burden of higher education through spiraling tuition charges and loan programs? Will increased federal support programs have the effect of reducing state, local, and private support? At what point should increased public support (as a percentage of the gross national product or of the total tax dollar) begin to level off? At what points and for whom does an increased investment in higher education cease to pay off? These are some of the unresolved issues that require greater understanding and consensus if we are to plan more intelligently for our educational future.

To move ahead effectively, we also need to develop a more efficient organization of higher education, and this we are already beginning to do. State-supported institutions are coming more and more under the jurisdiction of coordinating councils or commissions. Both public and private colleges and universities are evolving consortia. Nationwide associations and the federal government, in the effort to foster developments needed to solve nationwide problems, exert influences which emphasize the interdependence and coordination of educational activity. In short, social mechanisms for interinstitutional decision making are being developed.

Meantime, it is obvious that uncertainty and confusion still exist about which sorts of decisions are best made by centralized authority and which by localized authority. There is no consensus about how much voice the federal government should have in the planning, direction, and conduct of the total enterprise, or about whether the wide diffusion of authority in Washington itself is advantageous or disadvantageous from the point of view of higher education. Nobody has as yet made an objective assessment of the uses and abuses of statewide governing or coordinating bodies, even though they continue to increase in number. In many states, the question of the role of private colleges and universities is either bypassed or dealt with ambiguously in the development of statewide policies and plans. Whether the regional compacts will increase or decrease in importance, and what effects the Education Commission of the States will have upon state and federal legislation are not yet clear.

Aside from the issues and problems relating to interinstitutional organization and decision making, there are many concerns having to do with the patterning of individual institutions. Of vital concern to the public at large is the development of the right numbers and types of postsecondary institutions to accommodate the expanded college population between now and 1980. What is the most economical and effective division of labor among different kinds of institutions for handling students of different ability levels, for emphasizing varied programs, for providing general and special, professional and graduate education? Does the present tendency of too many institutions to imitate indiscriminately the largest and most complex institutions dilute quality and undermine diversity? How much uniformity of patterning is desirable from one state or region to another? Should lay boards and commissions be empowered to establish those patterns? Who should decide the relative emphases on teaching, research, and public service for a particular institution?

Our resolution of these public policy issues will be heavily influenced, of course, by the relative values we attach to freedom and order, to equality and excellence, to the particular and the universal, to present satisfaction and future benefit. To make the Great Society a reality, it is manifest that wise discernment and resolute action are called for if higher education is to be a main instrument for its achievement.

Governmental Planning
for Higher Education

Whether by drift or by direction, public policy issues do get resolved. In a rational society the resolutions of issues are responses not only to existing pressures but also to anticipated problems and to mental images of future states of affairs considered to be desirable. More governmental involvement in the outcomes of higher education therefore implies more governmental involvement in planning, and in a period of rapid growth present decisions and actions necessarily must be oriented toward the future. Through their elected or appointed representatives in government, citizens are in a position to choose those alternatives that appear to offer the greatest gains and fewest losses. But in realistic planning, as contrasted to utopianism, feasibility no less than desirability must be taken into account. Governmental or any other kind of planning is thus an idle enterprise without the means of realization; however, a special advantage of governmental planning is that the body politic can command greater resources than any other agency.

Moreover, political decision making is an effort to shape the future and can become a basis for prediction in human affairs. To be sure, no present decision is likely to have much effect on the size of the college-age population in 1980, for it has already been born. No legislative or other current deliberations can do much to alter the forecast that an increasingly complex society will have a greater need for highly trained individuals. Some things are already known about the needs to be met between now and 1980. The responses we make to these and other circumstances through planning will constitute an effort to "invent the future" of higher education.

Even though nobody can predict at this point in time precisely what the pattern of higher education will be more than a decade hence, we need to take into consideration as many important elements as possible and proceed with strategies of implementation. It can be anticipated, for example, that more adults, through continuing education, as well as young persons will have to be accommodated by colleges and universities. Proportionately more of them will live in highly urbanized environments—a locale where 40 percent of the college-age group already goes beyond the secondary school level, as contrasted to 14 percent in 1938. If we are not to retrogress educationally, our nation has no option but to enlarge vastly the scale of operations in higher education. Even without drastic alterations in the character of education per se, this change in scale means that a wider diffusion in the process itself is of considerable significance.

It is likely that the public sector of our economy will continue to expand at the expense of the private sector. Some economists assert that whereas governments in advanced, non-Communist nations now distribute about 30 percent of the national income, this proportion will go to anywhere between 40 and 50 percent. This general trend in turn will influence the movement in higher education toward increased public support and control.

During recent years many individual campuses have engaged in planning, but equally notable has been the rise of governmental planning for whole systems of higher education. To plan more intelligently, we need to know more about educational inputs and outputs of existing programs and institutions. What are the determinants of demand for higher education for a given institution? for a state or region? for the nation? Is a national testing program desirable, or inevitable? Do we take into account sufficiently the changing and improving technology of education? Will collective bargaining become a more prevalent mode of behavior in the academic profession? Should the changing attitudes of students be given more prominence in educational planning? To what extent can colleges and universities assume further obligations of general social reform and uplift without weakening their capacity to conserve, diffuse, and advance the traditional higher learning?

Although it would be helpful to know in advance the answers to these and similar questions, planning cannot be delayed until all relevant data are in hand. The exercise of planning, moreover, is useful as a means for reaching a consensus about goals and their implementation. As contrasted with "muddling through," planning is more likely to identify basic problems, anticipate changes affecting higher education, and appraise the predictable consequences of alternate modes of action. Through planning, appropriate strategies can be devised to achieve some outcomes and forestall others.

In a democratic society where higher education is heavily supported by government, and where progressively more people want to be heard on educational issues, it is to be expected that government itself should become a planning mechanism. As already noted, this is already happening on state levels, where commissions and coordinating boards project the lines of development for statewide systems of higher education. Although nothing resembling a master plan for American education has yet emerged in the nation's capital, past and present actions of the federal government have markedly influenced the directions of many institutions and of the entire system. By granting or withholding funds, the federal government makes its influence felt. Contracts and grants-in-aid have accelerated scientific research, added momentum to campus building programs, fostered graduate study, encouraged student borrowing, and in many other ways expressed political determinations of priorities for present and future development.

It would be an error to conclude, however, that federal support for higher education has been guided by a coherent set of principles. Federal funds have been used and doubtless will continue to be used to underwrite both expansion and improvement, the status quo and innovation, uniformity as well as diversity, and to supplement as well as complement moneys from local, state, and private sources. In no instance has federal involvement supplanted local or other control. The strength of public sentiments favoring a dispersed direction of higher education development is likely to continue in the foreseeable future, and hence it is improbable that a master plan emanating from Washington would gain much acceptance.

Out of deference to such sentiments, federal officials are careful to refer to central government as the "junior" or "silent" partner in the enterprise of higher education. Federal underwriting of the cost of higher education has already grown to an estimated one-fourth of the total outlay, nonetheless, and the proportion is likely to increase in the future. Under such circumstances, how long is the silent partner role likely to last?

With the general movement toward managerial forms of government and the spending of larger and larger sums of public funds, it is perhaps unrealistic not to anticipate more governmental voice in setting educational standards. A national testing program is already in the formative stage for lower levels of education, and the same arguments can be made for a similar program of higher levels. Those persons who are held accountable for the expenditures of public funds are likely also to insist on cost-effectiveness and cost-benefit analyses in an effort to further more rationality about spending procedures.

Aside from the prospects of more governmental involvement in the assessment of existing educational programs utilizing public funds, there is a growing interest on the part of politically elected representatives in shaping the future of American higher education. The President and many members of the Congress, for example, are committed to the promotion of more equality of educational opportunity. The U.S. Office of Education uses federal funds to implement civil rights legislation in such matters as the admission of students and the employment of faculty and staff. The virtually oligarchical control that scientists and other professionals formerly exercised through panels and other mechanisms over the expenditure of research funds for selected institutions is likely to be lessened by political pressures for a wider geographic and institutional spread of support.

As our nation moves toward universal higher education, with the vast sums of money required for expansion, it is probable that the federal government will assume even broader responsibilities of support and influence. But it is most unlikely that its support and control will ever become total, or even predominant. This means that the federal involvement will continue to be selective.

To maintain the assets of a pluralistic system of higher education and to avoid the liabilities of a monolithic scheme, the federal involvement should remain limited. Governmental planning for the future of education should stem from all levels of government, not just one level. The private sector needs to be maintained and strengthened, not submerged. On all levels and in both sectors there must be more joint thinking about the future, but no single agency can possibly have a monopoly of vision about what that future will be or ought to be.

Meantime, we should continuously remind ourselves that diversity of support and control are main strengths of the American system of higher education. They permit flexibility and experimentation. They foster a healthful competition among individuals and institutions. They forestall an irretrievable commitment to a single course of action which might in the long run be disastrous for all. Colleges and universities, to be sure, share heavily in a common obligation to create a greater society and a better world, but to do so they must be reasonably free to shape as well as serve, to criticize as well as innovate. To be of maximum value, they cannot become government agencies; rather, they must be upheld and improved as intellectual institutions.

On several occasions I have lectured on educational sub-jects before predominantly military audiences at the National War College. This lecture was given in Washington, D.C., September 23, 1968; in brief compass, it represents my attempt to cover a far-reaching topic suggested by the military.

Educational Systems and National Power

WARFARE, as this audience well knows, is a dramatic test of national power. Although the assessment of a nation's educational strength is never so starkly dramatized, the importance of educational outcomes for collective survival and well-being is now universally recognized. In the advanced nations, the demand for highly trained manpower and the public concern with institutions designed to produce it are unprecedented. Even in backward and impoverished countries, strenuous efforts are being made to extend and improve educational systems. If brief, there is almost everywhere an awareness that no nation can keep pace with the contemporary world without an adequate investment in formal education.

Until lately, however, economists and others have given little systematic thought to the question, What is an adequate investment in education? We have long known that more education increases individual earning power, and we have recently learned that it contributes substantially to gains in the gross national product. One research, for example, has compared enrollment ratios in three age groups (5–14, 15–19, and 20–24) with per capita GNP in a number of different countries and has noted striking correlations for the higher age groups.

Still another inquiry has formulated a composite index measured by enrollment at the secondary level of education as a percentage of the age group 15–19 and by enrollment in higher education as a percentage of the age group 20–24. It found that the average advanced nation is thirty-eight times higher in the index than the average undeveloped country. In the proportion of scientists and engineers, the discrepancy is even larger, with seventy times more of them in advanced nations.

The cost of education as a proportion of both government expenditure and national income has been rising in recent years in nearly all countries. Education expenditures as percentages of national income for some nations I want to compare run as follows: United States, 4.6; England, 4.2; France, 3.0; West Germany, 3.6; Russia, 7.1; and Japan, 5.7. Although I have no figures comparing the gross national products of these same nations, about ten years ago the United States and Russia were reported to be spending at about the same rate.

In our own nation education is the biggest single business; we lead all other countries in both the number and proportion of individuals engaged in educational enterprise. Notwithstanding this favorable status, we confront many unresolved issues relating to the expansion and improvement of our system. For purposes of later discussion, and without comment here, I mention some of the issues: At what levels of government should the various kinds of investment in education be made? Is diversity of support (and control) being undermined in this country? What justifications are there for allocating public funds to private institutions? To what extent should the federal government control the expenditure of federal funds for education? Are decisions about priorities becoming too politicized? Can there be an equal push for excellence and egalitarianism? Beyond high school, what educational costs should students themselves be expected to bear? At what points and for whom does an increased investment in education cease to pay off?

Turning now from investments in education, it is useful to look at some other salient features of our system and compare them with those of other advanced systems. My figures are not current but they are recent enough to be meaningful. For a recent year, the ratio of children in the age group 15–19 getting secondary education was highest in the United States (95.3) and in England (82.1), and lowest in the U.S.S.R. (33.9). Japan had a ratio of 79.4; France, 58.8; and West Germany, 55.3. Despite these figures, there is much concern in this country, as you know, about our dropout rate. Of the three million American students who leave secondary education each year, a million stop at high school graduation, a million go on to college, and the rest drop out before graduation.

In the matter of accessibility of educational opportunity, however, the United States has been and still is ahead of the nations being compared here. This comparative position prevails on the primary and secondary levels. The difference is even greater for postsecondary training, where the comparative higher education ratios of students to the total population aged 20–24 are 33.2 in the United States, 11.8 in the U.S.S.R., 9.8 in France, 8.4 in Japan, 7.9 in England, and 6.1 in West Germany.

The United States has long had universal primary and secondary education and now appears to be moving toward universal higher education for all who want it and can benefit from it. As we move in this direction, we confront a number of basic questions, such as the following: What should our guidelines be for the expansion of existing institutions and the establishment of new ones? How can a more economical and effective division of labor be developed for handling different ability levels of students, varied program emphases, general and special education, graduate and professional education? What can be done about the university syndrome? How much uniformity of educational opportunity should there be throughout the nation?

Variations in Educational Opportunity

Any comparison and appraisal of educational systems should involve inquiry into the nature as well as the accessibility of opportunity. In this regard, advanced nations show more similarity on lower levels than on higher. In commenting on higher education, one observer has noted that the United States seems to develop programs largely in response to consumer or student demand. Until quite recently, in England the substance of higher education was mainly determined internally by academic tradition. Soviet Russia, as one might expect in a totalitarian state, centrally estimates manpower needs, fixes academic programs in consonant terms, and channels students accordingly.

As the 1963 Robbins report commented about education in Russia:

> Education is constantly and directly used both as an instrument of social policy and to manipulate the supply of trained manpower in a deliberate and detailed manner quite foreign to the western way of thinking. Higher education is completely professional in aim. Each course earns a qualification entitling the holder to practice in some branch of the economy. The total enrollment of the universities and colleges in the Soviet Union is determined by the requirements of the nation for specialists.

Although France does not have a totalitarian approach to education, its Ministry of National Education controls practically all public establishments. On the higher education level, staffing and budgets are subject to detailed state control, most academic appointments fall within the minister's province, and there is a central determination of admissions policies, curricula, examinations, and academic awards.

In Germany, the pattern of school organization varies considerably from one state to another, and institutions of higher education are controlled in the main by the various states rather than by the central government. The tradition of *Lehrfreiheit* and *Lernfreiheit* in universities has made educational responses to changed national needs rather slow and has resulted in an overcrowding of existing institutions. Also, it has complicated the rational allocation of expensive research facilities—a problem common, incidentally, to many countries in recent years.

Higher education in Japan is provided in junior colleges and in a number of universities, the most prestigious of which is the University of Tokyo. About 43 percent of the universities are public, as are 23.6 percent of the junior colleges. All universities come under the jurisdiction of the Minister of Education, with government subsidies granted in limited amounts to private universities for special purposes only.

A *Harper's* article by John Fischer in May 1967 made some pointed comparisons between American and European higher education. In one section pertinent here, he wrote: "Europe is suffering a major cultural lag. It has fallen far behind both the United States and Russia in modern technology, and in the education which produces it. As a consequence, it is suffering a hemorrhage of talent, as many of its ablest scientists, engineers, doctors and managers seek wider opportunities in America."

In connection with Mr. Fischer's observations, it should be noted that England is now expanding its system of higher education and countering the conservatism of what is called "Oxbridge" by establishing new institutions more closely attuned to the industrial and commercial needs of a nation short in the highly trained manpower required to compete in a technological age. Also, since government contributions to university operational costs have risen from 35 percent to 75 percent in the last three decades, nationally determined allocations regarding faculty, students, curricula, capital plant, and research are beginning to affect local policies.

Aspects of American and Russian Higher Education

No foreign system of education approaches American education in either the accessibility or variety of educational opportunities afforded, even though we really have no formalized system of education in the United States. On the primary and secondary level, there are almost fifty thousand basic administrative units, each with a large measure of independent control of schools. On the higher level, there are more than twenty-two hundred colleges and universities, many of which have considerable autonomy.

In general, all levels of our system are more affected by outside social forces than they once were. State departments of education and the U.S. Office of Education, not to mention regional accrediting associations and other agencies, are counterforces to parochialism in primary and secondary education. The increased mobility of our population and the employment of increased proportions of our total manpower by nationwide corporations demand increased uniformization of scholastic standards.

American higher education has until recently been organized

largely in discrete units, with local boards, administrators, and faculties exercising considerable power, but this scheme is changing. Public institutions within the states are coming more and more under some degree of influence from coordinating councils or commissions. Public as well as private institutions are evolving consortia. Both national associations and the federal government, concentrating on national as distinguished from strictly local problems, are emphasizing the interdependence and coordination rather than the independence of institutions. This collective effort to achieve broad objectives inevitably results in standardization and politicalization.

Some of the problems and issues we now face in relation to the trends of change are these: What kinds of educational decisions are best made by centralized authority and by localized authority? How much of our traditional pluralism must we discard to achieve more efficiency and effectiveness? Which aspects of institutional autonomy must we safeguard for functional reasons? In a democratic society, to what extent are we justified in making education an instrument of social policy? What role should the federal government play in attempting to set directions for educational development?

In considering such questions as these, we need to remember that the public expects formal education to do many things. Institutions have an obligation to perpetuate and enrich our cultural heritage. Not only do we look to all of them to diffuse existing knowledge, but also to some of them to invent and discover new knowledge. We expect them to produce useful citizens, and to help solve a multitude of problems that beset us.

The pursuit of knowledge for its own sake is recognized as one proper function of colleges and universities, of course, but we are now stressing more than ever before the trained manpower functions of education. In this regard it is of interest to compare the United States with another major world power, Russia. In 1959, the latest year for which I found data, the Soviet Union had only two-thirds as many persons with partial and completed secondary education. At the professional level, the Soviet Union produced during the thirty-five years 1926–60, 4,525,000 graduates from higher educational institutions, or about 40 percent less than were trained in the United States (7,650,000) during the same period. But the Soviet Union graduated 1.8 times as many engineers, 2.4 times as many agricultural specialists, and 2.4 times as many medical doctors. In the same period, we produced about 795,000 graduates with majors in science, as compared with 485,000 in Russia. Different emphases in Soviet and American efforts in developing highly trained manpower over the period 1926–60 may be noted from Table 1.

TABLE 1: *Higher Education Graduates in the U.S.S.R.*
and the United States, by Field, 1926–60

Field	Percentage of All Graduates	
	U.S.S.R.	United States
Theoretical and applied science		
Engineering.................................	27	9
Medicine...................................	11	3
Agriculture.................................	9	2
Natural and physical science.................	10	10
Total...................................	57	24
All other fields (humanities, social sciences, business administration, jurisprudence, etc.)..........	43	76

Source: Study Group in the Economics of Education, *Economic Aspects of Higher Education* (Paris: Organisation for Economic Co-operation and Development, 1964), p. 142.

Also revealing is a projection of the percentage of the age group expected to enter higher education in 1968–69 in all fields of study and at all levels; this projection sets the percentage for the United States at 46 and for the U.S.S.R. at 32. A similar projection of the size of the age group expected to complete higher education for the years 1971–72 gives 3,453,000 in this country and 4,019,000 in Russia. Within five years, in other words, it is anticipated that the Soviets will be sending more students on to higher education and graduating more of them.

Although the Russians appear to be moving ahead of us in sheer magnitude of educational enterprise, there has in general been no diminution of effort in the United States in recent years. As a percentage of our gross national product, the figure for all education rose from 5.0 percent in 1960 to 6.3 percent in 1966. For higher education, the corresponding figures are 1.3 percent and 2.1 percent. (I have not been able to obtain recent figures for the U.S.S.R.)

Educational Inputs
and Outputs

Most of our states in recent years have greatly increased their expenditures for education on all levels. Private giving is evidenced in the success of some of our leading independent colleges and universities in raising unprecedented sums of money. The federal government has also been channeling greater sums into education and research. Several dark clouds, however, are beginning to loom in this otherwise bright picture. Last year, for the first time since 1957, gifts and bequests to institutions showed a decline. This year, for the first time in a number of years, there is every indication that federal assistance will level off; with inflation and increased numbers of students, this outlook portends a drop in real support.

The human as well as material input and output of our educational system in the United States has less centralized direction than in most other countries. Even though we have more planning and coordination than we once had, the determinants of demand for education for a single institution, a state, region, or the whole nation are influenced by many fortuitous circumstances. In a democratic society we use financial and other inducements (grants-in-aid, scholarships, fellowships, loan forgiveness, and so on) to attract human talent into certain fields, but we do not impress individuals into particular fields of study or into occupations (other than the military) where trained manpower is in short supply. Furthermore, as Frederick Harbison has pointed out, formal education is only one of several important components in a nation's development and utilization of its human resources. In addition to formal education, he has identified four other elements: employment generation, training and development in employment, movements of manpower with critical skills, and planning and strategy development.[1]

Applying what Harbison has said about the utility of a systems analysis approach to educational planning for underdeveloped countries, I would argue that the same mode of thinking would be fruitful in our own nation. One main objection to indiscriminate

1. "A Human Resource Approach to the Development of African Nations" (Washington: American Council on Education, Overseas Liaison Committee, 1971).

federal general aid to education on all levels, it seems to me, is that it tends to underwrite a laissez faire approach and to underestimate the importance of a coordinated outlook on national needs. Although I agree with Congresswoman Edith Green and others that superior judgment does not necessarily have its locus in Washington, I have more confidence in the wisdom of the Congress than in most state legislatures, and in the U.S. Office of Education than in most state departments of education. Another reason for my belief in the importance of continuing categorical aid is that it is more likely in the long run to supplement than to supplant private, local, and state support.

A federal concern for the input and output of American education, as you will recall from our history, goes back to the time of Washington and Jefferson. The Northwest Ordinance of 1787 set aside lands for the development of public schools. The Morrill Act gave us our land-grant colleges and universities. The Hoover National Advisory Committee on Education Report in 1931, Truman Commission Report in 1948, and the 1957 Report of the President's Committee on Education Beyond the High School are evidences of a national interest in problems that transcend any particular institution, locality, or state. The National Defense Education Act in 1958 and the Economic Opportunity Act in 1964 exemplify efforts to cement the close connections between national welfare needs and our educational system.

Planning
and Evaluating

All of these steps, however, stop short of anything resembling a master plan for American education. None of the schemes presupposes policy-makers with centralized authority to determine what our educational inputs and outputs should be for short-range needs and long-range goals. Instead, virtually every scheme is based on the assumption that our system will respond to social and economic needs. As we endeavor to peer into the future, we therefore might ask ourselves such questions as the following: Is consumer demand for education an adequate basis for programming? How can we achieve more compatibility between general and special education? Should student subsidies be more widely used in fields where trained manpower is in short supply? What balance should there be between general and categorical aid to education on the part of the federal government? Are there any dangers in heavy reliance on the trained manpower concept in educational planning?

Up to this point, I have said little about the comparative effectiveness of American education. I have commented on the adequacy of our investment, accessibility of opportunity, purposes in providing opportunity, pluralism of our system, and trained manpower output of educational institutions in response to consumer demands and centrally directed incentives. In the remainder of my remarks I shall try to make some valid generalizations about the quality of our whole enterprise.

A basic question is, How well is American education equipping our youth with the basic academic skills needed for advanced education and training? My answer is that we are doing a better job than before Sputnik. You are undoubtedly aware of the improvements effected in high school physics as a result of the work of Zacharias and his colleagues. Similar changes have been made in the conceptualization and teaching of biology and mathematics. Various education groups are also at work on other disciplines. From all across the country, the impression seems to be that entering freshmen are better prepared academically to do college work than ever before. And these changes are taking place at a time when vastly increasing numbers of youth are continuing their formal education beyond high school. One of our biggest unmet needs, in my judgment, as I suggested earlier, is to do a better job of education and training for those young persons who are really not college material in the conventional sense of the term.

In all candor, I acknowledge that we know less than we should about how effective our schools really are. Furthermore, as reflected in the recent resistance of many public school leaders to the proposal for a national testing program, there seems to be a good deal of antipathy to the gathering of data that would enable us to make a nationwide assessment. For purposes of international comparisons, UNESCO and OECD (Organization for Economic Cooperation and Development) are accumulating and exchanging data relative to "different patterns of educational organization, curricula, and teaching methods." One outcome has been the recently published work,

International Study of Achievement in Mathematics. According to this study, the United States has a higher percentage of the school-age population studying mathematics, but ranks at the bottom among the twelve nations compared in means scores of achievement in mathematics. (A colleague at the American Council on Education recently reviewed this study for *Science* and found enough methodological flaws to throw doubt on the validity of the conclusions.)

The American Council is now collecting comprehensive information from a representative sample of more than three hundred colleges and universities, including several hundred thousand students, in a long-range program of longitudinal research on student development. We expect the data to replace academic folklore about the effects of different institutional environments on student development, and to yield some national norms that will make possible meaningful quantitative comparisons among different types of institutions.

Although standards of academic achievement in American colleges and universities vary widely, it can be said emphatically that our best institutions are at least as good as any elsewhere in the world. Because of the large number and divergent character of undergraduate programs, it is difficult to compare American colleges. On the graduate level, however, the Council two years ago published *An Assessment of Quality in Graduate Education* which summarized and analyzed expert opinions of graduate departments in twenty-nine academic disciplines in 106 major universities.

Conflict and Change

You are all well aware that institutions of higher education in the United States and elsewhere are now in the midst of a tumultuous period. Several months ago the Council queried twenty-three hundred colleges and universities, and on the basis of a preliminary study of a sample of one hundred eighty-five institutions, it appears that about 58 percent of the nation's campuses have experienced some kind of student activism. Slightly more than 25 percent report quite a lot of activism or protest, generally conducted in peaceful and legitimate ways, and 21 percent say they have had at least one sit-in, obstructive picket line, or other disruptive protest. Less than 3 percent of them, however, have had violent protest, such as would be exampled by an attack on persons, the damage of property, or resistance to arrest.

Chaos and violence in some of our institutions is generating a backlash of public opinion that could be very damaging to the autonomy of American colleges and universities. If academicians are either unable or unwilling to put their houses of intellect in order and keep them that way, we can be certain that others will do it for them and a tribute to be paid to outside recriminatory forces will be a loss of freedoms our institutions have traditionally enjoyed.

Neither an authoritarian crackdown nor a business-as-usual posture is in my judgment a fitting response to student activism. The activists range from nihilists and true revolutionaries to those who have a legitimate interest in the orderly modification of existing policies and practices. Those who interfere persistently with the rights of others should indeed be expelled. When they break the law, they should not be shielded by amnesty. The nondisruptive activists, on the other hand, should not only be heard but also heeded for the reason that reform *is* overdue in some of our institutions of higher learning.

Whatever the responses of institutions may be to demand for change, that reform must take into account certain circumstances. One of these is that colleges and universities are created and maintained for the good of the larger society, and not just for the benefit of those directly connected with them. A second consideration is that change must be linked with continuity; basic functions and structures that have evolved over a long period cannot and should not be altered abruptly. Even the most affluent institutions have limited human and material resources and cannot meet virtually unlimited and often conflicting demands. I would urge, therefore, that decisions should be made, not as response to the most strident demands of the moment, but with view to the long-range best interests of our nation.

Every element in the university community certainly has a right to express itself about the ends and means of American higher education, but town meeting schemes for conducting the affairs of large and complex institutions are ill-adapted to the furtherance of teaching, learning, research, and public service as the main objectives of higher education.

The pluralism and diversity of American higher education already exemplify many ways of disposing and controlling power, and doubtless can be accommodated to yet untried ways. Enlightened self-interest ought to inform all of us, nonetheless, that a sensible division of labor in the academic community enhances the freedom and productivity of all its members. As we proceed with the reform of admittedly imperfect institutions, I trust that we shall bear this elemental principle in mind. The current public school situation in New York City and other places reminds me also that the complex and serious business of education on all levels requires the interested parties to work as partners rather than adversaries in a vast collective enterprise whose effective functioning is essential to the survival of our society.

Part Two

STUDENTS, PROFESSORS,
ADMINISTRATORS, TRUSTEES

In light of the student-centered campus upheavals that have taken place since the fall of 1964, it would be ridiculous today to speak of the student as a "forgotten man" in higher education. The address reproduced here, however, was given at Franklin and Marshall College, Gettysburg, Pennsylvania, October 27, 1964. My notes for it were put together even before the first Berkeley episode, which occurred just a few days earlier.

The Forgotten Student

WE ARE LIVING in an age in which our educational institutions are valued to an unprecedented extent. We hear daily—on spot radio and television announcements urging financial support for the "college of your choice"—that "college is America's best friend." The advertisements of insurance companies and banks enticingly describe the increased lifetime earnings for those who attend college. Such an expenditure of time, effort, and money, we are assured, is nothing less than a hardheaded "investment" with "practical dividends."

Local, state, and federal governments place the hope of the nation on institutions of higher education, both in creating the knowledge to maintain our economic and defense superiority in the world and in ameliorating the social disorganization induced by rapid technological change.

From the goals of "expanding and expounding knowledge" we have moved to the goals encompassed by the term "knowledge industry." Not only from our major metropolitan areas, but also from hundreds of communities across the land come the pressures to make colleges and universities mean all things to all people. The rest of the nation looks with envy at the economic growth of the California Bay region surrounding Stanford and the University of California, or at the mushrooming electronics industries on Route 128 from Boston, which lean on Harvard and M.I.T., and it is presumed that this is to be emulated everywhere, by everyone, for the good of all. In short, the pendulum has swung from expecting too little of our colleges and universities to perhaps expecting too much—of straining the essential foundation of higher education on the assumption that it can support a structure that will give solutions to all our problems.

The spate of new demands and new expectations, without carefully selected priorities, contributes to an increasing danger that the individual student may be crowded out of the picture. For some of us, there is a recurrent need to recall that colleges were created primarily for students. The many pressures and diversions that beset us could create a deplorable condition where the student is the forgotten man.

The need to make higher education available to all qualified youth is being met by our unique American system of mass education, and in the process the notion is discarded that college is for only a small, elite group. Individual responses to the challenge by the hundreds of junior colleges, colleges, and universities in our country have been laudable. Physical plant expansion, the growth of graduate education to provide the necessary faculty members, and creative fund raising for the support of all types of institutions have marked the past decade, and will, we must hope, keep pace in the future.

One danger inherent in higher education's new-found success, however, is that created by a seller's market. With 40 percent, or more, of our youth seeking admission to college, it is all too easy for those of us engaged in teaching or administration to avoid confronting some of the student issues that should be at the heart of our concern. Because others are standing in line to take the places of the dropouts, there is a danger of our becoming indifferent, if not callous, to the sources of discontent and the causes of failure.

We know that the rate of expansion of enrollments in the next decade inevitably will have a heavy impact on student life. Increasingly, students may have less personal contact with professors and staff members of their institutions except as they find themselves in serious trouble and have to be dealt with in some official way. With the advent of programed instruction may also come the faceless anonymity that IBM cards, drop cards, seat numbers, and ID numbers represent. The depersonalization of the student, if allowed to go unchecked or unchallenged, represents a grave threat to the very purposes of higher education. We must not only sympathize with the student's desire to make a human or personal connection with his college, we must also vigorously assist him in making such a connection.

This problem has become so critical that the organization which I represent, the American Council on Education, will devote its next annual meeting to a full-scale consideration of "the student in higher education." That meeting will bring together in Washington the presidents of some one thousand colleges and universities to analyze and discuss the place of the student in higher education; the quality of his educational experience; the degree to which higher education is reaching its objectives in the development of the individual student; and the student's learning needs that have yet to be met.

Let us take a brief look at three critical issues I believe we must confront and resolve.

Factors Affecting
Learning Goals

First, what factors obstruct or reinforce the learning goals of our colleges and universities?

Obviously, the first order of business in a college is learning. Yet we know that learning cannot be truly fruitful if it takes place only—and grudgingly—in the classroom and laboratory. A student spends most of his time outside the periods of formal instruction. Therefore, what happens during this time may well be crucial in the outcome of whether the goals of the college are obstructed or reinforced. The desire to learn, the cultivation of the mind and of individuality, the acquisition of literary judgment, aesthetic taste, and spiritual identity are goals for students that should pervade the atmosphere of the entire campus, not just the classroom.

Let us consider several factors which affect this issue—extracurricular activities, faculty and administration values, and the climate and environment of the campus.

We need to reexamine the extracurricular life of our colleges in light of present conditions. It may well be that certain of the adolescent preoccupations of nineteenth-century college life are no longer fitting. I do not mean, however, that any moment spent away from a book is a wasted or frivolous moment. Nor do I argue that entertainment has no place in institutions whose primary mission is edification. Everyone knows that leisure and diversion are necessary to keep our campuses from being grim, unsmiling, joyless places. But with the rising expectations and standards demanded of students and, I hope, the increasing level of student maturity, we can afford to drop the enervating and time-consuming activities that (on some campuses) preoccupy the energies of students and obstruct realization of the real goals of education.

Extracurricular life can be both enjoyable and constructive, and we should assist students in restructuring traditional student activities so that they have a more positive role in the campus environment. The pervading out-of-class values and climate of a campus are major factors in obstructing or reinforcing a student's acceptance of the intellectual mission of the college. In this sphere, too, the concepts of right and wrong, justice and injustice, truth or sham, are learned and reinforced.

Much has been said, but little done, about the publish-or-perish syndrome and the low value attributed by faculty and administration to the effective and committed teaching of students. Consultantships, outside research grants and contracts, and publications seem to score more points for faculty members. For this attitude, faculty and administrators must accept responsibility. Clark Kerr, in his recent book, *The Uses of the University*, summarizes it well in stating:

The undergraduate students are restless. Recent changes in the American university have done them little good—lower teaching loads for the faculty, larger classes, the use of substitute teachers for the regular faculty, the choice of faculty members based on research accomplishments rather than instructional capacity, the fragmentation of knowledge into endless subdivisions. There is an incipient revolt of undergraduate students against the faculty; the revolt that used to be against the faculty *in loco parentis* is now against the faculty *in absentia*.[1]

If the college does not reward faculty members for their devotion to teaching and relating to students, the student body can infer only that such activity is not considered terribly important. If the faculty itself regards *relief from teaching* as the chief reward for accomplishment, or as the highest status symbol, and relegates undergraduate teaching to inexperienced graduate assistants, we may be sure that the students perceive this situation too. Obviously, such matters can obstruct or reinforce whatever values a college seeks to attain.

In recent years, behavioral scientists have become interested in studying campus environments and climates as they affect student perceptions of college goals and values. This is a fascinating area of study, incidentally, which I urge colleges and universities to examine. Many of you are familiar with the work of Nevitt Sanford and the other contributors to the book, *The American College*. Simply, it points up evidence that the environment in which learning takes place—or is supposed to take place—is of sufficient consequence to merit our efforts to do everything we can to improve it.

The work of Robert Pace of U.C.L.A. and George Stern of Syracuse has a particular relevancy here. Dr. Pace and the Educational Testing Service have developed College and University Environment Scales (CUES) wherein some one hundred fifty statements about college life are rated by students as generally *true* or *false* with reference to their college. The results yield a highly interesting description of the college from the students themselves. Because they are a part of the institution—live in it—they presumably are able to judge or describe best what that environment is. The resulting environmental scales are labeled Practicality, Community, Awareness, Propriety, and Scholarship. I commend the significance of such research activities and hope that they will be helpful in reexamining the images we create, knowingly or unknowingly.

1. Cambridge, Mass.: Harvard University Press, 1963. P. 103.

Student
Behavior

A second issue that demands our attention is student personal conduct and behavior. Our newspapers and magazines are featuring, with increasing frequency, popular articles on the subject of student morals, rebellion, drinking, and general strife. Many self-styled experts are just discovering these problems, although those of us with long experience on campuses know that they are not of recent origin. Aristotle made a relevant comment when he said long ago:

They [youth] have exalted notions, because they have not yet been humbled by life or learnt its necessary limitations; moreover their hopeful disposition makes them think themselves equal to great things—and that means having exalted notions. They would always rather do noble deeds than useful ones: their lives are regulated more by moral feeling than by reasoning—all their mistakes are in the direction of doing things excessively and vehemently. They overdo everything—they love too much, hate too much, and the same with everything else.

A problem *does* exist in the area of student behavior. Colleges and universities cannot be indifferent to questions of honesty, integrity, and morality, but it is not easy to reach a consensus on expected standards of behavior and the means of enforcing them. In some of our "multiversities" the faculty has apparently disavowed any interest in student behavior outside the classroom or off the campus. Although individual faculty members may privately feel concern, the problems are so involved that they may adopt a hands-off policy and leave the worries to the deans of students. At the other extreme are colleges where the faculty take most seriously the *in loco parentis* concept; student life, both on and off campus, is regulated by a system of elaborate rules and regulations. Students need permission to leave campus, they must be in dormitories at specified hours, the use of automobiles is denied, and freedom of behavior is severely circumscribed. For most of our colleges and universities, however, the situation lies between these two extremes. Many of them are groping for answers to cope with the changing values and mores of our society and particularly those of our youth.

We readily acknowledge that the home milieu in which many

of today's students were reared is different from that of their teachers and deans. The postwar period of general prosperity, mobility,
and redefinition of values has witnessed a reduction in community
and family restraints. Some parents do not support the restrictions
which colleges have traditionally placed on students in matters of
personal conduct. Other parents, however, expect colleges to police
their sons and daughters in ways which they themselves did not, or
could not do. Our colleges, of course, cannot reasonably be
expected to accept responsibilities which really belong to mothers
and fathers. Given all of this, it is no wonder that the present tension exists between students and institutions regarding rules, discipline, morals, rights, freedoms, and responsibilities.

The overburdened college president, possessing the ultimate
responsibility, more often than not delegates matters affecting student life to other administrative officers, such as the dean of students, and the function of dealing with students in this crucial area
becomes a segregated and negative one. The dean may readily
become a scapegoat, for, without full faculty cooperation, he may
be forced to promulgate proscriptions which he alone cannot
enforce. This state of affairs is an open invitation to some students
to protest, of course, but legitimate modes of protest and ground
rules for settling grievances, both alleged and real, are unclear on
many campuses.

The student newspaper is often a symbol of the tension that
exists between undergraduates and local authority. Editors frequently want to be considered immune from responsibility or
accountability—as though the campus or the principle of academic
freedom provided a sanctuary from community standards of good
taste, propriety, or responsibility. College officials may counter this
situation, however, with a plea to the alumni and the community
to recognize that the student newspaper is not an official spokesman for the institution and that one learns by doing and having
to defend one's actions and words.

What are the answers to these and numerous other problems?
Shall we do away with all rules and regulations? Do students really
want to be left completely alone in nonacademic areas, as they are
in some European countries? Do they want enough control over
operations to be able to shut them down, as is the case in some

Latin American countries? There are no pat answers to these questions, and so we come back to the difficult job that each college or university must define for itself—the eternal question posed by freedom and responsibility. And the confrontation of this issue begins anew with each generation of students.

I believe that every college or university has a responsibility for what happens to a student outside the classroom, and this is especially true for the residential college. That obligation cannot be sidestepped, no matter how much we may wish to avoid it. Qualities of character, conscience, and citizenship are part of the educational development of our students. All of us, faculty as well as students, make a tragic mistake if we proclaim that this is not the proper business of the college.

Student
Attrition

Let me turn briefly to the third and final issue, which is of interest to me because it represents a waste of human potential. It is the continuing high rate of student attrition in higher education. Nationally, various studies show, only about four out of every ten entering freshmen are graduated from college four years later. Although one or two more of the ten may finish sometime later, or somewhere else, the total picture is one of waste, inefficiency, and probably considerable personal unhappiness.

Some of these students are outright academic failures, but we have made real progress recently in our selection and prediction instruments that should soon reflect itself in a rapidly decreasing attrition rate for academic reasons. Still other students find themselves out of step with institutional requirements, schedules, and unrealistic faculty expectations. The fact that they do not "fit" a preconceived mold or are repelled by the pressures and irrelevancies put upon them should give us pause for reflection.

There is some truth in Paul Goodman's statement that "for most students, the abstractness of the curriculum, especially if the teaching is pedantic, can be utterly barren. The lessons are *only* exercises, with no relation to the real world: they are never 'for keeps.' And many of the teachers are not practicing professionals, but merely academics, interested in the words, not the thing."

In the race for "excellence," too many students who would have been successes a decade ago are found in the tally of casualties. A great many colleges and universities have tended to denigrate academic adequacy in student capability and performance and over-emphasize a stringent definition of academic excellence. A substantial portion of youth seek and can profit from higher education. We can demand adequacy for all students, but excellence can be expected only from a few. The danger is that we will eliminate those whose motivation and capabilities are only average or slightly above. We do so at the peril of the nation, for by definition such young people make up the foundation on which our society rests.

I know that your faculty and administration is concerned with this problem of attrition. In your deliberations, I hope you will not pose a dichotomy between unrealistically high expectations and no standards at all. We should demand the best from each student. Despite that best effort, however, there will still be a bottom quarter in each class. In many cases that category should not be regarded arbitrarily as failures. We can be flexible without being lax, and we can treat students as individuals without having academic chaos. Each of us should be challenged by this problem.

I have attempted to pose for your consideration three critical issues which should engage the attention of faculties and students in our institutions of higher education. They are (1) the factors which obstruct or reinforce the learning goals of our colleges; (2) the problems of student personal conduct and behavior out of class; and (3) the continuing high rates of student attrition that cause waste of human resources.

Your college is fortunate in being homogeneous enough in size and purpose to retain that sense of community so precious in collegiate life. You have the opportunity for face-to-face discussion of these important issues and the possibility of achieving a consensus within the faculty and student body so that means of coping with your problems can be discovered.

What you discover here, in such deliberations, will not only aid you in achieving your goals but also should prove valuable to those more complex institutions that may not have the same opportunities for such discovery. There is much to be done, and you have my best wishes as you get on with the job.

This is a "then and now" view of the American university professor that makes some comparisons between 1942 and 1965. The lecture was given at the University of Michigan, Ann Arbor, September 15, 1965.

The Professor and His Roles

SEVERAL YEARS AGO I was asked to address a conference at the University of California on the topic "The Academic Man Revisited." It was suggested that I analyze salient characteristics of the present-day academician and the ways in which he and his roles have changed during the last two decades or so. The designated topic related to a book I wrote in 1942 called *The Academic Man.*[1] Since this title is on the reading list of background material for the present seminar, I shall again make some "then" and "now" comments about the professor and his roles.

Those of you who have read the book may want to challenge me, but in retrospect I shall begin with the assertion that basic patterns of behavior among professors in the campus milieu have undergone no great alteration and that many of the problems of the profession in 1942 are still with us in 1965. In making this assertion, I do not maintain that there have been no significant changes. Indeed, there have been. Higher education is not only an enlarged

1. New York: Oxford University Press, 1942; reprint ed., New York: Octagon Books, 1964.

activity today, but also a more important enterprise. A corollary is that teachers, scholars, and scientists are more important figures on the current scene.

Returning to my perspective of 1942, however, let me review my frame of reference for considering the academic man. I looked at the formal and informal organization of the university from the perspective of a typological individual. Factors having to do with recruitment were considered, and the academic hierarchy was viewed as it affects the student and apprentice, the staff member from the lowest to the highest rank, and the professor administrant—as I then chose to call him. My book deals with the problems of academic status in successive chapters from the anatomy to the physiology of the profession, the third section of the book deals with academic processes and functions and attempts to show the interrelations of prestige and competition, and of prestige with regard to the teaching and research functions. The last part gives conclusions.

My original reasons for choosing major universities as a focus of inquiry were that (1) these "wield the most influence in setting the pattern of higher learning," and (2) "it is only such centers which yield the kind of uniformity in which we are interested." With the growth in size and complexity of institutions of higher education in recent years, the pattern, of course, has become more prevalent, and I believe that the uniformities described are more commonplace.[2] In focusing on the influences brought to bear on the academician as a creature of his environment perhaps I anticipated what was later called the "organization man" of corporate enterprise.

Although my inquiry did not attempt to follow academicians from the cradle to the grave, I did look into all available information concerning the social origins and backgrounds of those who are drawn into college and university work. The findings revealed, as was to be expected, that intellectually superior individuals form the recruits. Because of the inherent nature of advanced teaching and research I am sure that this will always be the case, but whether

2. More than half of all students attending senior-grade institutions are now enrolled in these larger, more comprehensive places. Also the "university syndrome" is more conspicuous today than it was a quarter of a century ago.

the academic profession has been able to hold its own in recruitment alongside law, medicine, engineering, not to mention business and industry, is another matter. Certainly, until the last few years of marked improvement, its comparative bargaining position worsened during the intervening period.

The Academic Ladder

The situation I described then—the overproduction of doctorates in some fields, the "slave markets" at annual meetings of learned societies, the frantic individual quests for $1,800 instructorships—is today completely reversed. Prospective employers of all sorts now search out individuals possessing advanced degrees.[3] In short, even individuals with unexceptional records confront a seller's rather than a buyer's market for their talents, so that the problem of most graduate schools today is that of increasing their production rather than that of finding jobs for those who have been highly trained.

Another aspect of the changed market situation is that the fledgling academician is much less likely to begin his climb of the academic ladder on the bottom rung. If he already has his Ph.D. and has had any teaching experience at all, he is, in many institutions, likely to start his ascent with the rank of assistant professor. Furthermore, if his performance measures up to the average, he is less likely to remain as long in the intermediate ranks before achieving a full professorship. Viewed institutionally, in many places the occupational "pyramid" has given way to something resembling a square. This changed configuration indicates that, from the perspective of both individuals and institutions, higher ranks are being more freely assigned in order to pay higher salaries, particularly in the lesser institutions.

Although I have no comparative evidence, I suggest that a consequence of this easier vertical mobility is a lessening of the ten-

3. See Theodore Caplow and R. J. McGee, *The Academic Marketplace* (Garden City, N.Y.: Doubleday & Co., 1958); Paul Lazarsfeld and Wagner Thielens, *The Academic Mind* (New York: Free Press, 1958); and David G. Brown, *Market for College Teachers* (Durham: University of North Carolina Press, 1965).

sions in the lower academic ranks to which I made frequent reference in my 1942 commentary. Likewise, my guess is that gerontocracy in faculty government of university affairs is less prevalent today, but that "faculty politicians" may be no less active in faculty governance.

As to university government, it has, in general, become a more discrete rather than a more diffuse process. Despite proclamations by faculty about the desirability of wider participation in basic concerns of administration (or governance), the increased size and complexity of university operations has necessarily resulted in a more intricate division of labor. As departments and divisions have multiplied horizontally, so has administration grown vertically. Structure has adapted itself to function; in other words, deans, associate and assistant deans, and other specialized officers of administration have assumed new assignments or taken on responsibilities formerly spread among faculty individuals and committees.

In most institutions the faculty still has virtually complete jurisdiction over all matters pertaining to the curriculum, but even in this sphere it has been suggested by the late Beardsley Ruml and others that teaching would be improved and teachers better paid if this authority were shared with others, including trustees. Faculty attitudes toward encroachments on their traditional spheres, of course, are hardly less hostile than they once were, although a certain ambivalence is indicated by the reluctance of many teachers to be burdened with committee work and other tasks not having to do directly with teaching and research. One source of cleavage between faculty and staff is that many faculty look upon money spent for administration (beyond a bare minimum)—including "overhead allowances"—as money which otherwise would have gone into their own salaries.

All in all, it can be maintained paradoxically that the administration of universities—and of many colleges—is both more and less democratic than it once was. Even though the president continues to be the most important single officer in any institution, the man himself is much less commonly the father image, the authoritarian leader, and the king pin who formerly dominated the scene. Both he and the trustees are likely to be too busy in promotional work and fund raising to engage in much overt interference with the faculty. Thus, by default, educational leadership in the strict sense of the term can be more readily assumed by members of the faculty than in bygone days. Now as then, unfortunately, the ablest teachers, scholars, and scientists are too often unwilling to take much time away from their specialized pursuits to devote to the problems of the institution—and of higher education—as a whole. A recent study by my colleague, Allan M. Cartter, documents this tendency. In connection with a query responded to by some four thousand university professors in thirty different academic fields, most of them indicated they would prefer to spend more time on research and writing and less on their undergraduate teaching and administrative duties. They now spend 15–27 percent of their working hours in administrative tasks, but their preferences for such duties range from only 7 percent to 14 percent.

As I reflect on my 1942 observations about the academic hierarchy, it seems to me that I either overemphasized its influence as a conditioner of behavior then, or else it has become less significant as a factor now. It is possible, to be sure, that experiences that are sharply outlined for those directly involved may become blurred from a more distant and detached perspective. In any event, if I were redoing my original inquiry I should certainly pay more attention to the effects on the academician's attitude and behavior of such structures as the department, the college or professional school, the graduate school, and special arrangements for teaching and research.

With the growth in the size and complexity of universities, the department as an entity undoubtedly assumes greater importance for the average faculty member. In a large university, for example, the English department may have more members than are included on the entire faculty of a small liberal arts college and may contain virtually all of their professional concerns. The department and the field of specialization, rather than the institution, may thus be the occupational "universe" of the scholar or scientist. Moreover, there are noticeable attitudinal differences between individuals in the humanistic studies and the physical sciences, the fine arts and engineering, education and the medical fields, and so on. Some of these differences stood out quite clearly in faculty reactions to the recent student episodes at Berkeley. (I should like to see a study of the

Young Turks on faculties to ascertain whether they more typically emerge in some departments than in others.)

Since 1942, graduate education has loomed much larger in the university picture. Assuming that the percentage of bachelors who go on for advanced degrees will continue to rise from the present 19 percent (up from 12 percent since 1959) to 25 percent in 1975 as a proportion of all enrollments, now and in the future this level of academic activity becomes much more significant than it once was. In addition, in some places postdoctoral work is also taking on heightened significance.

Among the special arrangements for teaching and research to which I alluded earlier the campus-based research institute or center needs to be mentioned as an important development which has taken place largely since the last war. Before the war there were few, but now their number is estimated to exceed three thousand in approximately two hundred universities. Berkeley has more than 80, and a recent count at the University of Michigan disclosed 146. These centers, as Allan Cartter has said, "fall outside the usual educational chain of command." Some have very large budgets, involve persons from many departments and schools within a university, and represent a complete reorganization of traditional disciplinary approaches to problems, both theoretical and applied.

To the professor, attachment to a research center often provides a degree of freedom and flexibility which is not easily duplicated in the educational institution proper. To the university, the existence of such centers often aids in attracting distinguished scholars. This is a two-edged sword, however, for the allegiance of the faculty member is divided between center and department, and the retention of faculty may be as much a function of continuing university grantsmanship as it is of the quality and climate of the education enterprise.[4]

Problems
of Status

If research activity were motivated solely by the desire to seek the truth and teaching followed entirely from the wish to diffuse it, there would be no problems of academic status. My analysis of status does not make an opposite assumption, but it does employ a

4. Allan M. Cartter, unpublished MS.

motivational scheme in which the employee's status is necessarily of great significance both to him and to the institution. Twenty years and more ago there appeared to be a good deal of uncertainty, confusion, and misgiving surrounding the whole matter of status appraisal. Those of you who may have to engage in this kind of personnel evaluation will come to realize that it still involves what is known in navigation as blind reckoning.

Recently I thumbed through an American Council on Education publication, "Policies and Practices in Faculty Evaluation." I was struck by the fact that insofar as precision of method is concerned, not much progress has been made of late. Along the lines of an unprintable limerick, it looks as if many administrators are still not clear about who is supposed to do what, with what, and to whom when it comes to evaluating faculty performance.

During the last decade or two, as all of you know, many university professors have become heavily involved in research and public service. In response to pressures from business, industry, and government they are more frequently in their laboratories, secluded in their offices, or even away from the campus altogether for considerable amounts of time. Thus, one hears complaints about the neglect of undergraduate teaching and the divided loyalties of faculty persons between their traditional assignments and these enlarged functions. Institutions of higher education in general and universities in particular are now deeply involved in the most basic problems of our era, and Mr. Chips has almost disappeared from the campus scene. What the Germans term *Gemeinschaft* has been displaced by *Gesellschaft*, as the spirit of a homogeneous community gives way to the depersonalization of a heterogeneous society.

In most universities today, in contrast to 1942, there are lower teaching loads, larger classes, and more use of substitute teachers for the regular faculty. The choice of faculty members is more often based on research accomplishment than on instructional capacity. Between 1940 and 1960, our national investment in research and development grew by 3,714 percent, and the participation of our campuses in this phenomenal trend has inevitably affected them.

There is a rising tide of grumbling everywhere, and especially in the larger universities, about the lack of attention to effective teaching and the absence of systematic means of teacher improvement. In some instances, of course, careful study is being given to such pedagogical aids and devices as closed-circuit television, teaching machines, and what not, but the most essential element—the human ingredient in the person of the teacher himself—is largely ignored or taken for granted. A few universities do have procedures designed to evaluate and improve beginning teachers, and some use crude student-rating schemes for all teachers, but to the best of my knowledge there is not a major institution anywhere that has made a strenuous across-the-board effort continuously to evaluate and better its teaching productivity with the same diligence that virtually all of them devote to their research output.

Contrary to expert as well as popular opinion, the proportion of Ph.D.'s on most faculties has increased rather than declined. But relief from teaching has come to be regarded as a reward for accomplishment and one of the highest status symbols. Everywhere, of course, there is lip service to the importance of good teaching, yet in few places is there really systematic and rigorous attention to reinforcing rather than obstructing the values institutions claim to uphold in this regard. The average faculty man's research gets criticized and evaluated; not so his teaching, for his classroom is still regarded as being sacrosanct.

In my opinion, both faculty and administration must accept blame for permitting consultantships, outside research grants and contracts, and publications to score more points in the ratings of academicians than does dedicated and effective teaching. The much-discussed publish-or-perish dictum, however, is in actuality more fiction than fact in the average institution. More than a decade ago, I made a detailed analysis of the published research of three institutional faculties in a university system with which I was then associated and I found that on one campus 71 percent of the faculty had never published an article and 90 percent had not published a book; corresponding figures for the other two campuses were 40 percent and 90 percent, and 29 percent and 66 percent. More recently I had a tabulation made of the published writings of approximately a thousand faculty persons in a different university system and found that 32 percent had not published any articles and 71 percent had not published any books.

Among the two thousand cases in these two samples, let me

add, were some individuals whose personal bibliographies exceed in volume the collective output of a sizable proportion of all the rest of their colleagues. Since the data to which I refer were collected from large universities (both members of the Association of American Universities) and not from small colleges, they lead me to conclude that allegations about the emphasis on research and publication as *the* cause for neglect of teaching are unfounded. Other evidence I have seen reinforces my surmise that in all except a few leading institutions less than 10 percent of the faculty accounts for more than 90 percent of all published research. In brief, if the publish-or-perish dictum were fact rather than fiction on most campuses, the average professor would be dead!

Although our nation undoubtedly needs more genuinely distinguished, research-oriented universities, I doubt that the number can or should exceed forty to fifty. The kind of research that contributes to the advancement of knowledge should be a major emphasis in perhaps two hundred of our institutions, but I believe that on most campuses it is sufficient to expect the average faculty member to keep abreast of his field. Because talent for really creative research and writing is apparently a very scarce capability, it seems logical to conclude that time and energy would be put to better use if most academicians were encouraged to give more attention to their teaching. An urgent problem for the administration as well as the faculty, accordingly, is to find out more about the nature of effective teaching, establish means of identifying and rewarding it, and cease giving mere lip service of its importance.

In reviewing my 1942 treatment of academic status, it seems to me that my least satisfactory section is that dealing with professional status. My frame of reference was too closely tied to one organization, the American Association of University Professors. Although it is the one academic organization (excluding the American Federation of Teachers) that includes all kinds of specialists and that most closely parallels the trade unions or the broad professional associations in other fields, my present opinion is that it is less important for the average university teacher than his particular scholarly or learned society.

For the typical chemistry professor, for example, I suspect that the American Chemical Society is closer to his perennial concerns, and a corresponding relationship would also hold for the American Sociological Association, the Modern Language Association, and dozens of others. Through participation in the activities of these societies rather than in those of other types of associations (A.A.U.P., A.F. of T., A.H.E.), the academic man gains professional recognition by reading papers, being on committees, chairing sections, serving in offices, and otherwise rising to prominence. To use a labor union analogy, it would be the *craft* rather than the *trade* unions that are of most significance in determining an individual's status in the academic world.

Members of the academic profession in the 1930s and early 1940s typically considered their socioeconomic status as being depressed. Little did they realize that they were enjoying relative affluence compared with the deterioration to follow during almost two decades of inflation. The average salary figures I cited then have in many instances more than doubled, to be sure, and even the purchasing power of academic incomes has improved. However, per capita incomes in the whole society have increased at an even greater rate.

Within the last six or seven years, compensation rates have markedly improved almost everywhere, and even though these gains have been less widely proclaimed than the previous losses, the total incomes of many professors in large universities, as well as in some of the more affluent small colleges, are considerably higher than the public is aware. To be eligible for an "AA" rating under the A.A.U.P. scale for 1965–66, for example, an institution must compensate its full professors at an average rate of $23,290. Because of consultantships and contract research in science and engineering, in the professional schools, and in a few other areas, the outside incomes of scholars and scientists are appreciably more significant than they once were. The effect of income differences and of the wide variation by fields has been to enlarge the disparities between and within institutions and thus afford a new basis of disquiet in the academic profession.

Although I commented on outside earnings in my 1942 book, it contained little information about fringe benefits for the faculty. One good source of data on the subject is Greenough and King's *Retirement and Insurance Plans in American Colleges.* Another is

Mark H. Ingraham's *The Outer Fringe: Faculty Benefits Other than Annuities and Insurance.* In reviewing the latter volume, Allan Cartter comments:

And what a grab-bag it is! Sixty percent of the institutions queried are landlords for faculty families, 15 percent are mortgage brokers, 93 percent of private colleges provide taxfree scholarships in the form of tuition waivers, 75 percent provide emergency medical treatment to faculty and families, one-fourth grant personal loans to employees, two-thirds pay moving expenses for tenure appointments, one-third provide discount purchasing services on appliances, food, etc. Others, in varying numbers, provide family bonuses for children, free faculty lunches and morning coffee, free baby-sitting services, two-thirds of foreign travel expenses, and run holiday camps for faculty families. Over half of the institutions have regular sabbatical leave policies, and others have informal leave-with-pay arrangements. Six hundred institutions provide faculty parking spaces. Some, like Princeton, house half their faculty in university-owned property or in houses where the university has advanced all the money and requires no payments on principal.[5]

No single institution, of course, provides *all* of these services. Cartter estimates that these benefits may easily add up to six or seven thousand dollars a year—perhaps even ten thousand before taxes for the family at the "right institution" and with two children in college.

As to image and reality about the professor as a person then and now, I noted in 1942 that in the hotel lobby or lounge car it was difficult at a glance to differentiate the professor from the doctor, lawyer, or businessman. Today I would note that the traveling professor goes by jet plane and has little spare time to tarry in hotel lobbies. He is still more likely than his counterpart in medicine, law, or business to wear crepe-soled shoes, a tweed jacket, and occasionally to have a beard, but, unlike his earlier counterpart in the academic profession, he is seldom a reclusive scholar whose activities are confined largely to his own campus. Even more than most professional workers today, he is a frequent participant in meetings, conferences, and other collective endeavors which draw him away from the classroom, library, and laboratory, not only to distant cities in this country but also to remote parts of the world.

5. *Science*, Sept. 3, 1965, p. 1084.

In brief, it can be said that in many fields the professor has ceased to be a vaguely respected but unappreciated figure as he emerges in the role of the expert and true professional whose knowledge-ability has become a highly valued commodity.

Processes
and Functions

Turning now from considerations of status to academic processes and functions, it should be noted that my earlier analysis ties both individual and institutional competition to the quest for prestige as an ultimate value. The competitive processes I described then seem to me to be about the same now or, at least, they are no less intensive. As Berelson's *Graduate Education in the United States* reveals, the leading institutions of a generation or so ago are still in the main the leading universities today. Yet there have been some changes. The University of California, for example, is no longer just one of the top five or six universities; it now vies with Harvard for preeminence in first position.

Although major centers of advanced study and research are somewhat more numerous than they were a generation or more ago, the material and human resources required to build and maintain a truly great university are perhaps even more difficult to come by. One reason is the explosion of knowledge, especially in scientific and technical fields, and the considerable investments required to effect further explosions. To be sure, graduate study and research have undergone notable improvements almost everywhere, but, even so, I suspect that qualitative differences between the best and the worst universities are greater now than ever before. Curiously enough, some of the federal policies and practices widen this gap by concentrating grants in institutions which are already strong and others narrow it by deliberately attempting to encourage a geographic and institutional spread of activity.

The national need for greatly increased numbers of highly trained individuals and for more creative endeavor in all sorts of spheres suggests, moreover, that in the future many of these matters cannot be left to chance or to local determination. Under such circumstances it is indeed likely that interinstitutional cooperation and coordination, either on a voluntary or mandatory basis, will become more prevalent.

Student-teacher relationships are still central concerns in major universities, but the proportional amount of time the contemporary professor gives to classroom or laboratory teaching has steadily dwindled with the increased emphasis upon research. In fact, it has been sardonically noted that some professors in some universities appear to do no regularly scheduled classroom teaching any more. Professional novices even—when their bargaining power is enhanced as unusually promising researchers—have been known to insist on teaching loads not in excess of three to six hours per week. The same inadequacies in evaluating and improving teaching that were the subject of debate several decades ago seem to me to persist. Despite sporadic efforts here and there to improve teaching, the situation in most places can still be aptly described as one of laissez faire. My earlier generalizations about the comparative prestige of superior teachers and superior researchers are still valid today.

As I review what I originally had to say about prestige and the research function, my present judgment is that I overstressed the influences of ulterior motivation on research itself. Certainly now, and perhaps even then, there is less cold calculation of projects for what they may or may not do for the professional advancement of the individual directly involved. In the more dynamic fields of knowledge, research is pervasively such an integral part of what goes on that the young scholar or scientist of even average ability is likely to have a fairly wide range of choice among worthwhile possibilities for involvement, either working with others or on his own. Furthermore, in some fields today many research projects necessarily require team effort and leave less latitude for the virtuoso or solo performer.

Throughout my treatise on *The Academic Man* there is an emphasis on the social determinants of his behavior. This is to be expected in "A Study in the Sociology of a Profession," as the book is subtitled. The mode of analysis I employed did succeed, I still think, in getting at the sources of personnel stresses and strains in the university as a social system. Flaws in the scheme of coordinating effort, giving precedence to means over ends, institutionalized evasions, and conflicts between nominal and real ends are all, without question, at the root of many problems besetting the academician in his workaday world. The logic of sentiment and the logic of efficiency still need to be more unmistakably identified as such.

However all this may be, I find that I am less prone to be an adherent of social determinism than I was twenty years ago. Perhaps it is because during the interim I have come to know personally enough academic men in many kinds of contexts to realize more fully the importance of subtle and little understood variables in human behavior.

As a former academic administrator speaking to an audience composed largely of presidents, deans, and other institutional executives, I gave this paper at a conference of the Association of Texas Colleges and Universities, April 15, 1966, in Arlington, Texas.

The Leadership Function

FOR AN AUDIENCE of educational leaders, a discussion of "The Leadership Function in Higher Education" may appear to bring coals to Newcastle. As seasoned educational administrators, however, you are necessarily aware of the tendency among many academicians to minimize the importance of professional leadership in higher education. Some academicians like to hark back to a mythical past when institutions presumably ran themselves, and they tend to regard anything resembling management as a parasitical growth of recent occurrence. You have doubtless also encountered professors who, themselves autocrats in their classrooms and laboratories, nevertheless are extreme egalitarians in matters of college and university governance. You are hearing, too, about, and perhaps even from, student activists and others who would like to eliminate most administrators as such and bring about that idyllic state of campus anarchy which, Robert Hutchins once remarked, many seem to prefer to any form of government. On several sides, in brief, there is the fixed idea that academic institutions can and indeed should be conducted on a one-man one-vote basis.

In such circumstances, your occupation is indeed an onerous profession. As a one-time member, I feel for you. The purpose of my comments on this occasion, however, is not to sympathize with college and university officials, but to invite attention to some critical leadership problems which now confront American higher education.

Recruitment

Our first problem is recruitment. Unless we devise more effective means of attracting able persons into academic administration, the present shortage of manpower is certain to become even more severe. The haphazard methods presently employed in most places for developing administrative talent simply will not suffice. An institution searching for a new president, for example, is often uncertain about the kind of leadership it needs and uninformed about where to look for the best available prospects. Job "candidates," as they are commonly but improperly called, do not openly run for office, as in politics. Nor do they necessarily progress to the top, rung by rung on an occupational ladder, as in the military or in industry. Aspirants to administration may feel the "call" inwardly, but they have no clearly appropriate way to express it, as do those who wish to prepare themselves for the clergy. Moreover, educational institutions, unlike business corporations, seldom consciously groom younger faculty and staff persons for top administrative posts.

Many academicians are also reluctant to be drawn into administrative work. For those who teach only six hours a week, draw salaries of $18,000 or more on a nine months' basis, have their research projects fully underwritten, and supplement their regular incomes through honoraria and consultantships, this reluctance to forsake the security and freedom which come with tenure for the uncertainties of administration is quite understandable. Further, a recent report comparing the average salaries of presidents and of full professors, with the latter salaries converted to a twelve months' basis, revealed the difference to be less than 20 percent.

Not only do administrative posts entail less job security, unlimited working hours, and only slightly higher pay than professorial positions of comparable grade, but also the expectations held for those who occupy critical leadership positions are often unrealistic. The average institution looking for a new president, for example, often draws up a set of qualifications which could be met only by the Holy Trinity.

Aside from the exacting specifications drawn up, however, the procedures employed in the actual search for talent are typically haphazard and inadequate. Thus with thousands of administrative positions to be filled every year (including several hundred presidencies), it is not surprising that lists of vacancies grow steadily longer. Yet it *is* surprising, in view of all the hue and cry about the shortage of teachers and researchers, how little public attention has been paid to the equally critical shortage of qualified administrators.

If higher education is to avoid a real crisis of professional leadership, several things need to be done. The president and other key officials on each campus should assume a continuing responsibility for identifying promising talent and for testing interests in, and aptitudes for, pivotal leadership assignments. Coupled with this need for local identification of talent, better ways should be devised for giving visibility to such individuals beyond their own campuses. Scholars and scientists have done this for themselves through their professional societies and other agencies; there is no good reason why administrative officers, using their associations, cannot be equally successful.

Although the American Council on Education's internship program in academic administration and one or two others of its kind represent the beginnings of an effort to identify, train, and develop a pool of promising younger leaders, these programs are limited in scale and cannot meet more than a small fraction of the national need. Almost $5 million of Ford Foundation money is invested in the Council project, and it is off to a good start. Some institutions, however, have thus far shown a singular lack of interest in a venture which can be helpful to them and to the academic community at large. We are encouraged, however, by the favorable response of the many colleges and universities now participating.

Training

Turning now to another aspect of the leadership function in higher education, systematic training, indoctrination, apprenticeship—or whatever one chooses to call it—is a second problem warranting our concern. When the Council's Board of Directors first discussed the implications of the administrative internship program, somebody remarked, "Surely we must all recognize the need to perpetuate our kind." Another board member added, "No, I would put it as the need to multiply and improve the breed."

Regardless of how the problem is viewed, little concerted attention has been given to training programs for departmental chairmen, deans, presidents, and other key officers of college and university administration. Indifference on many campuses and resistance on others to the idea that something more than trial-and-error learning is required seem to typify our traditional attitudes. Although no respectable college or university would employ professors who had not been carefully trained for their tasks, they seem to have no hesitation about giving complex administrative assignments to individuals who have had virtually no experience designed to assess their suitability for leadership roles and to prepare them for the tasks.

Such helter-skelter approaches to development may have worked reasonably well in the past when institutions operated largely by tradition, changed very slowly, and were relatively simple in structure. Today's institutions of higher education are such costly and complicated enterprises, however, that their executive officers must do a great deal more than merely preside over faculty meetings. A respectable background as a scholar and a rudimentary knowledge of parliamentary procedures no longer qualifies a man for most of the tasks to be performed. Whether we prefer it that way or not, the part-time amateur is more and more likely to be displaced by the full-time professional with a career commitment to institutional management. As a corollary, we can no longer afford the expensive process of having the necessary knowledge learned in an ad hoc fashion on the job itself.

To employ an analogy from teacher training, we can no more produce the needed kind of educational leadership through a specialized curriculum than we can turn out good teachers by substituting courses in pedagogy for those of subject-matter content. I believe that we should continue to draw most recruits for administrative assignments from those who have had direct experience in teaching, research, and other prime functions of the college or university. I share the academic man's suspicion of leaders recruited from other walks of life, and suspicion of those indoctrinated as a professional class separate and apart from the colleagues whose cooperation is essential to their success. Despite these qualifications, it needs to be emphasized that we do a disservice to professors, administrative obligations, and above all, to our institutions, when we thrust men and women into positions for which they are unprepared.

Few individuals ever reach top executive posts without prior administrative experience, to be sure, but this does not excuse our confused procedures for the early identification of good prospects, our unsystematic methods for challenging their interests and testing their capabilities, or our inadequate scheme of incentives and rewards for the performance of functions that are central to the maintenance and improvement of higher education.

Performance

A third problem at the heart of our concern for the leadership of higher education is to define clearly what the administrative functions are. To begin at the level of the department, there is the mistaken notion in some institutions that the headship or chairmanship is merely a kind of recording secretary's chore to be rotated among the tenured professors who can be cajoled into accepting it. That strong individual leadership on this level may spell the difference over a period of years between a mediocre and a distinguished department seems in some quarters to be either unknown or disregarded. A professorial tendency to denigrate the importance of administrative roles in institution building is also seen in efforts to dissuade able young colleagues from accepting part-time assignments outside the department—as if teaching and research were the only activities worthy of the best energies of the best persons.

These attitudes suggest failure in institutional circles to recognize that the caliber of an institution's managerial talent is hardly less important to its present strength and future prospects than is the quality of its faculty. Despite the professorial quip that all a president needs is a head of gray hair to lend him an air of distinction and a peptic ulcer to give him a look of concern, most members of any academic community recognize the importance of having a capable leader at the forefront of the whole enterprise. This awareness is less widespread when it comes to defining the qualifications necessary for the other members of the administrative staff.

Among the various officers of administration, and between them and the other members of the academic community, it is vital that there be a clearly understood division of labor. In view of current efforts on some campuses to further the notion that the best way to conduct affairs is to have everybody undertake to do everybody else's washing, we need to remind ourselves that a pronounced division of labor is the mark of a civilized society and that its absence is a trait of primitivism.

The time-honored division of labor which defines the main job of students as learning, that of teachers as advancing learning and knowledge, and that of the administration as furthering the entire endeavor is ridiculed in some circles as hopelessly outmoded. College newspaper editors and other student leaders recently were urged by a prominent national figure to annoy academic official-dom and criticize the administration—presumably on the theory that wisdom about educational matters decreases with age and experience. In some quarters, duly constituted officials are by definition either stupid or stuffy and are derogatorily referred to as "The Establishment." Members of the faculty, who have always shared in the decision-making responsibilities of institutional governance, are in turn being exhorted to unionize and engage in collective bargaining—a movement which further splinters any academic community.

Under such circumstances there is a tendency to forget that without institutional leaders to draw discrete interests together in a common cause, many colleges and universities would soon be pulled apart by contending factions. Sir Eric Ashby, in an essay "The Scientist as University President," has said, "The function of the chief administrator . . . is to ensure that the decisions which are made to preserve the cohesion of the institution are consistent with its purposes and contribute to its integrity. He has to think in terms of balance and perspective." Even with clear definitions of authority and responsibility and with a well-understood division of labor, however, there can still be ineffective leadership. For want of tested and verified knowledge to guide their decisions and actions, the most capable leaders must at times rely mainly on intuition.

Systematic Knowledge

Accordingly, a fourth problem of institutional leadership is the need to develop a systematic body of knowledge about college and university administration. A few basic questions will illustrate. Looking at the total higher education market, how does a given educational institution logically decide on the fields and levels of study it will project? What does an institution need to know about its student input and output to determine whether it is operating efficiently and effectively as a productive enterprise? Assuming specified material and human resources, how can an optimum scale of operations be ascertained? How can alternative program costs be realistically assessed? What administrative devices are available to evaluate and improve teaching effectiveness? Is one pattern of organization and management better suited than another to a particular institution? Who should decide on the pattern, and on what grounds? In budget making—always an exercise in the allocation of scarce resources—what criteria should guide whose decisions?

These and other fundamental questions of educational policy and practice are now being answered largely on an ad hoc basis nearly everywhere, by reason of the lack of objective information and valid generalization to guide decision making. Academic researchers, over the years, have studied nearly every other environment more carefully than they have their own. Agricultural and labor economics, for example, are well-developed fields of long standing, yet only recently have economists given much thought to the economics of education. A few colleges and universities have established offices of institutional research, and the results of their inquiries are useful, but, in contrast to the advanced technologies found in other areas, the technology of higher education is still in a crude state.

In the American Council's operation of the Academic Administration Internship Program and the Institute for College and University Administrators, we are continuously impressed by the dearth of published material available for study. The scanty literature underlines our need to encourage this kind of reflection and analysis in your institutions.

Environment
and Viability

A fifth and final concern is the need to maintain an environment in which leaders are free to lead. Much has been said and written about freedom for professors, but little attention has been given to the corresponding need of administrative officers for leeway in which to discharge the responsibilities vested in them.

Four years ago Harold Dodds cautioned, "The presidential office well may go the way of the buffalo if it loses its traditional character of education leadership."[1] Allan Nevins, at about the same time, appeared ready to accept the compromised conception of the academic president as a "coordinator rather than a creative leader . . . an expert executive, a tactful moderator."[2] Other educators have argued that someone must be concerned with the whole institution, and that it is mainly the president's job to safeguard institutional integrity and cohesion.

I grant that there are different styles of successful leadership, but if our institutions are to be viable entities, I see no substitute for centering a large measure of authority and responsibility in their duly constituted leaders. I am disturbed, accordingly, by the current forces inside and outside our institutions that appear to be fragmenting authority and responsibility.

Without sufficient awareness of the possible effects on individual colleges and universities, we may be rushing into the creation of statewide systems, state commissions to allocate federal funds, anonymous task forces, and interstate compacts, and other schemes that may confuse the decision-making process in higher education. I firmly believe that traditional institutional independence must necessarily give way to new forms of interdependence, but as we devise these new forms I think it is a serious mistake to

1. *The Academic President—Educator or Caretaker?* (New York: McGraw-Hill Book Co., 1962), p. v.
2. *The State Universities and Democracy* (Urbana: University of Illinois Press, 1962), pp. 118–19.

bypass and undermine the established and locally responsible leadership of American higher education. I view with alarm any move that in effect displaces the most experienced institutional leaders and relegates them to the role of mere observers in public policy formation. Issues in higher education are too vital a concern to the public at large to be settled by professional educators alone, of course; yet it would be the height of folly to remove front-line leaders from the main arena of decision making and to replace them with politically constituted committees, commissions, and other agencies remote from the real scenes of action.

Let me express the conviction that individual leaders are no less essential than individual institutions to American higher education. Of course, we must have a better coordinated and more unified system to meet state, regional, and national needs, but never at the price of stultifying local and individual initiative. To maintain the diversity and freedom of our institutions, their chosen leaders must not be hamstrung by outside authorities. This has been our credo in the past, and it has served our society well. I know that individually and collectively thoughtful members of the academic community can be counted on to combat the forces that would erode the integrity of our institutions and the freedom of their executive officers. In the great enterprise of expanding and improving higher education, basic leadership roles must be maintained. I therefore conclude by saying to all who hold executive posts in colleges and universities, "More power to you!"

By the time of the Council's annual meeting in Denver during October 1968, my concern over the widespread abuse being heaped on administrators in general, and presidents in particular, was such that I felt impelled to speak out in their behalf.

A Few Kind Words
for Academic Administrators

CONSIDERING THE valiant struggles of academic administrators to maintain a balance between campus freedom and order, it is scant reassurance to note that as yet only a few of them have had their offices pillaged and burned, or their homes invaded. Even in the absence of strife and disorder, however, they are the men caught in the middle as the defenders— and, altogether too often these days, the beleaguered defenders—of institutional integrity. Few, if any, other members of the academic community have been as continuously badgered and abused.

I certainly do not agree with *Time* magazine's recent characterization of academe's executives as being in the main an exhausted lot. I do think, however, it is high time somebody said a few kind words in their behalf. I hope that the implications of my remarks will somehow reach those campuses where many students and professors appear to be singularly unappreciative of what constructive leadership means to them and their institutions.

Since I probably know as many top administrative officers as anybody else in the country, I speak with personal conviction in commending the ability and dedication of those who comprise what is dubbed with increasing aptness "the roughest profession." Despite the higher pay in business, industry, and some of the professions, I doubt that the leaders in any other line of endeavor surpass academic officials in general capability. Moreover, the equanimity that academic leaders are expected to display under the most trying circumstances is seldom called upon in other organizational settings.

The institutions over which they preside are now serving more individuals and serving them more effectively than at any other time in our history. The expansion and improvement of higher education have not come about, furthermore, as a spontaneous response of taxpayers and private benefactors to the need for more classrooms and dormitories, for more and better paid professors, and for other essential elements of betterment. Without strong executive leadership, many of these developments simply would not have occurred. In an era of rising egalitarianism, however, there is a tendency to forget how much the many owe to the few.

With rising expectations, memories also tend to be short about how far we have already come from where we once were. Even a cursory review of the past would reveal that faculties and students almost everywhere "never had it better." In my opinion this is not so with administrators, some of whom never had it worse. Although college or university presidencies are still highly respected positions in our society, growing numbers of campus malcontents seem bent on doing everything they can to harass and discredit the performers of these key roles.

To be sure, there is nothing new about a generally critical attitude in academic circles toward administration per se. Some members of the college or university community fancy that institutions can run themselves, and others countenance a festering nihilism in which anarchy appears preferable to any form of government. Still others seem to believe that complex educational enterprises should be conducted like clubs or debating societies where "participatory democracy" gives everybody a voice in all affairs.

Presidents, provosts, deans, and others have long been accustomed to divergent views among their constituents about what colleges and universities should be and do, and recognize that one of their functions is to resolve conflict in conflict-prone institutions.

Most of them sense the futility of trying to please everyone and the disservice to higher education of having mere popularity as a leadership goal. The best of them are aware, in addition, that the pursuit of truth and the advancement of learning call for leaders who are something more than mediators.

Wise, experienced, and strong leadership in American higher education was never more needed than now, and an apathetic attitude toward its denigration can indeed become a collective calamity. As a long-time academician, I am distressed by the number of recent instances of faculty and student majorities—majorities whose support is essential in democratic governance—standing passively by to watch nihilists and revolutionaries wreak disorder and destruction. The intent of militant minorities is often unmistakable, but the failure of many other members of the academic community to resist intrusions on their rights and to join forces with the upholders of academic integrity is baffling. I am even more at loss to understand why the immediate spectators do not realize that they can become the ultimate victims.

Overwork
and Underappreciation

Harry Truman's dictum about staying out of the kitchen if you can't stand the heat is well known to academic administrators. They have to be a hardy breed to survive overwork and underappreciation, but, fortunately for colleges and universities, the satisfactions they find in institution building more than offset the inherent frustrations of the roles they perform. Although academic administration, like every other occupation, has its misfits, few among them are thin-skinned egocentrics. Responsible leadership demands sensitivity as well as hardiness, however, and it will be a misfortune for higher education if thick skins ever become prime qualifications for top posts.

Despite the fact that nobody has either to go into academic administration or to stay in it, I doubt that there ever will be a dearth of available candidates. Our growing problem is more likely to be the unwillingness of outstanding men and women to subject themselves to the increased rigors and decreased rewards that may be in prospect. Unlike most other rationally organized enterprises, academic institutions too frequently treat their duly constituted leaders as being highly expendable. To use a military analogy, they send their officers into exposed combat positions while most of the troops remain safely in their bunkers.

As we all know, more and more administrators are retiring early and going into less frenzied endeavors. From my own vantage point with the American Council on Education, I can testify to the mounting difficulty of replacing them with persons of comparable capabilities. To reverse this trend so that colleges and universities can continue to attract and hold outstanding leadership, kind words and general understanding may help, but they will hardly be sufficient. Other changes are required.

To begin, understanding and support might be developed for something like an administrators' Bill of Rights. Most colleges and universities have long been guided by widely accepted statements about the rights and duties of professors. Some institutions have adopted a recently formulated set of guidelines about the rights and freedoms of students. The forgotten men and women among these components of academe have been the administrators. Their responsibility has been enlarged at the same time that their authority to discharge it has been undermined.

Seeing no prospect for lessening the burdens of top administrative posts, some observers suggest shorter terms of office, such as five to ten years. In 1960, incidentally, the average number of years in office of presidents was reported as being between ten and eleven. The 1968 roster for presidents of institutions in the Association of American Universities shows a median tenure of just under six years. Whether this signifies a trend, I do not know. If so, in my judgment, it means that we are losing some of the advantages of continuity in experienced, professional leadership—an advantage our institutions have long had over most colleges and universities in other countries.

To recruit and retain outstanding individuals for key positions, it seems to me that job specifications must be changed. Only a superman could match the qualifications set forth by most institutions in their searches for academic presidents. Once on the job, there simply are not enough hours in the day for administrators to do all of the things their varied constituents expect of them.

*Shared
Responsibilities*

With faculty and students demanding a wider participation in college and university affairs, some of the demanding duties of executives might be portioned out among them. It would be interesting, for example, to see what faculty and student committees would do with multimillion dollar fund-raising assignments. Faculty senate committees might be asked to share in the onus of deciding which individuals and departments get less favored treatment in the allocation of scarce resources. Other groups could be charged with specific responsibilities for the maintenance of campus order. Students and professors, however, should not be permitted to move in and out of these and other assignments at their pleasure. Like full-time administrators, they would have to accept a continuing share in the institution's accountability to the public at large.

Regardless of the division of labor, nonetheless, there is no substitute for capable and responsible leadership. Without it, our colleges and universities will flounder and no reasonable hopes for their future will be realized. All elements of the academic community are therefore under the necessity of reinforcing mutual understanding and confidence and of upholding the orderly processes that are indispensable to the forward movement of higher education.

This paper was prepared for the Special Committee on Campus Tensions, chaired by Sol M. Linowitz, and parts of it appeared in their report entitled Campus Tensions: Analysis and Recommendations, *published by the American Council on Education in 1970.*

The Concerns of Trustees

AMID THE CAMPUS HUBBUB over competing and often conflicting demands of special interest groups, higher education's main reason for being—the public interest—tends to be overlooked or pushed aside. Academicians like to think of institutional objectives in terms of their own professional prerogatives. In the name of academic freedom, they draw up unilateral promulgations defining their rights and duties. More and more students, in turn, are becoming restive about institutionally ascribed roles, and activists among them make "nonnegotiable demands" of college and university authorities. Administrative officers, responsible for both stability and change in ongoing operations, find themselves having to spend ever more time as mediators in situations from which they frequently emerge as scapegoats. Standing somewhat apart from the fray but inevitably drawn into it are the trustees or regents.

The trustees, who presumably represent the public interest and embody "lay control" of the institution, soon discover—if they did not already know it—that in time of crisis an academic community is not a readily coordinated enterprise. Although many boards of trustees or regents have the legal power both to oversee and manage the academic endeavor, most of them have the good sense to avoid laying heavy hands on the daily conduct of college and university affairs. In normal times and for those who regard their unpaid fiduciary positions as being mainly honorific, the mantles of ultimate responsibility and authority may rest lightly. Few difficult cases may have come their way as a court of last resort. Now, however, even those campuses not beset by conflict are caught up by the rapid and turbulent change sweeping through American higher education.

Conserving and increasing the material assets of an educational institution, overseeing the improvement of its programs, maintaining its coherence and integrity, and protecting it against destructive forces are tasks that try the mettle of trustees almost everywhere. Today, as never before, they are called upon to represent the public's interest to institutions, and the interests of institutions to the public. Among the thirty thousand or so Americans who are trustees of the nation's colleges and universities may be counted many of our ablest and most public-spirited citizens. By and large, however, they are busy individuals, and not many find or take the time to articulate for the public at large their attitudes about the current scene in academe. The mass media, moreover, are little interested in trustee opinion or behavior unless it assumes extreme forms.

To find out the concerns now uppermost in the minds of a cross section of trustees, a query was recently addressed to board chairmen of a variety of institutions across the country. More than fifty replied, and some did so at length. Their responses suggest that by no means all trustees are as stuffy and parochial as was implied in a widely cited survey conducted several years ago.

If the respondents queried more recently are at all representative, trustees are aware that in some quarters the legitimacy of their authority is being attacked, their qualifications and organizational composition questioned, their performance criticized, and the importance of their function denigrated. With reference to current disorders in colleges and universities, one observer (not a trustee) has noted that although "trustees are not a primary factor in creating campus tensions, . . . by doing certain things and failing to do others they do not exert their full potential to alleviate or forestall tensions." He goes on to assert that "it is the quality of most boards to react passively, aggressively, petulantly, cooperatively; but almost never constructively, imaginatively, or sensitively."

In a paper prepared for the Special Committee on Campus Tensions, one trustee began by showing sensitivity to the range of attitudes about the role as illustrated by his selection of quotations from the responses of fellow trustees to the survey query:

A board of regents, representative of the university constituency, is more important now than at any time in the history of higher education. (A business executive)

Boards of trustees and regents are an anachronism, and should be abolished, if not immediately, certainly over the next five years! (A graduate student from a West Coast university)

It's about time regents helped constituencies understand the revolutionary changes taking place in academic life and not simply interpret what they think are our wishes to the academic community. (An attorney)

Trustees are old, rich, totally out of touch with today's academic world and useless except for fund raising. (An undergraduate student leader in a private Midwestern college)

Students and faculties are now so irresponsible and militant that trustees have an obligation to demonstrate who holds the actual power. *We* hold it, not the faculty, not the president, not the students, and it is time we started making that clear! (Trustee of an Eastern college)

Although there is manifest disagreement about whether trustees are really needed, and, if needed, about their duties and how they should be executed, clearly the leaders among them are deeply concerned with a wide range of critical problems in American higher education. According to the recent survey inquiry, the six most common concerns of trustees (in descending order of frequency) are: (1) finances, including optimum use of funds and facilities, and threatened loss of support as a result of public backlash; (2) governance, including communication; (3) faculty, teaching, and innovative educational programs; (4) student unrest; (5) definition of institutional goals and higher education's relations to society; (6) institutional leadership.

Finances

Since the public interest in higher education bears directly on financial support, trustees, as representatives of that interest, are necessarily concerned with money matters. Advocates of faculty and student hegemony in governance tend to ignore the actuality that their institutions are heavily subsidized from the outside. Thus these institutional constituencies are fortunate that trustees and top administrative officials are never allowed to forget the hard realities of financial problems. Many trustees know that students and faculty often criticize them for not having more firsthand knowledge of educational issues, but they are also aware that these same constituencies would be even more critical if trustees diverted time to programmatic matters at the expense of the institution's solvency.

The most prevalent single worry of trustees and regents today is the growing public disenchantment with higher education and the prospective leveling-off or even decline in financial support as a result of reaction to campus disorders. Many of the proposed reforms that come before them call for added expenditures in a period of financial stringency; seldom do student or faculty recommendations for change suggest what their proponents would be willing to forgo in order to acquire the often expensive new goodies. Moreover, urgings that academic institutions develop action programs to help solve problems of environmental pollution, poverty, slums, the culturally deprived, and so on, come at a time when these very problems compete with educational needs for financial assistance.

Everywhere the trustees of independent colleges and universities are bothered about the future of private higher education. Board members in both the private and public sectors report being plagued by the consequences of inflation, loss of federal grants, student aid needs, soaring construction costs, and continued pressures to broaden services without regard to the limited means available. More than most members of the academic community, trustees also recognize the desirability of interinstitutional coordination to avoid wasteful duplication of facilities and programs.

Governance

Some trustees acknowledge uncertainty about how faculty and student participation in decision and policy making would be most useful. The prevailing sentiment seems to be that boards must retain ultimate authority and responsibility in governance, with delegation where appropriate. Some complain that presidential views tend to limit their province too exclusively to protective functions, fund raising, campus planning, and selection of the president. Whether plaintively or not, one trustee voiced the opinion that the board chairman is no longer a Triton among minnows! Another noted that trustees suffer frustration and discontent because they are not clear about what their responsibility is and how they should discharge it. He conceded that students and faculty are entitled to know where decisions are made and how action is taken. A different trustee claimed, however, that board members are at times disillusioned by the way institutions are conducted without either the knowledge or consent of relevant board committees or of the board itself. There was some sentiment in favor of more codification of rights and responsibilities of the various constituencies, but this was coupled with the realization that careful codification is no guarantee of mutual trust, improved consensus, or high morale.

Board members are cognizant that in some quarters they are criticized for being mostly successful individuals, past fifty years of age, and possessed of above average means. They wonder, however, whether adding resentful failures and young or impoverished persons to their ranks would increase their collective wisdom. They also doubt that their institutions and the public would be served better if board authority (and its related "impartial stewardship") flowed entirely from those being governed.

A regent of one of the largest and most prestigious state universities admitted that board members too often forget the distinction between formal and legitimate power, and are surprised when the university community defies or ignores their orders. While in general they oppose the inclusion of faculty and students in their membership because of possible conflicts of interest and the inherent cleavages in special pleading, many trustees acknowledged need for better bases of board selection and diversity among members.

A number of board members were bothered by inadequate

communication to them of knowledge about basic educational issues and programs. They felt that students, faculty, administrators, and trustees must somehow develop more effective means of rapport in complex institutions. Still others voiced a need for comparative norms to be used in deciding policy questions. Many recognized that, as intermediaries between the academic community and the larger society, boards serve as buffers and conduits, but none was willing to see trustees or regents become mere pipelines.

Insofar as relations between the board and the faculty are concerned, a trustee of a major university asserted that the rhetoric of faculty governance betrays a cultural lag. Intricate structures maintain a pretense of a self-governing "community of scholars" where there is no real community. Except in crisis, he contended, most professors do not want to be bothered by problems of academic government. They rise in protest and then lapse back into their own affairs, leaving day-to-day government to a small minority—mostly the bureaucrats and politicians in their midst. By implication, in large and complex institutions where the concept of "community" has lapsed, responsibility has to be assumed somewhere, not just for parking, money raising, and public relations, but for the "deeper requirement of any organization for central direction." Most trustees concur that they and their chief executive officer, the president, often have no option but to carry out this responsibility.

The Faculty
and Teaching

Trustees are concerned not only about faculty derelictions in self-governance but also by the high proportion of campus disruptions in which members of the teaching staff (mostly the younger and lower-ranked members) play leadership roles among the students. Trustees are also prone to interpret the first loyalty of many academicians to their discipline or field as a sign of disloyalty to the institution as a prime claimant on their services.

As one survey shows, more than nine out of ten trustees believe that the teaching function is more important than research. Many of them are correspondingly worried about the academic guild system that gives priority to research and publication as a basis for professional recognition, and are groping for ways to strengthen the significance of effective teaching in the institution's reward scheme. Likewise, they have increasing doubts about tenure, viewing it as a shield for neglect and incompetence as well as a recognized protection for academic freedom.

Some share with student dissidents a feeling that many faculty are opposed to innovation and change in their own areas, are not really zealous about the improvement of teaching and learning, and are reluctant to have their real productivity objectively evaluated. Alongside this belief that many faculty neglect their basic institutional obligations is a feeling among some trustees that a loose coalition of students and junior faculty is beginning to form against board members, administrators, and the more responsible sector of the faculty itself.

As someone has observed, the board's relationship with the educational program and hence with the faculty is probably its area of greatest confusion. Recognizing that their status as amateurs or laymen limits direct involvement with curricular matters and those who preside over these areas, trustees sense that everything else in an institution is subsidiary to the educational program. Hence they view the ultimate responsibility of a board as necessarily implying a deep concern for basic academic functions. Thoughtful trustees thus complain about having programs reported to them only in financial terms and about receiving information on educational developments that have already taken place. Even board members who wish to effect what they regard as constructive changes are uncertain how to proceed in the face of faculty indifference or opposition.

Other trustees are disturbed over the prospect that, in responding to change, the institution may lose its integrity. "The university must keep its integrity; it must maintain itself as an institution serving the present, but embodied in history and dedicated to the future."

Student
Unrest

It may surprise some that concern with student unrest ranked only fourth as a current worry among the trustees queried. The most irritated of the trustees would probably agree with a well-known writer on education, who, in an unpublished commentary, has remarked on what he calls "the schizophrenia of the student movement" as illustrated by students

driving totally unnecessary cars to meetings to protest air pollution, acclaiming a hedonist approach to life in a time of intricate inter-dependence and grievous need for systematic planning; denouncing the hypocrisy of others while exploiting everything and everybody in sight. In the absence of an understanding that the nation needs skilled profes-sionals and managers, students cannot begin to ask for a major role in planning educational experience. They are being permitted to feed parasitically on the productive labors of others because the society expects them to emerge from higher education ready to make some contribution, and all discussions of the university must keep that very obvious fact in mind.

There is a great deal that can be done to free up the colleges and respond meaningfully to student demands—but not in the framework of the students' presentation of them.... The student movement is in severe danger of becoming, to coin a phrase, irrelevant. But there are very real and important grievances behind the movement. If we allow them to fester untreated because the students can't articulate their problem—and the more I see the student leaders, the more impressed I am with how *inarticulate* they are, despite all the fashionable mouthings—we shall be cheating everybody.

Speaking for his trustees as well as for himself, a president has stressed the problem of "how to improve communication among the several constituencies, how to resolve internal pressures without destroying orderly procedures, how to minimize the tremendous wastage of time unproductively used in gamesmanship with those who claim they want dialogue but who mean they want control, and to do these things in a way that is rational and sensitive."

In one highly selective private institution, an uppermost con-cern pertained to pressures pushing that institution more and more toward serving "the alienated affluent and the alienated impover-ished." Several trustees expressed puzzlement over the lowering of admission standards to enroll disadvantaged students, and also doubted whether most institutions would or could provide the added funds, facilities, staffs, and special programs to meet their needs. One commentator, speaking broadly, observed that the large majority of institutions are designed to serve only one of three types of students—the 70 percent who adjust to the curriculum and instruction without being very creative or imaginative. The ill-served groups (approximating the remaining 30 percent) are the underendowed or disadvantaged and, at the other extreme, the highly intelligent and creative.

The specificity of attitudes about student unrest trailed off into expressions of astonishment and dismay about students' motives and philosophies, and a concern, already indicated, about whether adverse public reaction will be reflected in greatly curtailed financial support of both public and private institutions. One corporate executive felt that teachers are not giving students a fair picture of the free enterprise system of American society.

Many trustees would doubtless agree with a member of the Special Committee on Campus Tensions who has stated that students learn better in reciprocal than in one-way influence situations. He has gone on to note:

How to attain mutuality in a relationship that cannot appropriately be symmetrical?—for there *are* teachers and learners; the elders have greater experience, competence, and expertise. I don't think this one has been very well solved. We currently err on the side of squelching the student. I would not like to see us shove the pendulum in an uncritical swing toward permissiveness and student control. Student wants may be clear enough, but student *needs* can only be guessed at uncertainly. I am not saying that faculties know best, but I am certain that students do not fully know what they need in the long run.

Institutional Goals
and Societal Relations

In their capacity as overseers, trustees ideally have no vested interests as individuals, and most of them appear to be well aware of their obligation to help relate institutional objectives to the needs and aspirations of the supporting society. Their reactions indicate a rejection of the idea that the college or university is an organization intended solely to meet the needs of individual students as defined by the students themselves. As lay representatives, they also resist the syndicalist view of many professors that the academic profession should virtually control all of the educational aspects of institutions of higher learning. Some of them regard presidents and other officers of top administration as being primarily executives of broad policies formulated by trustees.

In the main, however, trustees recognize that many parties are involved in the development of policy and that every institution has varied outside constituencies. The campus as well as the outside constituencies likewise have competing objectives. Some would make the college or university a general-purpose institution; others would have it serve special purposes. For the national economy, meeting manpower needs is given primacy as an educational objective; from the perspective of the individual student, his own self-development may be uppermost as an educational aim. The variety of purposes is recognized by all institutional policy-makers, but the tension generated sometimes manifests itself in trustee ambivalence about priorities of effort.

Moreover, trustees, as one observer has noted, are more often validators than formulators of policy. "In fact, it can be said that most institutions operate by habits, by assumptions, by accumulated decisions—all acquiring in the course of time the force of common law. But the vulnerability of institutions to attacks by radical minorities has been dramatized by the revelation that boards have not adequately devoted themselves to the review and refinement of policies and to the effective communication of policy."

Trustee comments repeatedly show a conscious need to clarify the objectives of American higher education as a whole and the role of each institution within the system. Many realize that traditional programs do not always fit current needs, and that better institutional guidelines should stem from long-range planning and the establishment of campus priorities. They sense that not only the heightened importance of higher education but also the prospect of its becoming universal will thrust most colleges and universities into a closer relationship with the surrounding society. They have a growing awareness that in many places compromises will have to be worked out between competing conceptions of the college or university as a community of scholars, a community of students, a corporate enterprise, an agency or arm of the state, a public service agency, and so on. Charged with maintaining the solvency and protecting the integrity of their institutions, they are also worried about upholding these responsibilities while simultaneously responding to an increased variety of internal pressures and being party to the allocation of scarce resources to social problems of the larger society. Furthermore, they are not inclined to accept the notion that change for its own sake is invariably a good thing.

Institutional
Leadership

By and large, trustees are of the opinion that individual leaders are no less essential than individual institutions to the welfare of American higher education. Trustees of public institutions, in particular, view with some alarm the tendency of politicians and bureaucrats in the national capital and in state capitals to bypass and undermine the traditional powers of trusteeship and to erode the leadership responsibilities of the executive officers the boards have chosen. Observing egalitarian movements on many campuses, a number indeed wonder whether many of the denizens of academe do not prefer anarchy to any form of government. Board members, being for the most part successful business and professional men, are understandably resistant to the notion that colleges or universities can and should be conducted like clubs or debating societies, with all sharing equally in the determination of ends and means.

Trustees and regents are aware of the reluctance of many academicians to be drawn into administrative work and of the mounting harassments to which top executive officers are subjected on some campuses. Their perception, however, is that now as never before strong leadership is needed to bring divided interests together in a common cause. They see a main job for themselves and the presidents as being creative leadership and not just mediation, moderation, or conciliation.

Some board members concede that a reexamination of trustee functions is overdue. They acknowledge their shortcomings in dealing with many of the complexities of institutional governance, and believe, further, that better liaison is required with faculty, students, and other constituencies. They also acknowledge the need for improved methods of selecting board members, better devices for effecting change as well as continuity in their membership, more effective operating structures that would bring to the fore of their attention the values of asking the right questions and insisting on the right answers about the institutions they oversee. Even though they grant that their changing assignments may call for more diversity of talent and experience, they oppose the idea that a governing board should be a collection of special representatives.

As one prominent board member has put it, "Trustees should not run the institution, but should see that it is well run." Accepting this truism of academic governance, most trustees realize the need to delegate many of their powers to the president, and to hold him responsible for the execution of basic policies. In this same vein, nine out of ten trustees view the president as a leader rather than mere mediator. Although they sometimes feel that presidents and other administrative officers are not sufficiently firm-handed in what they regard—in corporate terminology—as "management," many are aware that the central direction of academic enterprise must depend more upon persuasion than upon other control devices in situations where shared power, consultation, and the development of consensus are the most effective means to institutional ends.

On all sides there seems to be a growing awareness of the necessity for more clear-cut accountability in the conduct of academic affairs. A number of trustees, for example, articulated the importance of performing better a "function that lies between hiring and firing—the function of evaluation." They also express a need for more objective means of assessing institutional management and accomplishment. As the recent public statements of some prominent university presidents indicate, this sentiment is shared by executive officers, who are increasingly dismayed by the uncertainty and confusion surrounding their authority and responsibility.

In conclusion, many trustees and regents are puzzled by criticisms from within and without the academic communities they believe themselves to be serving. Some resent the lack of appreciation often shown for their supportive efforts and the openly expressed view in some quarters that boards at best are supernumeraries and at worst hindrances to collegial endeavor. They are disturbed by the illusory notions of those members of the academic community who speak as if institutions had the option from taxpayers, legislators, private donors, and others of forgoing all semblance of outside direction and control of campus activities.

As informed critics of academic governance have virtually all concluded, despite its shortcomings, the lay board is still preferable to other methods of control. Realistic consideration of the alternatives strongly suggests that the reform of board organization and procedures is preferable to an abandonment of the board concept. No mere redefinition of trustee roles will eliminate existing frictions, but failure to make lay boards more effective participants in the total enterprise is certain to increase the tensions now disturbing much of American higher education.

Part Three

HIGHER EDUCATION'S
VARIED OBJECTIVES

On June 1, 1964, I gave the commencement address at Mercer University in Macon, Georgia. Adopting a critical attitude toward certain widely shared American complacencies, I held forth on some false cults of the time.

Education for Adversity

M Y REMARKS to you today are intended primarily for members of this graduating class. You may wonder why on such a happy occasion I have chosen such a doleful sounding subject as "Education for Adversity." I do so because I believe it is a matter you graduates need to do some hard thinking about.

Before I go to my main points, however, I will state that I do not appear before you as a "prophet of doom." To speak colloquially, I doubt that any other generation of college graduates "ever had it so good." Without having yet contributed much to what we call "the American way of life," you will enjoy the cumulative benefits of the labors of generations that have preceded you. You will inherit a standard of living which has improved more in the last fifty years than in all the previous centuries of Western history.

If the least fortunate graduate among you achieves merely average economic success in this prosperous land of ours, he will enjoy a per capita income more than five times that of the world average. On your jobs, in this age of mechanization and automation, most of you will never engage in enough manual labor to make the term "sweat of your brow" anything more than a figurative expression. You will be a member of a free society in which much of the activity of the marketplace is designed to make life easier and more pleasant for the public at large. In your homes you will be surrounded by conveniences and comforts undreamed of by your forebears. If you choose to travel afar, the prediction is that you will reach your destinations at supersonic speed. The probability is that you will be healthier and will live longer than any previous generation.

Educational Outcomes

Since you have already successfully completed sixteen years of formal education, you are familiar with the statistics on the increase in earning capacity that results from every year spent in school. Perhaps I should warn you that those of you who are successful in your vocations are likely not only to work harder but also for longer hours than those of more limited capacities and aspirations. The predicted decline in the work week to thirty hours or less is not a prospect for executive and professional men and women, for our society is rapidly being dichotomized into two categories. It is rather ironic that the so-called laboring classes are the ones getting more and more leisure time, whereas persons in positions involving high ability and great responsibility never worked harder or longer. Those of you who choose careers that are not too demanding may find some solace, accordingly, in the outlook for more leisure for the pursuit of your avocations.

There are those who feel that the American people live a little too comfortably. It is in the upper income brackets, curiously, that we find most of the critics who believe that the masses have been demoralized in recent years by having their incomes and living levels greatly improved. I do not share this view. I see nothing ennobling about poverty and no virtue in unnecessarily enduring discomfort and deprivation. One of the measures of the success of our economy is the extent to which it has elevated not just the privileged few but the citizenry at large. A major challenge ahead is to eliminate the "pockets of poverty" which are still to be found in every region.

One lesson to be learned from our kind of society is that we have achieved our high plane of living largely because we are better educated and more productive. We can consume more because we produce more. We can have more leisure because we get more done in less time. Our labor-saving devices and comforts are not the consequences of laziness, but of ingenuity. Thanks to the advancement of science, technology, and better ways of thinking and doing, we have found solutions to many problems which baffled earlier generations and still baffle the great masses of illiterate and semiliterate peoples in many parts of the world.

Many of you will agree, I trust, that American youth today is, in the main, well educated both to maintain and to further our life of relative abundance. Those who claim that higher education in the United States has undergone a decline in standards and accomplishments simply do not know what they are talking about. Formal education in classrooms and laboratories, however, should not be held accountable for the entire development of the individual. Many attitudes, interests, and skills are necessarily shaped outside the schoolyard and off the campus. Much that we must learn can be learned only through a process of self-education. When I speak of education for adversity, I am talking principally about self-education.

Student counselors, guidance experts, admissions officers, and prospective employers well know that many important aspects of an individual's total personality do not lend themselves readily to formal education and cannot be evaluated by the usual rating procedures and transcript notations. Character development is a complicated process. It is not merely acquiring a body of knowledge that can be taught directly as such in our schools and colleges. As Woodrow Wilson once noted when he was president of Princeton University, character comes as a by-product—and, I would add, a by-product of cumulative life experience. We long ago discovered that youth is not made tolerant, courageous, truthful, honest, and persevering by being compelled to memorize and write down high-sounding copybook maxims. Strength of character is acquired in more subtle and indirect ways. Formal training and discipline imposed by others can aid us in following through on jobs and in avoiding discouragements at first failures, but true discipline must come from within.

An old maxim says that "Adversity introduces a man to himself," and still another states, "Gold is tried in fire, and acceptable men in the furnace of adversity." Along with your sixteen or more years of formal education, all of you graduates have acquired, I hope, the character traits that will enable you to meet the tests ahead. For many of you, your degree will be a ticket of entry to a job, but you should remember that no institution can provide you with a passport to worthwhile living. Somehow you must find this for yourself. I trust that you have by now developed some helpful guidelines, and, in any event, I should like to caution you against dependence on some of the misleading cults of our time.

Misleading Cults

The first of these cults stresses the physical self—security, conformity, and the avoidance of discomfort at all costs. Its ideals come less from the enduring values of the ages than from fads and fancies of the moment. Its adherents are more concerned with being like everybody else than with developing their own individualities. Avoidance of doing the wrong thing is more important to them than doing the right thing. Many of this cult's devotees confuse the search for security with the pursuit of happiness: still others identify happiness with the escape from discomfort. Although avoiding wherever possible anything that might be personally painful, they are hardly moved by the plagues and woes of mankind.

As long as these latter-day hedonists are healthy, and feel secure and prosperous, they have no quarrel with the world around them and are perfectly content to take it as it is. Except for the complication of their lives by the quest for status symbols, their psychology is essentially that of the larger order of primates. I trust that none of you graduates expect to cushion yourselves against life's adversities through membership in this basically animalistic cult.

The second cult which ill prepares us for adversity has to do

with the mind. It is the cult of softheaded thinking, of impression-
istic judgment, of misplaced values. Despite our zeal for careful
examination, analysis, and experimentation in the spheres of science
and technology, we are frequently reluctant to use logical methods
in the conduct of our personal and collective affairs in social,
economic, and political areas. Many who are acutely aware of the
importance of a balanced diet for the well-being of their bodies,
for example, seem strangely oblivious to what goes into their
minds. Parents project their own laxities and shortcomings as failures
of the educational system in developing a sense of responsibility
in youth. Without regard to what could be learned from the
humanities and social sciences, presumably educated individuals
continue to make important life decisions as if relevant knowledge
were nonexistent. In our attitudes toward mental and emotional
disorders, criminality, chronic poverty, the culturally deprived,
large-scale unemployment, international conflict, and a host of other
problems, we likewise very often proceed foolishly and irrationally,
as if nothing had been learned in the last two thousand years.
It is no wonder, then, that we are surprised and poorly prepared
for some of the adversities we encounter.

Several centuries ago, in his *Novum Organum,* Francis Bacon
remarked, "Knowledge and human power are synonymous, since
ignorance of the cause frustrates the effect. For nature is only sub-
dued by submission, and that which in contemplative philosophy
corresponds with the cause, in practical science becomes the rule."
We usually follow this rational principle in dealing with the phe-
nomena of the physical sciences, but when it comes to thinking
about ourselves and our fellow human beings we often prefer to
rely on sentiment and prejudice to the exclusion of reason.

Aside from the need for clear, hard thinking if we are to
minimize the consequences of ignorance and error, our thought
needs to be attuned to the problems at hand, however unpleasant
they may be. At times, pessimism may be a more sensible outlook
than optimism, but more than either of these we require a constructive skepticism in confronting the brute facts of life. The
highly educated have a special obligation to know the facts, to
marshal them as a basis for decision and action, to avoid bias and
prejudice, and to show courageous leadership in facing up to the

critical personal and public issues of our era. I therefore wish for each of you graduates the mental framework that makes this kind of thinking possible.

In addition to those cults of the body and mind which handicap us in coping with the inescapable—and often harsh—realities of life, I add a third: that of the spirit. It has been asserted that psychologically the largest single problem facing the average person now and in the future is alienation—a kind of social malaise characterized by lack of identity, isolation, powerlessness, and a sense of meaninglessness. The stresses and strains of living in an increasingly complicated society are evidenced in such manifestations as neurosis, psychosis, alcoholism, delinquency, broken homes, and other readily observable forms of behavior. Other evidences which are less amenable to measurement are social indifference and moral and political apathy. Even on some of our campuses, there is a growing sentiment to the effect that "academic brightness is moral goodness, and academic dullness is evil," with the corollary belief that the personal behavior of students in all other respects is really nobody's business.

In our misguided efforts to escape the consequences of alienation, we can, as someone has said, minimize freedom itself by trying to eliminate some of its costs. Conflict is one such cost, and we can count its price too heavily and its worth too lightly. If too many of us wish to escape the hazards of conflict and seek private and public lives of complete harmony, unity, and peace at any price, the road can lead, as it has led historically, to the omnipotent church of the Middle Ages, or the totalitarian state of modern times. To offset having all our choices and decisions ready-made, we must discharge our own duties and be prepared to pay the price of maintaining individual integrity. For all who weary of the unrelenting effort necessary for self-discipline and spiritual independence, I would recommend reading or rereading George Orwell's *1984*.

Another manifestation of cultism of the spirit is religiosity in contrast to real religion. Because of the inability of many of us to take the sour along with the sweet, the worse with the better, we have been witnessing a rise of what theologians have called the dogma of reassurance—a contemporary effort to make religion over into magic. For some, this takes the form of surface manifestations of the traditional sort, and for others movements of a secular nature are substituted. In any event, there is the common desire to escape from worry and failure, and to find a panacea for personal and social harassments.

As Robert M. Hutchins recently said, education itself is in danger of being regarded as the answer to every prayer and the means of realizing every dream. He has mentioned that orators on unemployment, peace, technology, delinquency, divorce, democracy, developing nations, and race questions almost always bring their remarks to a stirring conclusion by asserting that education is the "solution." From our former stand of asking too little of education, we have now, perhaps, moved to a position of expecting too much. I agree with him that some things education cannot do, and many more it should not attempt.

Reinhold Niebuhr has pointed out that our misguided efforts to find complete reassurance about all of life's difficulties lack the realization that all human effort, no matter how noble, contains within it an element of failure. Even the Christian doctrine of salvation implies a good deal more than merely wanting to be saved.

In essence, to be ready for life's adversities, we must first transform ourselves. Just as some try to escape through various cultish beliefs, others become alcoholics or live in a mental and spiritual world of fantasy. If we will make our selfish aims secondary to broader and higher objectives, then we shall be on the path to leading happier as well as more useful lives. As A. N. Whitehead has put it, "There stands the inexorable law that apart from some transcendent aim the civilized life either wallows in pleasure or relapses slowly into a barren repetition with waning intensities of feeling."

In conclusion, I want to urge the members of this graduating class not only to avoid the false cults of body, mind, and spirit, but also to face the uncertainties ahead with courage and determination. Whatever may be in store for you, I trust that you will make big plans and not be content with little schemes. By aiming high and realizing that struggle is the law of growth, I believe you will be truly prepared for the worst as well as the best, and I sincerely wish each of you Godspeed.

Having concluded in 1967 that all the talk about the importance of excellence in American higher education was causing the equal importance of adequacy to be slighted as an objective, I chose this topic for my commencement address at the University of Houston, June 3, 1967, in Houston, Texas.

Education for Adequacy

LET ME START by saying that adequacy, in the sense that I am using it, means sufficiency for a purpose, or being fully equal to a requirement. It does not denote mediocrity or minimum acceptability. I choose this subject because the great amount of attention given to education for *excellence* in recent years has resulted in a neglect of emphasis on the importance of adequacy as a worthy goal. Entering freshmen, no less than graduating students, might readily get the impression that they are destined for leadership, and that they would be derelict in their duties and a discredit to their institutions if this later proved not to be the outcome. To be sure, those who go beyond competence to excel others in any line of worthwhile endeavor are our most precious human resource. But other levels of achievement are also important to our collective well-being, and education for adequacy or competence is no less essential to our national welfare than education for excellence.

We need to remind ourselves that excellence is, by definition, a status to be achieved by the few rather than the many. We compete for things or values that cannot be equally shared by all of

146

the competitors, with the highest kudos and rewards presumably going to those who excel in their accomplishments. Competitive enterprise is thus an activity in which one of the aims is to outdo others. Our team sports, for example, are contrived to result in wins or losses of games, and the victor emerges as the national or international champion. Even in an individualistic sport like golf, there is a pecking order for amateurs and professionals, ranging from the Arnold Palmers to those who play so badly that they are beyond the pale of handicaps.

Rank orders of capability and performance in other and more basic human endeavors are seldom so easily perceived, but there too the participants necessarily distribute themselves over a wide spectrum. College-bound young persons display a considerable range of aptitudes, and once on the campus, their performance ranges from the first-semester flunk-outs to the small number of those who are later graduated with straight *A* records. Moreover, the qualitative variations in standards among institutions are extensive.

I mention these variations not only to illustrate the meaning of excellence but also to demonstrate its inappropriateness as the sole objective of endeavor. If a consistent golf score of about seventy were a prerequisite for country club membership, most of our golf courses would be virtually deserted; if top academic talent were essential for all educational enterprise, most of the nation's twenty-two hundred colleges and universities would be empty. Fortunately for most of us, something short of excellence is both necessary and sufficient in most human affairs.

By making a fetish of excellence in spite of the growing egalitarianism in higher education, we can readily denigrate the importance of adequacy. It has been observed that although the British system of higher education, with its highly selective admission policies, did a very good job in the past of educating those being groomed for leadership posts, it also tended to bypass that nation's growing need for well-trained individuals for a large variety of other positions. Great Britain, incidentally, is now following our example of providing a much wider range of educational opportunities.

In the United States, we are now moving toward universal

postsecondary education, with higher education no longer an elitist enterprise. In some parts of our country, 80 percent of the present generation now finishes high school, and more than half of those go on to college. To encourage all of these youth to believe that they must somehow outperform others in order to be considered successful in college and later in life is a mistaken fostering of false hopes that may lead to frustration and bitterness.

Within the pluralism of American higher education, a wide variety of educational opportunities are available—from the very selective, special-purpose institutions such as the California Institute of Technology to the open-door junior colleges. One characteristic of the large public institution is its provision of a learning environment attuned to the needs and aspirations of a very diverse group of students. Despite current criticisms of the comprehensive university, it affords many advantages on a single campus. Students benefit from contacts with others who differ markedly from them in abilities and interests, and they are mutually stimulated by an environment that includes a mix of backgrounds, ideas, and aims. The experience of the atmosphere of such surroundings is, in my opinion, good training for the conditions of modern urban living.

Importance of Realistic and Eclectic Objectives

In view of the range of human talents and socioeconomic needs, we need to be both realistic and eclectic in our educational objectives. To do so does not imply, of course, an acceptance of slipshod performance, a watering-down of academic standards, or a nurturing of mediocrity. It does not imply a lowering of admission standards merely to accommodate the social aspirations of those who lack the native capacity for college or university work. More positively put, it does mean that the culturally deprived, the underachievers, and others who may have latent capacities should somehow be brought up to performance levels adequate for the tasks at hand.

Institutions of higher education, as you well know, are not supported by the public primarily to promote student self-enjoyment or egocentric development. Furthermore, every accredited college or university is required to uphold academic standards of sufficiently recognized worth to command a universal currency. The credits given and the diplomas and degrees awarded are expected to signify satisfactory levels of subject-matter mastery. The possessors of technical, professional, and advanced degrees are assumed by society to be capable of performing certain complex tasks. Reputable colleges and universities thus have an obligation to educate for adequacy in all instances, with the achievement of excellence as an added dividend wherever possible.

It is altogether reasonable also that in return for its heavy investment in higher education, society has a right to demand, as well as to *expect*, competence of college and university graduates in their fields of specialization. Even in private institutions, student tuition never defrays the entire costs of instruction, and hence the payoff from the subsidies enjoyed by all students should be gauged in large measure by their increased individual usefulness to society.

In many of the services that the university-educated perform for society, certainly nothing less than adequacy is good enough. Employers do not brush aside repeated errors by accountants who also happen to be college graduates and very personable fellows. We all depend on the complete accuracy of optometrists and pharmacists, and rely on architects and engineers for technical knowledge that we cannot and need not understand. It is cheering to have a doctor or nurse with a pleasant bedside manner, but it is essential to be able to depend on their unswerving competence.

Although there is a French proverb which says the best is the enemy of the good, many collective undertakings call for both kinds of performance. Flights in outer space, for example, would be inconceivable without the best efforts of the ablest scientists and engineers, but, as the recent disaster at Cape Kennedy demonstrated, adequacy on the part of a great many other individuals is also indispensable. Even in routine flights on commercial airlines, we are continuously reminded of the extent to which our convenience, comfort, and safety depend upon the trained competence and complete reliability of master mechanics as well as crew captains.

To achieve both excellence and adequacy in our nation, education has the task of guiding individuals into roles suitable to their aptitudes. As Pliny once noted, "No man possesses a genius so commanding . . . that he can attain eminence, unless a subject suited to his talents should present itself, and an opportunity occur for their development."

Freedoms
and Obligations

Let me go on to say that we ought to appreciate more fully the benefits of the American system of higher education. Not only does this system provide educational opportunities for virtually all individuals who deserve them, but also it permits students more freedom of choice than does any other system. If you had grown up in a totalitarian society, perhaps 10 percent of you could have received an advanced education entirely at government expense, but the price you would have paid would have been the loss of freedom to choose the kinds of education suited to your own needs and wishes. Upon graduation, furthermore, you would have no option but to become employees of the state. For those students who chafe under the reasonable restraints necessary for the orderly conduct of our own colleges and universities, it would be a good object lesson for them to experience a year abroad as students under some totalitarian regime.

The freedoms we enjoy have their corollary obligations, however, and in our society there are entirely too many individuals satisfied merely with getting by, on the theory that, somehow, society owes them a living just because they exist. Although a college degree is increasingly being required for entry into many occupations where trained manpower is at a premium, still it is no guarantee that its possessor "has it made" thereafter. As you are aware, in many fields, the knowledge you have acquired will rapidly become obsolete, and unless you keep pace with new knowledge your degree will be worth less and less as time goes on. As you also know, erudition and brilliance are of little utility unless accompanied by initiative, diligence, and perseverance. Even in the bestiary of a fast-paced society, the tortoises sometimes still overtake the hares.

Despite recent allegations that our colleges and universities are encouraging technical competence at the expense of personal character, they do inculcate such important values as orderly work habits, a rational approach to problem solving, and career motivations related to the application of knowledge and skill. Whatever your fields of specialization, either now or later, these qualities will stand you in good stead. Our era, someone said, is not quite an heroic epoch, but we do live in an achievement-oriented society, where individuals, in the main, are judged by what they can do.

As our society becomes more bureaucratized and the division of labor enlarges, more and more tasks may be defined with greater precision and their performance assessed more accurately. Under such circumstances, the capable and ambitious young college graduate needs neither influence nor brilliance to demonstrate his sufficiency for many worthy purposes. Few jobs are so routinized that one cannot rise above meeting the minimum demands by a willingness to work longer hours, display initiative, or otherwise show qualities indicative of adequacy for more important assignments.

My truisms, I realize, may sound to many of you like a latter-day version of *Poor Richard's Almanac.* If you are not at all moved by them, perhaps a statement from George Bernard Shaw will be more evocative. Shaw once said:

> Every person who owes his life to civilized society, and who has enjoyed since his childhood its very costly protections and advantages, should appear at reasonable intervals before a properly qualified jury to justify his existence. This existence should be summarily and painlessly terminated if he fails to justify it—and if it develops that he is a positive nuisance and more trouble than he is worth. Nothing less will really make people responsible citizens.

Although Shaw's exhortation arouses no more than fanciful consideration, probably nearly everyone has his own list of people who are nuisances and trouble-makers and whose disappearance would make life pleasanter for all who have to suffer their presence. A difficulty in thinning them out, however, as Dr. Samuel Johnson grimly remarked, is that "If everybody got his just deserts, nobody would escape hanging."

Gallows humor aside, the task of education is, fortunately, the positive one of providing opportunities for as many human beings as possible to lead happier and more useful lives. I am confident that all of the graduates assembled here are to be counted as beneficiaries who now stand ready to make their contributions to a better world for all.

My Honors Day remarks at the University of Texas at Austin, in April 1966 (a variation was also given on a similar occasion at the University of North Dakota, at Grand Forks, in February 1968), tried to make the case for time-honored means of influencing student learning. In spite of the growing vogue of permissiveness and the scorn many persons now have for "carrots and sticks," I still think that they serve very useful purposes.

Carrots and Sticks
in the Higher Learning

ALTHOUGH CAMPUSES may be regarded ideally as places where knowledge is unrelentingly pursued for its own sake and truth is sought because it makes men free, we all know that colleges and universities are rooted in the world around them. The zeal for learning is often restrained by the law of laziness and other curbs on accomplishment, and no one should be surprised to find that formal education has evolved its own carrots and sticks in a systematic effort to influence student behavior in institutionally desired directions. Since some of my remarks about this generation of students may seem to malign them, I must say immediately that I agree with those who judge them to be in the main the best motivated we have ever had on our campuses.

As Kenneth Keniston has pointed out in his perceptive article, "Faces in the Lecture Room," higher education is no longer merely a pleasant interlude for sons and daughters of the well-to-do. In a technological society such as our own, higher education has to be a serious enterprise, and the status of individuals must, in general, be determined by accomplishment rather than inheritance. Coupled with this logic, these is also the egalitarian sentiment that young people from all social strata are entitled to as much advanced—and subsidized—educational opportunity as their capabilities warrant.

It is no wonder, then, that on most campuses the competition has become stiffer and the work harder. With a growing emphasis in our whole society on the principle of "what you can do" rather than of "who you are," it is to be expected that institutions of higher education should place a premium on cognitive efficiency, intellectual competence, and specialized knowledge. For serious students, diligence and performance displace popularity and polish as traits yielding the most carrots from academic endeavor. For those individuals whose achievement is mediocre, campus recognition and rewards tend to be meager, and for those who fail, the sticks of attrition may be felt as heavy blows.

Although intensified campus competition is producing the best-educated college graduates in history, it is also resulting in some problematic types. Dr. Keniston describes at some length, for example, the minorities whom he tags as the activists, the disaffiliates, and the underachievers. Just how prevalent these symptoms of disaffection are I do not claim to know. Some of the activists, of course, have attracted wide attention by acts of violence on the campus, and, ironically enough, often in protest about issues quite remote from the groves of academe. Those disaffiliates who have sought escape by way of pad, pill, and pot have likewise not escaped public notice. And even the underachievers are at last being recognized as problems not to be ignored or wished away.

Stress
and Strain

To attribute student tension and disquiet solely to the bureaucratization, impersonality, and bigness of the modern university is an oversimplification and an evasion. I would also add that the removal of all stress and strain, were it possible, could render the collegiate environment an unrealistic training and proving ground for life conditions in a complex society. Despite all the talk about an affluent society's indulgence of its young people, I do not believe that students are a coddled lot. As a well-known physicist has put it in *Science* magazine, "Students are probably the most overworked and underpaid class in our society . . . [and are often treated like monks] with a vow of poverty, austerity and over-work . . . given cafeteria fare in cinder block buildings" in an "affluent-society parody of medieval monasticism."

Aside from the psychological and physical stresses caused by heavier intellectual demands on students, vocational and other pressures of specialization diminish their chances of being liberally educated. Not enough time is left for the joy of learning for its own sake, for exploratory reading and study, or for personality enrichment. In short, while a college or university education is presumably being made into a more useful experience, it also may be turning into a less happy one.

We continuously need to remind ourselves, however, that the main purpose of higher education is not to further the contentment of students but to foster their intellectual growth. If it were otherwise, cues might be taken from the television networks and an academic equivalent of the Nielsen rating system devised to determine which courses and professors would be dropped, kept on, or given prime time—that is, time between ten and twelve o'clock on Mondays, Wednesdays, and Fridays. Student stress could also be reduced rather easily by lowering academic standards, slowing down the pace of work, and conferring degrees on all persons who stayed around for specified numbers of years.

Elsewhere in society, as a well-known sociologist has noted, there are many accepted ways of protecting the inept, as may be witnessed in labor union practices, business collusions in restraint of free competition, public school teacher promotions through seniority alone, professorial permanent tenure, civil service job security, and so on.

Even so, a competitive, open-class society must necessarily give more than lip service to the principle that individual status should be determined according to merit, and I could not recommend compromising it in the field of higher education. Let us acknowledge to ourselves, nonetheless, that adherence to it exacts a price in personal tensions.

An initial strain for many young persons, and their parents, is the matter of college admission. This is most acutely felt, I suspect, by those who seek entry into the Ivy League institutions and their counterparts across the nation. High school standing and the SAT score, as Louis Benezet has commented, are passports determining whether the student lands in "the college egg-crate marked 'Grade Double A.' The life that the student will live, the job he will attract, the graduate school he will get into, the people he will know, the girl he will marry—these depend much upon the particular college that admits him." The difference in the quality of student bodies is, of course, enormous in the institutional diversity represented by American higher education. A study by Alexander Astin, one of my associates at the American Council on Education, has shown, for example, that the dozen most selective colleges in the country could choose their entire student bodies from the top 2 percent of the student population, whereas the 176 with the least power of selectivity recruit virtually no entrants of this standing.[1]

Matching Capabilities and Opportunities

Although it is important that student abilities and interests be carefully matched with institutional opportunities, most people are prone to exaggerate the values of attending prestigious schools. For some students, a small, liberal arts college may be the best place to go, and for others, a large complex university will be more suitable. With 50 percent or more of all secondary school graduates going on to college in many states, it is a good idea, in my judgment, to have some open-door institutions which accept any high school graduate. Specialized and highly selective institutions, such as the California Institute of Technology, also have essential roles. In general, I do not favor a rigid institutional segregation of students according to their abilities, and I agree with Sir Eric Ashby that there can be a "peaceful coexistence of mediocrity and excellence" in higher education, just as there is elsewhere in society.

To minimize unnecessary frustrations in higher education, we should not let egalitarian sentiments delude us with the notion that everyone can benefit from the experience. In a cross section of one hundred persons, according to the Army General Classification

1. "College Preferences of Very Able Students," *College and University*, Spring 1965, pp. 282–97.

Test, there are eight or nine whose intelligence quotients fall between 70 and 80, and seven more of lesser mentality. Although a suitable education can enhance their limited capabilities, *higher* education is simply beyond their grasp. It is estimated that about thirty-four out of every one hundred persons, those with IQs ranging from 80 to 100, have "normal intelligence." Not every institution accepts such applicants, but many of them would be admitted somewhere and some of them would succeed in college and later.

In brief, I would argue that we should keep the doors of advanced educational opportunity open for all who can benefit themselves and society by utilizing it. This definition means, of course, the removal of all discrimination because of race, sex, class, creed, or other irrelevant criteria. It means an avoidance of institutional arrangements which relegate impecunious young people to vocational or other specialized schools for the poorer classes, as is done in some European countries, and an avoidance of corruption by selling college admissions and passing grades, as is the case in some countries of Latin America, Asia, and Africa. The other side of this coin is that we should avoid making higher education a fetish to the extent that a person must have gone to college to qualify for a job as a filling station attendant, retail sales clerk, or other position where secondary schooling would suffice. After all, intellectual capability is not the only quality needed by our complex society; persons of limited formal education but with more than their share of honesty, compassion, ingenuity, and simple diligence are to be counted among the most useful members of every community.

Despite the current concern about the dropout problem in this country (and the erroneous assumption that dropouts have by definition "failed"), in fact our schools and colleges have greater holding power than those of any other nation. More than 60 percent of all young Americans now finish high school, and by 1980 that figure is expected to rise to 80 percent. Of these latter, it is anticipated that by 1980, 60–70 percent will seek a still more advanced education, with the likelihood that more than the present percentage of those entering will be graduated.

The tendency for higher education to become universal, however, does not imply the disappearance of conventional carrots and sticks. Continuous testing—a present source of much uncertainty, anxiety, and criticism—promises to be intensified as we improve our ability to evaluate individuals more systematically and objectively. With further refinements in standardized testing and the use of computers in the interpretation of results, we can foresee more assessment and placement of individuals through national use of evaluative and predictive tests.

Testing
and Evaluating

In view of the debates in recent years about the virtues and vices of the unrelenting testing that young Americans are subjected to from nursery school through college, something about its rationale is in order here. Whether, as elitists, we want to single out the most promising achievers, or as egalitarians, we want to provide appropriate opportunities for all who participate in education, in our kind of society we cannot logically opt for eliminating continuous testing and evaluation.

As the anthropologists have observed, a society can ascribe statuses on such arbitrary bases as family background, skin color, sex, age, susceptibility to epileptic seizures, and other traits, or it can leave statuses open to individual achievement. With some qualifications, our ideology in this country is now identified with the latter alternative, and the result is clearly evident in our educational system. Evaluative as well as predictive testing of student progress is thus unavoidable in contemporary education and reliable information is essential in the administration of our educational institutions.

Even though testing is still fraught with hazards, we do have widely accepted means of measuring general intelligence and special aptitudes. The results of such tests, alongside course marks, often determine whether a child is in a slow or fast track in school, whether his secondary education is primarily academic or vocational, and which colleges or universities will accept him for admission. Still more testing is used to ascertain his capability for graduate or professional education, and even after he completes his formal education, many potential employers use standardized testing in placement and promotion.

Commenting on all of this, the *Carnegie Quarterly* a year or so ago observed:

Considering the role such tests play in determining who goes where and does what in our society, it is not surprising that there is widespread concern about them. Most of the concern, however, has focused on the tests themselves—whether they are valid (that is, whether a given test measures the thing it is intended to measure), whether they are reliable (does the same person get the same score on the same or comparable tests if he is retested later?), whether they fail to pay attention to important qualities such as creativity and motivation, whether they tend to measure slickness and quickness but not depth or subtlety of mind.

Orville Brim's report on American attitudes toward intelligence tests discloses that the following issues are currently prominent: inaccessibility of test data for feedback purposes, invasion of privacy, rigidity in use of test scores, the selection of certain types of talent, and the fairness of tests to minority or culturally deprived groups. In a talk before the College Entrance Examination Board, James A. Perkins, president of Cornell University, asked whether most of the objective tests in use had been designed to tell the student where he can or must improve, or whether they were designed primarily to help the school and college sort the talents in their charge. His conclusion was that in the United States, as contrasted with more authoritarian political and educational systems, we must maintain a balance among the desires of the student, the requirements of the program, and the judgments of the institution.

Those of you who have read Michael Young's provocative book, *The Rise of the Meritocracy*, will recall that his projected "classless society" is one in which no single human characteristic, such as intelligence, would be the basis for evaluating individuals. Instead, there would be plural values to determine social status: imagination, sympathy, generosity, and other qualities would be evaluated beside intelligence, education, occupation, and power. The aim would be for each individual to have a high status in at least one respect, just as the Army General Classification Test tries to identify at least one activity in which each recruit can excel.

The college or university must function in a real rather than an imaginary society, however, and in the real world human capabilities range from idiocy to genius. A premium is necessarily placed on the kinds of performance that are valued, and sanctions must be provided to differentiate between approved and disapproved forms of behavior. To prepare individuals for useful roles, institutions of higher education cannot abandon their responsibilities as testing agencies. Their challenge in the field of testing is to develop a climate of assessment in which the temptation to fake or cheat is diminished and the punitive aspects of failure are minimized. We need vastly improved testing techniques, improved methods of recording and interpreting test scores, and a more positive approach to break the lockstep in education and to enhance the counseling and guiding of students. Wise testing programs, in other words, can function as carrots no less than as sticks in the higher learning.

The Significance of Symbols

Let us look now at the carrots and sticks used as categorical rewards and punishments—the familiar marking system, with grades ranging from *A* for excellence to *F* for failure, and class ranking practices. These designations have long been bones of contention in academic circles, but of late there has been even more growling than usual over them.

A recent American Council on Education study of some two hundred thousand entering freshmen showed that the majority of them sensed a sharp competition for grades. A working paper used in 1966 at the National Convention of Students for a Democratic Society called grading practices "the direct cause of most student anxieties," and asserted that "grades are, at best, meaningless, and more likely, harmful to real education." The student author demanded that the society work for the abolition of the grading system. As yet, I have not heard of any colleges and universities that have done away with grading, but I know of many where there is limited experimentation with pass-fail schemes of evaluation.

You will recall that student protest was quite vehement a year or so ago about the use of averages and rankings by the Selective Service. Despite the fact that professorial judgments have long influenced the life chances of millions of young persons, some professors joined in the general rebellion against the conventional grading system. As of last July, Selective Service changed its deferment policies, but most colleges and universities have not drastically changed their marking system, and the argument about them is lively on some campuses. During January of this year I noticed a news report to the effect that the Yale Law School was considering a proposal to abolish the scheme of grading by letters, and more recently that a George Washington University professor was in difficulty following his announcement that he would give all *A*'s to students in his introductory course and all *F*'s to those enrolled in an advanced class. His purpose, he said, was to provoke thought about the grading system, and this he certainly did. (He has since been assigned to other duties on the campus.)

Perhaps college marks are less significant than is commonly thought, and it certainly can be argued that grade-point averages are too pervasively used as measures of the student's "general worth." Yet is it sensible to contemplate their abolition? As a Harvard dean has remarked, "I don't know where else in life you're not graded in one way or another." Max S. Marshall, a professor emeritus at the University of California, has recently suggested a scheme that he calls "triangular grading." Instead of being restricted to one letter symbol, the teacher would use three; the student "who applies himself well and seems to be worth encouraging gets his first *A*. If he performs well on assignments, he gets a second *A*. Considered to have a good brain and to be talented, leading to an estimated good potential, he adds a third *A*. His *AAA* would express this with at least some specificity and definition. A grade of *CAA* suggests a satisfactory immediate performance by a student with talents, but one who made poor use of his opportunities."

In the so-called free universities established here and there by dissidents, none of these issues is of any great moment. (According to a count we have made at the Council, there are more than fifty of these student-run experimental universities.) The curriculum can be anything desired, no testing is necessary, and no grades are indicated. Since most of the knowledge they disseminate is not marketable, they can ignore any equivalent of a gold standard in the higher learning, can forget about such mundane things as credit hours, and can thumb their noses at all forms of accreditation and certification. My assumption is that such establishments hold nobody accountable to anything or anyone except himself.

I do not argue, to be sure, that our customary ways of educating and evaluating students are sacrosanct. To caution you honor recipients and to console your friends who did not make it, let me pass on to you some research findings about the significance of grades.

One of these is that teacher ratings are potentially more useful predictors of further academic achievement than they are of creativity. Another finding is that academic achievement—knowledge—and other types of student growth and development are not closely related. It may disturb those of you who are primarily interested in making money to learn that there is little relationship between grades made in college and incomes earned later. It will cheer those of you with less than straight *A* averages to hear about a study of a thousand or so business, education, and government leaders selected at random from *Who's Who in America*. The investigator's conclusion was that the "stuff of leadership is not necessarily scholastic excellence, but rather, drive and a determination to get ahead added to an ability to communicate."

Do these observations mean that grades are unimportant? Of course not. In the first place, academic performance must be at least satisfactory to obtain a degree, and, increasingly, a degree is a ticket of entry into the most desirable occupations. As two examples, a high-ranking medical school graduate has a wider choice of internships and the top law graduate has a better chance of getting into a leading firm.

Even in business, a field where self-made men or those who were born to wealth formerly tended to monopolize the highest positions, 91 percent of the top executives now are college products and only 11 percent are sons of wealthy fathers, in contrast to 36 percent in 1950. Perhaps the last place one would expect to find accomplishment outranking inheritance would be in such a listing as the *New York Social Register*, but a study made of it several years ago concluded that education is now more important than family background as a key to social status.

And speaking of status, I do not want to conclude without paying tribute to the university's importance as a place where the truth may be pursued for its own sake and because it makes men free. If these were the only motivations of higher learning, then the carrots and sticks I have discussed here would be of much less importance. The contemporary university in our highly competitive world has other legitimate objectives, however, and I have tried to show how current practices in student selection, testing, and grading relate to them.

Some of you will recall that when Margaret Fuller loftily announced her decision to accept the universe, Thomas Carlyle said, "By God, she'd better." Fortunately for all of us, both higher education and society can be changed. To those of you who are disaffected or alienated, I suggest that before you reject existing practices or attempt to change them, you begin by making an honest effort to understand why things are the way they are. To those of you who are complacent about the status quo because you have done well in it, I would point out that higher education cannot remain viable without undergoing continuous adaptation and constructive innovation.

The American Council on Education's annual meeting
subject in 1968 was "The Campus and the Racial Crisis."
Viewing the existing situation in terms of a dialectic
process, I treated meritocracy as the thesis, egalitarianism
as the antithesis, and suggested a synthesis that could
emerge.

Merit and Equality

THE CURRENT RACIAL CRISIS on many campuses is a reminder of responsibilities thrust upon educational institutions to transform American society from a caste to an open-class system. Civil rights legislation formally removed many of the impediments to this transformation, to be sure, but the common expectation is that education must do the main job. Since an individual's life chances admittedly are influenced more by his own educational attainments than by the nation's laws, this expectation should not surprise us. In an era of rising egalitarianism, moreover, we can expect nonwhites as well as whites to demand more equality of opportunity. Whether, without vastly increased public understanding and support, educational institutions can meet the demands placed upon them is open to question. About the growing aspirations of the American people, however, there can be no question.

Some of these circumstances are by no means new. As noted a quarter of a century ago in the Harvard Report, *General Education in a Free Society*, American higher education long has had the dual obligation to further the Jacksonian principle of elevating the people at large and to advance the Jeffersonian principle of drawing upon all strata in training a natural aristocracy of leaders. More successfully than any other nation, we have indeed reconciled the demands for quantity and quality in higher education.

In light of this accomplishment, there would seem to be no basis for posing a fundamental antithesis between quantity and quality in our educational enterprise. Although disadvantaged members of our society have not received their fair share of educational opportunities, the consensus is that this nation is headed toward universal postsecondary education. Furthermore, the quality of opportunity has steadily improved and doubtless will continue to do so.

Forward movement in higher education has always been fraught with uncertainties, however, and some of the uncertainties now confronting us may prove to be particularly hazardous. Elsewhere I have commented on the perils of overextended institutional involvements without concomitant increases in resources, but the problem on which I wish to focus here concerns a growing contradiction of guiding principles behind educational endeavor.

This emerging contradiction or paradox stems in the main, I believe, from a general reluctance to acknowledge that in organized educational activity, the principles of merit and of equality often appear irreconcilable. Since the American system of higher education as we know it today is essentially meritocratic in function and structure, impulsive responses to modify it to accommodate egalitarian pressures are necessarily producing confusion and conflict. Of these I shall have more to say, but first let me review briefly the meaning and significance of "merit" as it applies in and to colleges and universities.

Meaning
of Meritocracy

The functional underpinning for a meritocratic structuring of the higher learning derives logically from the fact that nobody becomes educated by inheritance, gift, or decree. Even when provided with unrestricted opportunity, every person is limited by his own will, desires, and capabilities. The main virtue of the merit principle when applied to educational processes, however, is that it couples individual advancement with ability and effort. Thus it was no accident of history that led the founders of our nation to recognize the importance of universal and free education in maintaining the viability of a democratic society. This recognition began with the common schools, extended to high school, and is now moving rapidly upward to include advanced levels of education. In short, higher education, once regarded as a luxury for those who could afford it, is coming, under meritocracy, to be viewed as a right for the many rather than a privilege for the few.

In terms of numbers at the various learning levels, our educational system still resembles a pyramid. Correspondingly, the sustaining ideology—at least until now—has included the concept that the system should sift and sort as well as retain and advance the millions of individuals it encompasses. Impacts of the educational process are judged most immediately, of course, by fairly standardized procedures of testing, grading, and certifying. Although these routinized tests of human worth have long been criticized, it is generally conceded that in an open society evaluation of individuals based primarily on what they know and can do is more equitable and certainly more functional than assigning status according to "who they are." In sum, whatever its defects, the meritocratic principle in higher education does have the virtue of emphasizing *achieved* rather than *ascribed* status.

In a society as complex as ours, higher education has to be a serious enterprise, and a significant proportion of the student population must be prepared in institutions that place a premium on cognitive efficiency, intellectual competence, and specialized knowledge. The competitive rewards for brains and effort are attended by deprivations for dullness and laziness, of course, and the consequent frustrations admittedly produce stresses and strains within the educational system.

You may recall that Michael Young's book, *The Rise of the Meritocracy*, a satire intended to describe what happened to English education between the years 1870 and 2033, sets forth the presumed consequences of an educational system that eventually succeeded in sorting and training all members of that society to the point that the dullest were at the bottom and the brightest at the top. The final outcome was no longer an open society with high levels of native ability born into all social strata, but in effect a closed society where everybody was objectively evaluated on his contributions to social productivity and then placed accordingly.

Even in the perfect meritocracy, however, popular demand for a classless society, based upon the denial that one man is in any fundamental way superior to another, finally asserted itself in what Young identified as the "Chelsea Manifesto." The "Manifesto" states:

> The classless society would be one which both possessed and acted upon plural values. Were we to evaluate people, not only according to their intelligence and their education, their occupation, and their power, but according to their kindliness and their courage, their imagination and sensitivity, their sympathy and generosity, there could be no classes. Who would be able to say that the scientist was superior to the porter with admirable qualities as a father, the civil servant with unusual skill at gaining prizes superior to the lorry-driver with unusual skill at growing roses? The classless society would also be the tolerant society, in which individual differences were actively encouraged as well as passively tolerated, in which full meaning was at last given to the dignity of man. Every human being would then have equal opportunity, not to rise up in the world in the light of any mathematical measure, but to develop his own special capacities for leading a rich life.[1]

The problem of equality and merit in American life and education was dealt with eloquently by John W. Gardner in his widely discussed book *Excellence*. In general, he gave an affirmative answer to the question, "Can we be equal and excellent too?" The author acknowledged, nonetheless, that there are no easy and ready-made solutions to such problems as: Does our devotion to equality condemn us to a pervasive mediocrity? How can one honestly explain or justify the slovenliness that is so often accepted as normal in our schools, in trade unions, in industry, in government—in short, everywhere in our society?

Aspects of Egalitarianism

Turning now to the meaning and significance of the equality principle, we can hark back to the preamble of the American Dec-

1. Baltimore: Penguin Books, 1961, p. 169.

laration of Independence which asserted almost two hundred years ago that "all men are created equal." Despite the irony that some of the signers were slave owners, they were in the main egalitarians rather than elitists in their views about the kind of nation they wanted the United States to become.[2]

Because of the inherent impracticality of radical egalitarianism as a working principle of social organization, however, no major American leader has ever seriously advocated it. And, among the others, few would argue that differences in ability, effort, occupation, and civic service can or should be ignored in the social status accorded to individuals. Not many would contend that problem-makers and problem-solvers should share equally in the fruits of human productivity. Even so, radical egalitarians do hold that social inequalities—whether political, legal, or economic—can and should be eliminated.

Other kinds of egalitarians differentiate between justifiable and unjustifiable inequalities. Their varying conceptions give rise to such maxims of distributive justice as: "To each according to his merit," "To each according to his work," "To each according to his need." They hold that where nature or society imposes individual or group handicaps, the state has a moral obligation to attempt to compensate for the impediments, as with the physically handicapped, the culturally deprived, and the economically disadvantaged. Moreover, the majority of our citizens support a system of taxation that is in part a mechanism for taking money from the less needy and turning it over to the more needy in the form of cash, goods, or services.

Although some of these conceptions of equality find little acceptance today, most Americans accept the idea of equality of opportunity. Without implying that everybody can or will succeed, this principle assumes that everyone has a fair chance. Nearly all parents want to gain special advantages for their own children, to be sure, and not many would be willing for the sake of complete equality of opportunity to have all children reared in orphanages. Nevertheless, we give at least lip service to the federal gov-

2. Some of my comments on the equality principle are derived from contributors to *Equality*, ed. J. Roland Pennock and John W. Chapman (New York: Atherton Press, 1967).

ernment's program to equalize educational opportunities by region, race, class, and other differentials that now relate to discrepancies in learning opportunities. In most colleges and universities, scholarship programs have for many years made special financial concessions for deserving but impecunious students.

Yet, as one writer points out, the usual formulation of equality of opportunity can be misleading; the runner with weak ankles has little chance against a Roger Bannister. Our society, like every other, admires and rewards some abilities more than others and encourages those pursuits it values. Nobody gets paid for "doing his own thing" unless it also happens to be the thing other persons want to buy. (A colleague has pointed out that some tenured professors are obvious exceptions to this rule.) The formal system of education is thus more likely to be geared to the pursuit of success than to the pursuit of happiness; and with schools and colleges for the most part heavily subsidized, there is also an understandable public reluctance to invest in persons or endeavors that offer scant "pay off" prospects.

Some critics of equality of opportunity as a guiding principle in society and in education further point out that it heightens social competition rather than cooperation, stimulates too many individuals beyond their real potentials, and results in countless frustrations. One man's gain is too often another man's loss, with success taken as proof of personal worth and with human relations turned into a contest for superiority.

If excellence, or excelling others, is the common goal in education, then by definition the vast majority must necessarily fall short of that objective. It seems important, therefore, to emphasize that equality of opportunity need not mean identity of opportunities. Education for competence or adequacy in a wide variety of undertakings is also an essential purpose in our system of higher education, and we can offset the sense of failure for large numbers of young people by adjusting opportunities to fit their capabilities.

By confusing equality of opportunity with identity of opportunities, we can mistakenly homogenize the rich diversity of American higher education. Sir Eric Ashby has noted with approval that Great Britain is now pursuing the American example in colleges and universities of setting up educational equivalents of assembly lines to produce Fords as well as Lincolns. With the pluralism of the American system, many educational opportunities are available—from the very selective institutions to the open-door junior colleges. In view of the range of human talents and socioeconomic needs, and the rising egalitarianism, one might logically conclude that, as a whole, our colleges and universities are admirably suited to the new demands placed upon them.

However this may be, under the growing pressure on institutions to become all things to all kinds of students and other constituencies, many are on a collision course. The collision would occur when the demands of meritocracy and of egalitarianism become irreconcilable. Taking some liberties with the Hegelian dialectic as it might be applied to current trends in higher education, I think that meritocracy might be regarded as the established thesis and egalitarianism as the rising antithesis. The outcome or synthesis, of course, is as yet unknown.

Although historical evidence of how and why meritocracy came to be the dominant motif in American higher education is abundant, there also are now at hand ample data to support the view that the antithetical forces are gaining ascendancy. Egalitarians are attacking admissions policies, testing and grading practices, standardized curricular requirements, long-accepted modes of certification, and many hierarchical arrangements, particularly in some of the more elitist institutions. Current policies and practices are criticized as anachronistic, elitist, undemocratic, irrelevant, and even dysfunctional.

As Jencks and Riesman point out, for both social and economic reasons the college diploma has become a virtual union card for membership in the middle and upper social classes, but opportunities to acquire the card have been severely restricted for lower-class young people, and especially for Negroes. Rising costs and rising standards, coupled with long-standing discrimination against blacks, have diminished their chances overall. Even though almost half of all high school graduates now go on to some form of advanced education, in contrast to one in every six in 1940, Negroes and other minorities have lost ground proportionately while increasing in numbers. According to one study, "From elementary school on, the meritocratic system tests, measures, grades and culls, to the progressive advantage of affluent whites."[3] Institutions created for Negroes have assumed most of the burden for educating blacks, and the opportunities for them in white institutions have been minuscule. Within recent years, to be sure, "high risk" and Upward Bound programs, financial aid packages, and special recruitment have constituted serious efforts to improve the picture.

This same study of state universities blames faculties for their reluctance to make changes in the composition of the student body, the nature of the curriculum, or "the prestige level of their own ranks." Faculty members, the survey asserts, more often talk of "strict nondiscrimination, merit, quality, and color blindness" than of compensatory measures to offset past discrimination. The survey asserts further that black demands for entrée, relevance, recognition, and dignity coincide with the need to cure such common institutional ills as "bureaucratic impersonality," "the equating of excellence and prestige with elitism and exclusiveness," "the feudalism and fragmentation of academic departments, the arbitrariness of certification and credentialing systems," "high student attrition," "the protection of incompetence by tenure and academic freedom," "ivory-tower detachment from the surrounding society," and so on. Thus, many things regarded as wrong about American higher education are presumed to relate to its meritocratic elements.

Merit in Admissions

In their zeal for changing the status quo in higher education, however, egalitarians apparently forget that historically it was the rise of meritocracy which enabled democracy to supplant elitism. The merit principle, for example, led to the disappearance of the *numerus clausus*, or quota system, that set admissions ceilings for various ethnic minorities. Laws in a number of states and the Civil Rights Act of 1964 added a legal requirement to the trend toward institutional "color blindness." Ironically, a contorted racialism is now demanding that some institutions restore quota systems, but with quotas *for* rather than *against* particular groups. (The conse-

3. John Egerton, *State Universities and Black Americans* (Atlanta: Southern Education Reporting Service, May 1969), pp. 93–96.

quences of such a policy, as Moynihan and others have noted, can result in serious repercussions, not only among the WASPs but also, in some of our most prestigious colleges and universities, among Jewish, Japanese, and Chinese Americans.)

Another merit principle in admissions has been the use of uniform criteria, with no favors granted to applicants because of their social status. Of late, however, a double standard of entry is being used overtly or covertly by some institutions to admit larger numbers of disadvantaged students. Although this change has been quietly effected in most instances, the recent experience of City College in New York illustrates the furor that can occur when the issue becomes publicized and politicized.

Pressures for open enrollment are being accompanied by attacks on standardized tests. Even though nobody has yet demonstrated how such tests are less meaningfully predictive of *academic performance* for the disadvantaged than for middle- and upper-class students, they are increasingly regarded as unfair to the culturally deprived. The real target, I suspect, is the meritocratic model of sorting and grading human talent.

In an unpublished paper, William W. Turnbull, vice-president of the Educational Testing Service, has pointed out three competing views about the roles of educational institutions and the rights and privileges of individuals in society. First, he notes that the conception of graded abilities to perform is quite foreign to some fields of endeavor. In some labor unions, for example, a standard of output is set for all members, with a presumed dichotomy only between the qualified and the unqualified. Second, the "remote criterion" concept aims simply to maximize the supply of trained persons in some posteducation category—as more black lawyers or more male elementary school teachers. Under this view, the educational objective is purely instrumental. Third, the "student-centered" view adjusts educational programs to suit student needs or wishes rather than fitting students to resources and programs. Even though the third view is not entirely new, according to Turnbull, "what is new is the proposition that each college, and therefore all colleges, including the most selective, should adopt this philosophy."

Revolutionary and radical reformist attitudes toward traditional values in American higher education are also evidenced in efforts to abolish letter grading, grade-point averages, and class standings. Although few, if any, institutions have responded by eliminating all performance comparisons, in some, pass-fail ratings are being adopted. A recent survey conducted for CBS News shows that, whereas 89 percent of all parents and 80 percent of all youth believe that "competition encourages excellence," only 31 percent of "youthful revolutionaries" and 66 percent of "radical reformers" have similar attitudes. The influence of these minority dissenters on institutional policies is thus quite apparent.

Another evidence of the rising egalitarianism among the young, as expressed in views on participatory democracy, was brought out recently in a nationwide survey conducted by the Gallup Poll. In reply to the question "Do you think college students should or should not have a greater say in the running of colleges?", the "Yes, should" response was 81 percent for all students, 92 percent for student demonstrators, and only 25 percent for the general public. Similarly, in answering the question "Do you think college students should or should not have a greater say concerning the academic side of colleges—that is, the courses, examinations and so forth?", the "Yes, should" response was 75 percent for all students, 86 percent for the demonstrators, and 33 percent for the general public.

One academic commentator on the egalitarian push sees it as a collision of objective judgments and subjective demands, with the amateur (as contrasted to the professional) "exalted as a kind of democratic culture hero, subject to no standards or restrictions." He wonders what has happened to the conception of the campus as a place where those who know communicate with those who do not, and why the faculty is willing to abandon its authoritative position to placate the young. The advancement of knowledge and learning, he fears, is becoming "less important than self-expression."[4]

Lest it be thought that egalitarianism in academe is confined largely to students, however, one should also observe indications here and there of faculty movements away from meritocracy, as

4. Robert Brustein, "The Case for Professionalism," *New Republic*, April 26, 1969, pp. 16–18.

signified by professionalism, and toward a leveling down as well as up in the system of recognitions and rewards. Although the threat of collective bargaining has not reached most campuses, unionization is a reality in a considerable number of community colleges and urban institutions. With unionization, seniority rather than merit tends to become the main criterion for individual advancement, and teacher welfare rather than professional improvement the goal of the collective enterprise. In matters of governance, the one-man, one-vote basis of decision making displaces earned competence as the dominant mode of participation.

Still another kind of opposition to meritocracy in higher education is illustrated in the recent article "Diplomaism: How We Zone People." Brushing aside the widely accepted idea that a certificate, diploma, or degree is a useful symbol attesting individual achievement, the author asserts, "We are well on our way to repealing the American dream of individual accomplishment and replacing it with a system in which the diploma is the measure of a man; a diploma which usually bears no relation to performance."[5] He goes on to charge our system with being a credentialing rather than a humanizing agency, and with fostering a diploma aristocracy.

Responses to Egalitarian Pressures

This gamut of strictures, ranging from criticism of a particular aspect of meritocracy in higher education to rejection of its basic rationale, exemplifies what is at best a competition and at worst a conflict between meritocratic and egalitarian principles as determinants of policy. An individual institution that has traditionally selected students to fit its resources and programs, for instance, may feel strongly impelled to accept a more widely representative group of young people and adjust its programs to fit their professed needs and wishes. Since the college honestly desires to maintain its autonomy and distinctiveness while also seeking to extend its usefulness to society, it may be caught in a real dilemma. Where the institutional status quo is highly resistant to change and the push of opposing forces is strong, the campus can become an arena.

5. David Hapgood, *Washington Monthly*, May 1969, pp. 2–8.

Insofar as the whole system of higher education is concerned, the nation's twenty-three hundred or so campuses afford enough diversity of opportunity to accommodate almost any variety of needs and wishes, and thus to offset the prospect of wholesale conflict—or, at least, so it would seem. On both the state and national levels, nonetheless, public resources are not unlimited and hard choices must be made in determining allocations. State legislatures and state boards or commissions of higher education often try to simplify their tasks by resorting to formula methods of allocating funds to competing claimants. Comparable programs tend to be given common denominators of student credit hours as measures of dollars to be provided without regard to qualitative differences among institutions. This approach, of course, implies egalitarianism rather than meritocracy.

Although some institutional stratification of individual opportunity in public higher education is evidenced everywhere, California is thus far the only state with a planned system based explicitly upon the meritocratic principle. Originally looked upon by many educational authorities as a model for other states, the California plan is now widely criticized within that state for the alleged inequities in the distribution of educational resources it is said to perpetuate. Thus, an already unresolved issue rises afresh: whether master planning or the marketplace is the better mechanism for promoting equity and excellence in higher education.

On the federal level also, a consensus is lacking about guiding principles and priorities of effort. Federal aid to higher education, until recent years, was quite limited in amount and selective in emphasis. Public reactions to Sputnik and the resulting questions about this nation's capabilities in science and technology encouraged Congress to make unprecedented funds available for specialized manpower training and research. Although the initial thrust was meritocratic in its mode of allocating support, federal aid to higher education has become progressively more egalitarian. Partly in response to widespread criticism of the concentration of federal support for particular types of programs, for selected kinds of institutions, and for certain geographic regions where the more prestigious institutions are clustered, Congress has been correcting "imbalances." The federal government has gone even further by underwriting programs intended specifically for needy students and underdeveloped institutions. Federal aid is in the main still selective, to be sure, but there is no mistaking the recent movement toward egalitarianism.

Touching upon this trend in a recent speech at Rockefeller University in New York City, Julius Stratton warned, "As one watches the actions of Congress, I cannot help but fear that the status of institutional *equality* has become more important than the concept of *quality* itself. We seek the highest mean level in the world, but we must never forget that the pace of progress is set not by the mean but by the best."[6] He also expressed the judgment that too few institutions are distinctive today, and too many show marks of a common mold.

In the current stress on egalitarianism, highly selective colleges and universities do, indeed, find themselves increasingly on the defensive. Although nobody as yet has proposed open admissions for all of them or advocated dividing up the Harvard and California faculties and libraries to spread around the country, many persons seem to believe that pluralism in American higher education is yielding to uniformity. Other observers maintain, however, that the financial circumstances of private institutions will orient them even more in the future than in the past toward middle- and upper-class clienteles and objectives.

In Great Britain as well as in the United States, concern is being expressed about alleged erosions of quality in higher education. The novelist Kingsley Amis, for example, has asserted that there the major cause of campus unrest is "the presence in our universities of an academically unfit majority, or large minority." Lord Snow has charged that England is in danger of neglecting her most gifted children because of an obsession with egalitarianism during the last twenty years and a lessened regard for academic excellence.

On the other hand, egalitarians argue that the modern economies of abundance flourish through maximum development of the abilities of all their members. In affluent societies, with potential plenty for everybody, the widest development of individual capa-

6. "The Importance of Being Different," October 9, 1968.

bilities adds to national wealth while raising the general cultural and social level. The egalitarians also contend that modern technology's expansion of wealth encourages the have-nots to demand their share by force and violence if necessary, and thus governmental promotion of equality of educational opportunity serves as a countermeasure to revolution by furthering social mobility and serving as a solvent of rigid stratification.

The growing competition and conflict over priorities in American higher education is certainly one manifestation of the unstable equilibrium of contemporary society. On individual campuses and throughout the educational system, debate spreads about what the mix of people and purposes should be within and among institutions. The meritocratic thesis and the egalitarian antithesis, under whatever guises, become more sharply opposed, and in most places, the synthesis is not yet in sight. Meritorians are charged with being mere elitists; egalitarians are charged with being anti-intellectuals. Ignoring the hard realities of resource allocation, optimists try to comfort everyone with the easy assurance that somehow we shall arrive at the best possible education of the gifted while simultaneously achieving the highest possible level of the great number.

Possible Outcomes

In a rapidly changing and free society, nobody can predict a certain outcome or impose a common resolution of the issues we now confront in higher education; the synthesis that will emerge in our historic dialectic is thus anybody's guess. It seems to me, nonetheless, that educational leaders have an obligation to bring their informed judgments to bear as much as possible in shaping the course of events. Our main job is to see that our society gets what it needs rather than what some of its more vocal members may want at the moment.

To clarify means and ends, it might be useful to conceptualize our complex situation in terms of game analogies. The name of the game is formal education; in a competitive world all nations must play it and the desired outcome is survival and well-being. Although every nation has its own system for training citizen participants, among them the United States has the largest proportion of its population engaged in higher education. Many foreigners regard our scheme as wasteful of resources, but our justification is that every individual—rich or poor, black or white, gifted or not—benefits society as well as himself through the maximum feasible use of educational opportunity.

Game strategies also differ markedly from one nation to another. In totalitarian states, for example, the purposes of higher education and the participants in it are centrally determined. Our system, in principle, allows considerable latitude in both respects. Unlike athletic team coaches, at least insofar as the whole system is concerned, American educators cannot focus effort solely on the most adept. Demands for universal postsecondary education are such that, by virtue of their sheer numbers, the less and the least adept get more time and attention in the aggregate than the most adept. The rationale is that advanced opportunity is a right rather than a privilege. And who is to say that it does not also have functional justifications.

Every society consists of all its members, not just some of them. Using the game analogy, all contributions—good, bad, and indifferent—count in the total effort of the collectivity. If cultural deprivations and economic disadvantages permit educational inadequacies among ethnic minorities and other groups, the whole society also pays a price for the neglect. If the talents of the gifted and creative are slighted—whatever their race or creed—the nation's progress is handicapped. The moral imperatives of egalitarianism and the functional imperatives of meritocracy thus coincide in justifying the most effective possible system of higher education.

As we go about modifying our system to meet changed needs and to build a better society for all, it would be, in my judgment, a serious error to undermine its pluralism and diversity in the belief that this would further the purposes of a democratic society. On the contrary, I believe that we should make more postsecondary options available—including those of a notably vocational emphasis—to the growing volume and variety of students. Moreover, I believe that the division of labor among institutions should be made much more explicit than it now is, with no college or university undertaking functions it cannot effectively perform. Some form of postsecondary education should be available for everybody, but it is time to emphasize what traditional higher education can and cannot do for the society that supports it. With these qualifications in mind, we can resolve our differences over merit and equality and have in this nation a system of higher education that not only serves the best interests of our own people but also of all mankind.

Although I have long been a proponent of formal education beyond high school for everybody who wants it and can benefit from it, at the Council's annual meeting in St. Louis in 1970, I pointed out toward the end of the meeting that professional educators need to examine carefully the impediments to an endless proliferation of the status quo and to consider also the development of sensible alternatives to conventional higher education.

Alternatives to
College for Everybody

AT THIS ANNUAL MEETING of the Council it has almost gone without saying that American higher education has ceased to be a *privilege* for the chosen few, or even an *abstract right* for the many. Instead, the popular sentiment that our nation has an *obligation* to provide postsecondary schooling for virtually everybody has in the main been reified. I have not heard anyone argue for compulsory advanced education, but I have noted the incongruity of frequent reference to the supposedly "involuntary" presence of young people in our institutions, alongside the intimation that somehow things will be better as we move toward universal higher education.

As members of the establishment in higher education, we should all acknowledge the necessity for change and improvement. More than that, we should unite efforts to move ahead rather than merely defend the status quo. Before we proceed further on the assumption that higher education for all is both inevitable and desirable, however, I think we must take a hard look at present impediments and future alternatives. Various commentators in our sessions have touched on present obstacles and have pointed out that the shape of educational things to come is not likely to be simply a large-scale extrapolation of what we have known in the past. To begin, let me review some of the impediments to universal higher education.

We need no reminder that the growing demand for higher education is accompanied by a mounting public reluctance to face up to the costs entailed. In some states, the rate of increase in legislative appropriations is being reduced. Various federal programs have been cut, and some have been phased out entirely. Private contributions to colleges and universities continued to rise this past year, but many institutions are pessimistic about the future. Blame is often placed on campus disruptions, public disenchantment with educational results, and increased competition for funds to meet other urgent societal needs. With hard questions now being asked about institutional outputs, or the dividends yielded by the nation's huge investment in its educational system, opinion is widespread that the bull market for higher education probably reached a peak in the 1960s.

Since the Council's annual meeting theme in 1971 will be specifically concerned with funding increased numbers of persons in higher education and more varied programs for them, I shall not comment further here on the financial problems to be solved and the issues to be settled.

Aside from money problems, there is another difficulty that we are prone to talk about only indirectly and in euphemistic language. This is what John Fischer a few years back bluntly termed "the stupidity problem" in a book having that title. The real dimwits form a small fraction of any age group, to be sure, but if all high school graduates should go on to college there is no gainsaying that the average level of intelligence among college-goers would decline. As Trow and others have mentioned, it would be a mistake to design and prescribe the same programs for all comers that are now offered to selected groups.

Still another discouragement to higher education for everybody in anything like customary forms is an already discernible erosion of the certification functions of colleges and universities. We *now* make distinctions in the values of degrees according to fields of study and institutions awarding them, and, ironically, egalitarian pressures may increase rather than decrease such invidious discriminations. Moreover, if academic standards are compromised in an effort to equalize social privilege and status, existing modes of "credentialing" may lose much of their content and significance. The further possibility is that occupational associations and employing organizations will take over from professional educators the function of assessing educational outcomes.

Some Implications

The movement toward college for everybody may shortly encounter a deterrent resulting inadvertently from the relaxation of requirements and the growing tendency in some places to let everybody do his own thing. Although these measures may reduce campus tensions and make the higher learning a pleasanter and less rigorous enterprise, they may also have the net effect of reducing the marketability of much that is learned. This relinquishment of the institutional function of sorting human talent for socially valued forms of endeavor will tend increasingly to produce graduates who possess neither a mastery of any body of useful knowledge nor enough trained competence to fit them for gainful employment. Under such circumstances, it can be anticipated that individual and collective disillusionments will be reflected in the curtailed patronage of institutions themselves.

Finally, the principle of limits is already operating in the labor market's capacity to absorb college and university graduates and use their capabilities appropriately. This spring, new Ph.D.'s found themselves confronting a buyer's rather than a seller's market, and many employing organizations drastically curtailed their on-campus recruitment of young persons completing baccalaureate and other programs. Recent studies reveal increasing numbers of individuals in jobs requiring less education than they possess, and show that promotions in many occupations depend less on education than on experience, seniority, and various personal traits.

In brief, academic degrees are no longer—if they ever were—guarantees of upward mobility. To be sure, the malfunctioning may be the fault of the market itself, yet the mounting frustrations of college and university graduates in finding the rewards they expected from their educational aspirations and accomplishments not only causes the number of malcontents in society to multiply but also debases the values everybody attaches to higher education as a worthwhile individual and collective enterprise.

Almost everyone agrees that functional illiterates do not meet the minimal educational achievements needed for effective participation in our society, but there is no consensus regarding what is optimum. Some occupations now require twenty-four years or more of formal education as a qualification for entry, and hence the prospect that formal education may "eat up" the best years of our lives is already being realized. Aside from questions relating to the individual's benefits from education and its costs to him, there are also those relating to the society. Are there, for example, more benefits in reducing illiteracy or in improving advanced education? From the differing points of view of equity and efficiency, quite divergent answers may be given to the same questions. And apart from the utilitarian aspects of higher education, with calculated economies and diseconomies, there is also a host of considerations relating to learning for its own sake and the pursuit of truth because it is presumed to make men free.

To summarize, it will be a mistake for us to opt for college for everybody if this means neglecting other alternatives that might in many instances yield greater individual and societal benefits. Some of these alternatives have already been set forth at this meeting, but others have received little mention. Let me briefly list them for your consideration.

Alternatives

First, the alternative of no further formal education after high school ought to be maintained. Is any useful purpose served by making social pariahs of those individuals who go directly into jobs and whose further education is largely self-education? If more and better education were infused into the K–12 period of schooling by cutting down on prolonged summer vacations, extending the curriculum, and improving instruction, two or more years of post-secondary education would be neither necessary nor desirable for some youth. We are told repeatedly that young people mature much earlier now than in bygone eras, and this would seem to justify shifting much of the subject matter of the first two years of college down into the last two years of high school. My guess also is that some of the vocational training projected for community colleges and technical institutes could be handled quite adequately and more economically in beefed-up and enlarged secondary school programs.

For those who change their minds after working at gainful employment, reentry to further formal education ought to be made easier at those institutions where little, if any, provision is now made for the beginning student who is not a recent high school graduate. Keeping open the individual option of not going to college or going later would undoubtedly free our campuses of the presence of many young people who either do not really want to be there or do not know why they are there.

Second, there ought to be more emphasis on equivalency programs that stress knowledge acquired and competence gained, under whatever conditions, rather than a continued insistence on arbitrary accumulations of credit hours, grade points, and semesters in residence. Taxpayers, customers, and clients—not less than students themselves—are entitled to complain when the increased time and money costs of unduly prolonged formal education are coupled to specious or arbitrarily imposed credential requirements that merely up the price of goods and services without enhancing their quality.

Third, I am of the opinion that individual institutions should strongly resist pressures to proliferate the curriculum endlessly. Reform of the curriculum is indeed overdue; deletions as well as additions should be considered. But students wishing to pursue their own lines of study need to be reminded that books in the library are often better suited to their particular demands than professors in the classroom. Campus nonconformists should be encouraged rather than impeded in their efforts to establish and maintain so-called free universities. In such places—and there are already at least three hundred of them—the curriculum can be anything desired, with tests, grades, and credits ignored. Free-wheeling endeavors of this kind would be well advised, furthermore, to find quarters off the campus and to forgo the inherent constraints of outside financial subsidy.

Fourth, if we really mean what we say about widening access

and broadening opportunity in higher education, members of the educational establishment—including those on campus who attack the establishment—must cast aside the notion that they alone are entitled to decide the alternatives for and in postsecondary education. The greater spread of postsecondary opportunities as desirable alternatives to a monolithic structure implies an involvement of the outside public in policy making. Campus radicals no less than conservatives will have to concede that citizens in general also have a stake in what happens. More cooperative work-study programs and on-the-job training projects, not to mention community betterment projects, will necessitate a more effective mutual relationship between the campus and the larger society. Such a relationship necessarily implies some changes in traditional institutional autonomy.

Finally, I believe that further education for nearly everybody should be encouraged as one of the ways to achieve a healthier society, but that it should not be promoted as a panacea for most of our social ills. Undue preoccupation with mass education as the only road to social salvation can become an excuse for neglect in other areas. It can blind us to the complex interrelatedness of modern society. Indeed, requiring ever more formal education as everybody's purchase price for the better things in life can become a stifling rather than a liberating element in human progress. In our efforts to achieve greater equality of advanced educational opportunity, we should, therefore, examine with care every major proposal to make certain that it will aid rather than impede our long-range pursuits. In any event, we should strive for the kind of future in education that will keep individual options open and social alternatives freely available to all.

My reactions in the spring of 1971 to a news release from Harvard College, a syndicated article in a large number of alumni magazines, an article in Harper's, *and a commentary in the* Washington Post *prompted me to put together some thoughts for a piece entitled "Diplomas and Jobs." Variations of this theme were used for commencement addresses at the University of Texas at El Paso, May 12, and at Nassau Community College, June 13, that year.*

Diplomas and Jobs

DESPITE THE STATE of our world and the depressed job market for college graduates, I congratulate those of you who are about to receive diplomas. Successful completion of your educational experience here should enable all of you to become happier and more useful members of society than if you had never gone to college. Let me remind you, however, that even though a college diploma is increasingly regarded as a ticket of entry to a good job and a good life, it carries no guarantees. The inscribed paper you will soon possess may open some doors that otherwise might stay shut, but its real significance depends largely on what you do with it.

This trite truism came to mind recently when I read a press release about the 1971 senior class at Harvard College. The news story said that the beneficiaries of higher learning at Harvard "are increasingly unsure of what they want to do after graduation." More than twice as many of them today as in 1967 are uncertain about their eventual careers. With graduate and professional education less appealing, desirable jobs harder to get, and world conditions not to their liking, quite a few of them stated an intention to

185

try out different life-styles. Just how many expect to take up sandal making, communal living, or mere loafing was not stated, but considerable numbers seem unwilling to take traditional jobs. They were especially turned off by the idea of going to work in large organizations where, as they saw it, "their identities would be subsumed and their energies misdirected." After graduation, some of the seniors will assuage their anxieties through travel, and still others have no immediate plans.

Although I share some of the uncertainties and misgivings of American young people, I find nothing heartening in the tendency toward the kind of aimless alienation reported from Harvard. When I took my doctorate there a good many years ago, neither I nor most of my classmates could afford such self-indulgence. Indeed, I felt lucky to have in prospect a $3,000, lower-ranking teaching job in a university of middling repute. The thought that my corporate employer undoubtedly would impose certain work requirements in return for my pay and that my identity might not be very conspicuous as one of a large number of employees never really occurred to me.

Higher Education
and Work

I cite my own case because it illustrates the kind of work ethic a viable society must require from most of its adult members. In an advanced economy, we earn our living by providing goods and rendering services for which other individuals are willing to pay. The young, the old, and the disabled are exempt from this requirement, of course, and an affluent society may even tolerate a leisure class. To the best of my knowledge, however, the only social systems that reward people just for being themselves or doing their own things are all utopian figments of imagination.

Since my remarks today have to do mainly with higher education and the work ethic, let me say emphatically that I do not want to be misunderstood about the broad purposes of formal education. Some of its basic objectives are not directly utilitarian and certainly not narrowly vocational. The cultural heritage it seeks to transmit vastly transcends any such limitations. The opportunities for self-realization it should afford to individuals ought to relate to recreation as well as to work. Institutional obligations to improve the quality of life should, in my judgment, have a higher priority than those to increase the gross national product. Acknowledging the importance of these and other purposes of American education, I want, nonetheless, to focus your attention on the public's reasonable expectation that the beneficiaries of higher learning should become more useful members of society. In brief, the taxpayers and other constituencies expect some pay-off from their investment.

Unfortunately for all of us, public confidence in the benefits of higher education appears to be eroding. In the current issue of several hundred alumni magazines appears a syndicated report entitled "Are Americans Losing Faith in Their Colleges?" which highlights a growing dissatisfaction with the way things have been going on many of our campuses. The report points to evidences of the backlash against campus protest and violence, permissiveness, disciplinary breakdowns, the rejection of traditional values, the politicalization of some campuses, and the generational clash of life-styles. It goes on to note that the public loss of confidence threatens the financial welfare of institutions—including faculties and students—and threatens their freedom as well. Legislative and other governing groups are tightening controls to the extent that in many instances institutional autonomy and independence are being seriously curtailed.

If time permitted, I should have liked to discuss with you some of the measures needed to restore public confidence and to accomplish overdue changes in many of our colleges and universities. Their structures do, indeed, stand in need of modification and their missions ought to be made more relevant.

John Fischer observed in the March issue of *Harper's* this year that one of our difficulties is "the life-style currently favored by many adolescents of the affluent middle class." It is, he points out, not only "hedonistic, hairy, impulsive, anti-rational, anti-organization, and contemptuous of the straight society," but also it is counter to the work ethic as we have known it in the past. Adoption of Charles Reich's Consciousness III cult, as set forth in *The Greening of America*, is unlikely, Fischer asserts, to foster the hard work, sacrifice, and the self-denial our nation must have to solve its most serious problems.

The work ethic, the Puritan tradition, or whatever one wishes to call it, undoubtedly has been the moral basis for much of our past economic progress and present well-being. At the same time, the structural basis of our prosperity has been our skill with large-scale organization, with its concomitants of hierarchy, discipline, and long-range planning. Coupled with these features has been a willingness among many citizens to practice self-denial and post-pone immediate gratification for the greater ultimate good of themselves and the society of which they are a part. The current corrosion of these values, particularly among young hedonists—not to mention their elders who fuel inflation by advocating the quick and easy dollar—does perhaps spell an end to an Age of Affluence that was built on generations of hard effort.

Inasmuch as the largest source of increase in the American labor force during the 1970s will be in the group aged twenty-five to thirty-four, whether our standard of living goes up or down depends heavily upon the young. You members of the graduating class will, of course, be among this group of workers. If you dis-approve of conspicuous consumption, see no need for three cars in every garage, and believe that the work ethic needs to be harnessed to some objectives other than affluence alone, I say more power to you, but I hope you will agree that we shall not have a better world without working toward it.

Although some of you may be fascinated by the thought of more than two hundred million Americans returning to a simple pastoral life, your education should enable you to sense the absurdity of such a notion. As someone has said, since Rousseau's time two hundred years ago "too much water has gone through the turbines," and now there are too many of us for any significant proportion to have a real alternative to life in a complex, technological society. To be reasonably tolerable, moreover, life in an advanced society requires a broadly educated populace and a large contingent of professional and technical workers to keep it going.

Despite the wide variety of jobs to be manned and the educational opportunities provided for individuals to cultivate their talents, our society does not conscript its members for civilian occupations, and even the most highly educated may choose to cop out on their obligations to be useful. And whereas mere withdrawal is less destructive than nihilism, both kinds of behavior erode the social order and contribute nothing to its improvement. We might remember also Thomas Hobbes's grim observation that life in a state of nature tends to be "nasty, brutish, and short."

What I have had to say up to now about the alienation of some American young people is not applicable, I assume, to most of you wearing caps and gowns here today. The findings in the news release I referred to at the beginning of my remarks pertain mainly to the scions of affluence whose privileged positions enable them to disdain traditional jobs in business, industry, or government. They may opt out of the competition but they do not, by that action, eliminate it. The downward mobility that inevitably awaits them means more room at the top for the able and ambitious graduates of a wide range of other colleges and universities. Because stratification of jobs according to difficulty and responsibility is inherent in any complex social system, the recent growth of equality in educational opportunity means that larger numbers of individuals will qualify for higher level assignments.

Work
and Rewards

Barring revolutionary chaos, which prospect appears remote, I agree with a view recently advanced that our nation is more likely to undergo a "bluing" than a greening if our most privileged young men and women turn their backs on conventional job opportunities. The upper and upper middle classes have no monopoly on native ability, and there are plenty of youth from blue-collar classes and other levels to assume positions of responsibility. This manifestation of the new egalitarianism was analyzed at some length by Peter L. and Brigitte Berger in an April 11 *Washington Post* article, "Youth 'Greening' May Turn Blue." The authors show that the personnel requirements of a technological society will continue to expand, with proportionally greater demand for scientific, technical, and bureaucratic workers. Their prediction is that if such places as Yale become hopelessly "greened," young persons with a more realistic view of work and society will move forward in increased numbers to take society's command posts and keep its engines running. This forecast, let me say to you graduates, should be particularly pertinent for your future.

To those among you who are inclined to dwell on the shortcomings of our society, I want to stress that, as we eliminate racism and promote equality of educational opportunity, our nation will continue its progress toward an open-class system in which nobody's social status is permanently fixed by the accident of birth. This fluidity implies, of course, *downward* as well as *upward* mobility. To avoid equal rewards for workers and drones, together with the consequent societal stultification, there can be no substitute for individual achievement as the primary basis of social recognition.

In the past, we have indeed placed too much emphasis on financial gain as a measure of individual success and have been too obsessed with increase in the gross national product as a gauge of our collective enterprise. I do not believe blind devotion to annual increase in the GNP is a proper goal of our society. Nor do I believe that its failure to increase signals retrogression. Alongside this conventional index, we need some social indicators of what is happening to the quality of life, with more incentives for the investment of money and manpower in those endeavors that would improve it.

To get on with all of the tasks at hand and ahead, moreover, we should not underestimate the satisfactions inherent in work itself. In some educational circles these days there is a lot of talk about self-realization as the aim of education, but, unfortunately, not much mention of the great satisfactions resulting from work well done. As a noted psychiatrist has said, "What man actually needs is not a tensionless state but rather the striving and struggle for some goal worthy of him."

Although the shorter work week is an understandable objective for those persons whose tasks are essentially monotonous, other kinds of meaningful involvements are needed for them to offset the boredom of idleness. Automation is displacing many of the monotonous jobs once performed by human labor, however, and the further development of our postindustrial society undoubtedly will open up more tasks that are intrinsically interesting for more highly trained workers. When this happens, the cleavage between work as what one does to earn a living, and living as what one does with earnings will be minimized.

Notwithstanding this prospect, automation and social reform

can hardly be expected to eliminate the necessity for human effort. Plumbers and philosophers alike will have to work at their jobs to accomplish anything, and the most difficult tasks will continue to be those for which advanced training and education are most relevant. To make your own education relevant, I hope that appreciable numbers of you will find out for yourselves that vocational achievement is one of the most satisfying forms of self-realization. And this is true, I would contend, for positions of lower as well as higher responsibility.

Although gaps exist between my generation and yours, I am encouraged that much youthful discontent is attended by an earnest desire to do something about the unsolved problems before us. For altogether too long, mankind has suffered war, race and class conflict, poverty, injustice, and other social plagues. In addition to these, we now confront urban deterioration and environmental pollution. To those of you who want to make careers in these areas of concern, I would say, "Have at it." The monetary rewards for jobs in these fields are often meager, but the psychic satisfactions and potentials for human betterment are unlimited.

My words of caution are that there is not much hope for improvement if appreciable numbers of our best educated young people cop out, merely protest, or become destructively nihilistic. Building a better social order calls for all the disciplined intelligence and joint effort that your generation can bring to bear.

The gospel of education and work I have tried to lay before you at this time probably has not made many converts of dissidents, but I want to say again that your educational experience at this institution should enable all of you to become happier and more useful members of society than if you had never gone to college. These outcomes, I would stress, can and should be closely related. Even though the pursuit of happiness is worthy as an end in itself, I have never known a man or woman who achieved it except through service and sharing. Living and making a living, in other words, are at their best when they are intertwined.

In closing, I want to contradict the frequent popular assertion that you are the brightest generation our nation has ever had. Since there has been no notable change in human intelligence during recorded history, this manifestly cannot be so, no matter how much you may like hearing it. Evidence does suggest, nonetheless, that you are our best educated generation yet to come along. We professional educators, together with your parents and friends, take special pride in this accomplishment. Many of us still have a lot of faith in your potentials, and we hope for your sakes and for the welfare of all that you will realize them in productive ways. Wherever you go and whatever you do after these exercises today, you carry with you our best wishes for the future.

Part Four

COSTS AND PRIORITIES

This paper, first presented at the Council's annual meeting in 1960, was published as a journal article in 1961 and in book form (1962) among a series of pieces by twenty college and university presidents. I include it here to illustrate that some of the problems and issues of today are virtually the same as those of earlier years. Plus ça change, plus c'est la même chose.

Analyzing and Evaluating Costs

A LTHOUGH MANY of the purposes of higher education transcend monetary considerations, colleges and universities are not exempt from influences of the marketplace. We sometimes proceed as if they were, however, and there is some truth in the allegation that professional educators are not a very cost-conscious lot. Because money has somehow been found to establish and maintain an astonishing number and variety of educational institutions in the past, it is a common assumption that future needs will somehow be met.

Everybody knows that educational costs—like almost all others—have gone up rapidly, but dividends from our investments have not even begun to level off. As long as this situation holds, some would argue, higher education is worth whatever it costs. Others contend that a college or university is not a business, does not lend itself to cost accounting procedures, never has all the money it needs anyway, and, hence, why bother with cost evaluation?

It would be impossible to put a price tag on the value of higher education to our society, but the hard fact is that the public

195

must pay for whatever it wants from colleges and universities. Faced with rising operational costs, rapidly growing numbers of students, and new and more complex demands for services, educators are caught in a fiscal bind. Unlike most other producers of goods and services, many have felt it unwise to pass all of these increased costs on directly to the immediate beneficiaries. Such a pricing policy, it is believed, runs counter to basic educational objectives and would be detrimental to the general welfare. Thence comes the stepped-up appeal for funds.

Our financial plight is now well known, but what the money is needed for is not so clear in the public mind. Present and potential supporters are beginning to ask how available funds are being spent and where the added dollars would go. Many are unaware of the increased number and complexity of educational responsibilities. Others do not know that only a small fraction (estimated in 1955 as being 1.14 percent) of the national income is allotted to all higher education. Everyone believes in its importance, but few sense that giving it the higher priority our urgencies require necessarily means less money for other desired goods and services.

The Appraisal of Efficiency and Effectiveness

Educational institutions cannot, of course, enforce demands for a larger share of the national income, even though they do more than any other institutions to enhance the productivity of those responsible for that income. To get increased support, we can resort only to the powers of persuasion. But how? A first step is to make certain that our colleges and universities are both efficient and effective. Second, this bettered productivity must be demonstrated to our constituents. And third, in view of other rising demands upon the public and private purse, we can show that an increased investment in higher education will yield greater dividends than virtually any other allocation of capital. None of these objectives can be achieved without a better knowledge than many of our institutions now have about the evaluation of costs.

If we do not wish others to perform the evaluative job for us, we must do it ourselves. In state after state, budget officers, legislators, management consultants, and other "outsiders" are already coming to grips with some analytical problems that educators have for the most part sidestepped or ignored. As the Western Interstate Commission for Higher Education has noted, it is hardly surprising that pressures grow for handy means of reducing complex educational matters to understandable and manageable proportions. Diffuse and uncoordinated processes of decision making, which may have sufficed in a period of slow change and stable costs, are being forced into sharper focus to meet the urgencies of curvilinear development. More and more, there is a realization that the economy of higher education, no less than other essential aspects of the total economy, warrants careful management and coordinated planning.

Although I am convinced that colleges and universities are, in general, as well run as most other organizations, we should acknowledge that merely spending more money is not necessarily going to improve the quality of higher education. There is certainly food for thought in a claim that despite our emphasis on research per se, we allot less than one-tenth of 1 percent of the educational dollar for research designed to improve the processes and outcomes of education. As many of us emphasize, education is not a business, but we do spend sizable sums of money, and even our most adequately supported institutions never have enough of it to enjoy the luxury of making educational decisions without regard to costs. Furthermore, none can afford the inefficiency and possible waste of uninformed decisions: hence, our common obligation to work continuously for improved efficiency and effectiveness.

Our fundamental consideration in the matter of evaluating costs is not whether we shall employ admittedly imperfect methods, but merely which kinds we are going to use. To be sure, the skepticism in educational circles regarding cost yardsticks and formulas is justified. As someone has said, they may confuse as well as clarify; they may obscure needs instead of pointing them up. To avoid being pressed into fiscal procrustean beds which others will inevitably devise for us if we default, however, educators must give this whole problem more attention than has been their wont. We must take into account the fact that a good deal of college and university policy making and administration is diffused—by delegation, by necessity of specialized operation, and so on. Hence, the faculty, as well as full- and part-time administrators, need to be more keenly aware of processes and developments, needs, and specific methods of cost evaluation.

Since the worth of an educational institution is its service to society, its performance cannot be accurately appraised by a simple balance sheet or even an elaborate financial report. Like business firms, nonetheless, colleges and universities must balance expenditures against income. In some way or other, their costs are controlled; the only real question is how this is to be accomplished.

If educational, rather than merely fiscal, ends are to be served, then costs must be identified and classified in a functionally significant manner. More than twenty years ago a useful set of common categories was devised for the allocation of costs to such functions as general administration, instruction, organized research, extension service, the library, physical plant, and maintenance. Yet it is probable that a good many institutions still have a clearer idea about whence their money comes than where it goes. And here, I might add, I am not thinking about such hotly disputed items as "institutional overhead."

Even so, we have made progress in developing and utilizing standardized classifications. (Every college and university president must know that for many intents and purposes he is to be counted an "indirect cost.") There are standardized taxonomies, for example, which tell us how to classify such miscellaneous activities as glass blowing, book buying, grade recording, atom smashing, and convention attending. Of course, some elements lend themselves more readily to classification than do others, and there is an unavoidable arbitrariness in the sorting process. Just as Corvairs and Cadillacs are both defined as automobiles, so do the basic classifications of institutional costs frequently disregard the qualitative differences they embody. Still—to apply the "input" concept of economics to the campus itself—we have learned that books and buildings, laboratories and lecturers are cost factors to be identified, classified, and, for some purposes, thought about in purely quantitative terms. We have found that "student mix" is just as important as the total number of students in any really significant calculation, and in most states administrators have even succeeded in getting legislatures to recognize that there may be very good reasons why an institution of ten thousand students may justifiably cost more than twice as much to operate properly as one of five thousand.

In short, taxonomic knowledge regarding educational costs has been developed to the point that formulas can be derived for different types of programs, levels of instruction, and degrees of institutional complexity. All of this makes it possible for educational planning to proceed with a better understanding of the means required to achieve desired ends. It also enables those who must provide the material resources to have more confidence in the validity and reliability of the requests presented to them.

Methods
of Cost Evaluation

Educational costs usually cover diffused functions rather than discrete entities, and classifying them properly is not always a simple problem. Still more difficult is the problem of quantifying or measuring them. The two procedures commonly employed are the percentage distribution method and the unit cost method. Each has its advantages and disadvantages.

The percentage distribution method serves its purpose best when applied over a period of years to a single institution in which role and scope have remained relatively constant. It yields those pie-shaped visual aids with which we like to relieve the tedium of our verbiage in presenting reports to the trustees, alumni, and others to show what a small slice of the educational dollar goes for general administration.

Although the percentage distribution method has its valid uses, the unit cost method seems to be preferred by those who wish to understand the physiology, rather than merely describe the anatomy, of institutional expenditures. One of the favorite functional elements in getting at complex interrelations is the student-credit-hour. In short, the budget analysts have taken us academicians at our word in making this a common denominator, except that they are thinking of dollars instead of learning. Just as we equate large and small, green and overripe "apples" (not to mention lemons, potatoes, and cabbages) in calculating hours for graduation, transfer, and what not, so do they. The principal contrast is that different grades are not assigned by educational cost analysts to good, average, or poor teaching. Being honest as well as analytical, they make no pretense of doing so. In brief, the unit cost method gets at quantitative rather than qualitative aspects of institutional functions.

Nonetheless, the unit cost technique has proved to be a very useful device. When rightly employed, it shows the extent to which teaching costs are affected by such factors as instructional method, size of class, faculty loads and salaries, total volume of teaching activity, and so on. Some of the results obtained merely pin down what common sense would suggest, but others run counter to widely held educational beliefs. The recently published California and Western Conference study, for example, found that high or low costs are not peculiar to specific subjects, fields, or institutions. It also ascertained that teaching salaries appear to bear no fixed relation to cost per student; thus it is possible to raise academic salaries and lower unit costs at the same time. This study and others of like nature suggest that thoroughgoing cost analyses have many positive implications for educational policy decisions.

California, Texas, Oklahoma, and a number of other states now employ rather involved statistical schemes to arrive at norms and formulas which are used as bases for legislative appropriations for all state-supported colleges and universities. In Texas, for instance, the Commission on Higher Education recommendations and legislative appropriations are categorized according to such basic functions as general administration, resident instruction, library, physical plant, and so on, with the student-credit-hour rate as a determining factor in several categories. Formulas have been devised in terms of programs, with teaching salary rates based on sixteen different programs and three different levels of instruction.

As yet, I am not aware of the development anywhere of units, reliable or otherwise, to gauge the presumed or real costs of such functions as public service and research. Implicit in much of this effort is the attempt to quantify a bewildering array of variables and to formulate norms of productivity. Perhaps the greatest success has been achieved in assessing and comparing plant utilization, but performance in teaching, research, and public service with regard to qualitative achievement has thus far eluded real measurement. Russell and Doi, in their extended series of articles on this whole subject in the journal *College and University Business* took pains to point out in conclusion that low unit cost may indicate efficiency or it may equally suggest low quality, and, conversely, high cost does not necessarily mean high quality.

To recast a familiar quotation, obsession with costs can lead us to know the price of everything and the real value of nothing in higher education. The use of averages as norms, for example, carries with it the virtue of standardization, but it also may lead to the vice of leveling down to mediocrity. In some of our institutions and public school systems with set appropriations per pupil, fixed salary scales, rigid seniority rules for promoting teachers, and standardized class size, we can already witness the adverse effects of a uniformity which can be disastrous to the rich diversity of higher education. Averages, units, and norms can be highly useful concepts, but they can also be dangerous. When applied indiscriminately, without regard to institutional differences in role and scope and heedless of quality, they can nullify the meaning of the one adjective in the phrase "higher education."

Some of the factors we need to get at most in the educational process, we have not begun to reduce to manageable terms. As some of the literature mentions, there is also a tendency of unit methods, formulas, and other pat criteria to become frozen. The slowness of political processes affecting public institutions is such that criteria are often based on outmoded data to begin with, and, once accepted, there is a reluctance of governmental agencies to make upward revisions of rates and ratios. Moreover, these devices are merely aids in making what are often very involved decisions, and should not be treated as substitutes for the exercise of careful judgment. Decision-makers who are one or more steps removed from actual educational operations need especially to be aware that statistics often reveal little or nothing about the factors making for excellence in higher education. Unless we know these factors, as various analysts have observed, there can be no firm assurance about how any given institution should be operated or how much it should cost.

Regardless of shortcomings in available methods of cost evaluation and fairly common abuses resulting from their improper application, there can be no question about the offsetting value of their discriminate use. Every institution needs to know with some degree of precision how much time, money, and energy it is giving to various objectives, and it also ought to have expenditure norms for similar activities elsewhere. The uses to be made of this information will depend, of course, on the purposes of the college or university and who determines those purposes and their implementation.

Through the application of unit and percentage distribution cost analyses, an institution may ascertain, for example, that plant operation and maintenance expenditures are rising at disproportionate rates; or it may learn—as did some independent liberal arts colleges which participated in the Sixty College Study—that increased sums being spent on counseling, public service, and administrative and recruitment programs were eating away the resources left for basic teaching. Whether it would then wish to adopt some of the drastic measures proposed by the late Beardsley Ruml and others to conserve more funds for teaching salaries would become a conscious policy decision.

To be sure, some institutional costs are subject entirely to outside determination (for example, utility rates), and most inquiries are directed toward operating expenditures, without reference to capital investment or depreciation. As long as everybody concerned understands the hidden element of largess in most educational services, there can be no objection to the prevailing practice. Yet those who make educational policy, and more especially the faculty, must realize that an uncoordinated multiplication of programs and services in any institution may seriously diminish its efficiency and effectiveness, and eventually threaten its solvency.

Cost criteria are more useful when their purposes are understood and when they are based on adequate data and are sensitive to situational differences. They should be changed when circumstances warrant and should be applied with skill and discrimination. As I implied earlier, some of our methods are so subject to error that identity of labels is no guarantee of similarity of content in making either intra- or inter-institutional comparisons. Many of the presumed "measures" of institutional efficiency are, at best, educated guesses. Aside from the fact that basic qualitative features of the educational process have thus far not been expressed in quantitative criteria, we still have a lot to learn about the effects of overall size alone.

Instead of resisting the effort to refine and extend this kind of appraisal, however, educators should encourage it, as many are already doing. Where there is interinstitutional equivalence, comparisons should be made and the similarities and differences evaluated by those who are close to actual operations. Even though many consider institutional comparisons of any sort to be odious, how else can the effectiveness of some policies be judged? For instance, Russell and Doi concluded from their comparative analysis that a wide spread of salaries within professorial ranks is a good device for getting and holding a strong faculty. And yet, majority faculty sentiment, not to mention some administrative opinion, runs in the opposite direction. Or, to cite another comparison, the A.A.U.P. attaches much more importance to minima and averages than to maximum figures of faculty compensation in its published salary gradings of colleges and universities. It would be both interesting and useful to know which of these three desiderata is *actually* most important for a long-range policy of faculty improvement.

To get more empirical evidence about the educational consequences of various policies and practices, it is apparent that we need more interinstitutional studies. The aim of such studies should be the unleashing, rather than the leashing, of educational enterprise; and a broad, rather than a narrow, perspective is required. In view of the complexities involved and the ends to be served, actual conduct of the research and its application is an endeavor worthy not only of our concerted attention but also of our best effort.

Although there are more unanswered than answered questions in the whole matter of institutional costs, we already know enough to be aware that concern with efficiency of operation means taking a hard look at some areas. One of these is proliferation of the curriculum and another is the plethora of small-size classes. We know that low student-teacher ratios and individualized teaching methods are costly; if we think they are worth the price, our task is to justify them. Also, as analyses of medical education costs have specifically demonstrated, there is a serious waste involved in avoidably high student attrition rates. This finding suggests the relevance of cost data to institutional policies regarding selective admission versus selective retention of students for particular programs. In the instance of physical plant maintenance, many institutions are irrevocably stuck with past mistakes, but enough useful knowledge is already at hand about this phase of institutional operations to avoid similar errors in the future.

Insofar as most of our state-supported institutions are concerned, cost evaluations are commonly used on the outside by central budget offices, legislative committees, commissions, and governors' staffs. Internally, they are utilized principally by key administrative officers and trustees. In private colleges and universities, the uses, naturally, are largely internal. Some criteria are more appropriate for one level of review than for another, of course, but basic criteria should be suitable for all levels. On every level, it is encouraging to note, there appears to be a growing desire to concentrate resources on what is most productive.

The Objective:
Educational Effectiveness

Since the pursuit of knowledge for its own sake is seldom an aim of cost evaluation in higher education, the fundamental consideration is the use to be made of knowledge. In my judgment, the most important use is to get maximum utilization of available resources and to secure badly needed increases in them for the momentous tasks confronting our colleges and universities. To make our case persuasively, I believe we should rely less on rhetoric than on all the facts we can muster.

In conclusion, I want to make a number of generalizations:

1. Like all other human enterprises, colleges and universities are not 100 percent efficient. Some of the unnecessary expenses and wastes in American higher education have been created by public pressures, which have resulted in the indiscriminate establishment and inadequate maintenance of particular institutions. Others have come about as direct responses to lay demands for unwarranted program proliferation and duplication, both within and among institutions. These and other manifestations, over which educators sometimes have little real control, are in large part inherent costs of the localized freedom in decision making which goes with decentralized support and control in an educational system.

2. Educational institutions are under no less obligation than other institutions to operate as efficiently as possible. But it should

be remembered that they do not produce standardized products. Their costs should be scrutinized and compared, but more to the point would be a comparison and evaluation of their educational effectiveness. The two processes should be joined in planning and in administration.

3. Appropriate criteria for evaluating some of the costs of higher education are already available; more and better ones doubtless will be developed. Their utility and improvement deserve our close attention. Of even greater importance, however, is the continuous experimentation required to economize effort and improve results.

4. Institutional planning is too often merely a matter of campus planning. The entire educational program ought to be projected in time and space with reference to student enrollment, types and levels of programs to be offered, emphasized, and deemphasized. We must have more operations analysis and improved operations reporting. Planning should go on among, as well as within, institutions. The laissez faire of former times is no longer adequate to the urgencies of our total society, and there must be more statewide, regional, and indeed nationwide planning. Likewise, within institutions, faculty, administration, and trustees all need to work toward centralized planning and better coordination of effort.

5. Moreover, the urgency for maximum utilization of educational resources should not result in false or misplaced economies that stand in the way of improving education. The Problems and Policies Committee of the American Council on Education rightly asserts that many of our criteria must transcend those of commerce and industry, with the end in view so important to both the individual and society that true economy dictates choosing the most effective, rather than the least expensive, means. Although the price of excellence is high and inevitably rising, the committee goes on to state, it is less than the cost of settling for educational mediocrity. In the final analysis, therefore, the price of educational adequacy is not really a cost but an investment promising rich returns.

Given as an address at the Chicago meeting of the Association for Higher Education in 1965, this paper has already been reproduced four times in print, but it seems to me that the problems it deals with are perennial and must be answered anew at least once a year in colleges and universities.

Setting Institutional Priorities

THE ERA of the Great Society is also an era of great expectations for higher education. Most of us are doubtless pleased by this enhanced status for our institutions and ourselves, and why not? For many years we professional educators have urged the public at large to raise both the level of support and the level of expectation for educational enterprise. At long last, perhaps more as a result of changed circumstances than of our own persuasiveness, the American people are sold—and perhaps oversold—on the values of higher education.

Within a single generation, we have witnessed a remarkable transition. The opportunity to go to college, traditionally regarded as a prerogative of the few, is now widely viewed as a right for all high school graduates and, indeed, as a duty for the majority. Those who teach them were once looked upon mainly as schoolmasters and schoolmarms for a privileged class of adolescents, but now professorial counsel is eagerly sought by business, industry, and government. Formerly, the preferred places for carrying on the higher learning were isolated groves of academe in rural settings, but currently the favored sites are bustling centers of teaching, research, and community service closely intertwined with the life of an urbanized society.

Even though some of us may look back nostalgically to the more halcyon years, from our vantage point in the mid-sixties it is clear that higher education confronts unprecedented opportunities and is being asked to assume unparalleled obligations. Not only are colleges and universities expected to transform youths in attendance, but also to play key roles in an effort to uplift the population at large. Whether it be eliminating poverty, reducing unemployment, improving morals, or getting a man on the moon, institutions of higher education are being drawn into a multitude of public concerns. In a complex and growing society, this greatly expanded role is understandable. Colleges and universities cannot stand still in purpose and scope; they have an inescapable obligation to provide better education for greater numbers, to enlarge and improve knowledge, and to serve society in unanticipated ways. They must be viable institutions, and they cannot ignore current problems and issues without losing their significance in a dynamic social order.

Even so, I would caution that neither our whole system of higher education nor any of its institutions should engage in the futile endeavor of trying to be all things to all men. If we permit our institutions to become saddled with responsibilities they cannot effectively discharge or to have shifted to them burdens which more logically belong to other agencies, we run the risk of damaging the integrity of academic endeavor and fragmenting its basic purposes. I hope we are beginning to realize that multiversities, like small colleges, can be overextended too, and that it is essential for us to set priorities of effort among and within institutions of higher education.

Scope
of Responsibility

In the matter of priorities, let me first mention some things that higher education cannot do. One of them is to transform native ability. In an ever more complicated social order where there are fewer and fewer jobs for individuals with limited intelligence and little education, it is unfortunate that an impediment of birth should remain a lifetime barrier, but in a random sample of 100 persons there are about nine with intelligence quotients between 70 and 80; another seven of every hundred will be of still lower mentality. Although the right kind and level of education can make most of them into more useful members of society, it must be emphasized that *higher* education is simply beyond their grasp. Between these individuals and the brighter members of our population, it is estimated that about thirty-eight persons, with IQ's ranging from 90 to 110, come within the range of "normal intelligence." Many four-year colleges would not admit youths with this apparent potential; most of them could enroll somewhere, however, and some of them would do quite well, both before and after graduation.

Thus far, we know of no better mechanism than an open educational system for distributing the members of a society according to their aims and abilities, but we must bear in mind that the bright learn more readily than the dull and hence formal education on advanced levels does not necessarily foster egalitarianism. Those who mistakenly believe in higher education as an equalizer of individual differences must, therefore, find other grounds for upholding the notion that everybody ought to go to college.

No matter how much we may increase our support of formal schooling on all levels, it is unreasonable to expect classroom influences to substitute for families, neighborhoods, and churches, to bear the main burden of transmuting caste into class, and to reconstruct the whole society morally and esthetically while leading it intellectually. We must recognize that the mass media, including advertising, and the values they implicitly or explicitly endorse supply youth with many of its behavioral patterns. Other institutions must share importantly in the development of our human resources and in overcoming poverty, delinquency, and immorality.

Although it may be infra dig in academic circles to suggest that formal education can be overdone, it may be possible to have too much of a good thing even when the "good thing" is higher education. Human resources, like material resources, are subject to the law of diminishing returns, and at some point additional investment in education may make a lesser contribution to society than other forms of private or public expenditure. In many parts of the world overpopulation is a more serious immediate problem than undereducation. Even in a relatively affluent society, the extension of the years of formal schooling on the one hand, and the earlier retirement and longer life of the older generation on the other, impose increasing costs on society; as more of these public service costs are borne by public agencies, some difficult choices will have to be made among alternative uses of resources.

Turning now from these disclaimers about education as the Road to Utopia, I want to emphasize my conviction that it is undoubtedly our most effective single way to improve the general welfare. Our colleges and universities do indeed have important roles as servants and shapers of the Great Society. To this knowledgeable audience, I need not detail the past performance and tremendous potential of higher education; many others have already described fully the services of academic institutions. Various national committees and commissions in recent years have drawn up specifications of goals for all levels of education, and President Lyndon Johnson, more than any other president of our time, has committed his leadership to a positive educational program for the entire nation.

American higher education assuredly does not lack objectives, but one of our major current problems is what to do about pressures and priorities. What do the pressures and priorities mean to the twenty-one hundred campuses throughout the nation? At this meeting you have discussed pressures from such sources as local, state, and federal governments; the growing and changing student population; demands for continuing education; increasing costs; industry, labor, business, and professional groups; the disadvantaged; women; the various academic disciplines; international needs—and a variety of other sectors.

Since even our so-called private institutions are really public service agencies, and since all colleges and universities are supported by the larger society in one way or another, they can hardly ignore all of these pressures. Their real problem is how to serve contemporary society without becoming subservient to it. If they become mere knowledge factories geared solely to increasing human productivity and improving standards of material living, their time-honored commitment to the pursuit of truth, the advancement of higher learning, and the enrichment of our cultural heritage may fall into neglect. Are the institutions not obligated, as Harry D. Gideonse has suggested, to offset many of the influences exercised by the society itself in order to develop men and women fit for intellectual and moral responsibilities in an even better society?

When I spoke of the integrity of academic endeavor, I had in mind the historic fact that our leading institutions have been dedicated to high purposes, including transmission of the best that men have thought and said in the past. Colleges and universities serve by playing a contemplative and critical role, and if they become too enmeshed in daily affairs of the community at large, this function is bound to be eroded. One evidence of what is already happening is the growing phenomenon of the faculty in absentia, and the fragmentation of intellectual effort and professional loyalties. Student loyalties also appear to be falling away in some places where centrifugal forces are not sufficiently countervailed by institutional cohesion and consistency of purpose.

As we confront the diverse and sometimes conflicting pressures surrounding us and try to set worthy priorities for endeavor, we should remind ourselves that colleges and universities are the main trustees of civilization. Adherence to this trusteeship has undoubtedly been a prime factor in their enduring quality as human organizations.

In addition to consistency of purpose (without which there can be no integrity), institutions of higher learning also have leadership obligations. If they are to help create a greater society and a better world, they must be able to criticize as well as to comply, to shape as well as to serve. These desiderata in turn imply a reasonable freedom of choice with respect to the means and ends of higher education.

With these provisos ever in view, let us now focus attention on the broad problems of setting institutional priorities. Here I think we should reverse our usual approach and start with higher education as a whole rather than with individual institutions. Our past assumption has been that the separated aims and activities of existing colleges and universities would somehow add up to the best educational interests of the nation. In my judgment, this is no longer a valid assumption. Higher education has become too complicated, too costly, and too important in the national welfare for its basic decisions to be made haphazardly.

Some Matters
of Assessment

For a number of years I have had the growing conviction that one of higher education's most urgent needs is for coherent, unified planning. My conclusion is that we have entered an era when colleges and universities must cease to be a mere aggregation and that they must somehow become a genuine system characterized by unity no less than diversity. In my opinion, there is no other way to expand and improve our institutions without an enormous waste of time, money, and effort. I set forth some of the particulars of this matter several years ago in a paper on "Basic Premises for a National Policy in Higher Education," and I have noted with interest that James Conant's recent book, *Shaping Educational Policy*, deals with similar considerations.

Although I endorse Dr. Conant's proposal to use state governments as units to form an "Interstate Commission for Planning a Nationwide Educational Policy" for our public schools, the private sector's importance in higher education suggests to me that on upper levels it would be more feasible to work through a non-political arrangement. This approach has advantages: it would build upon existing structures, and utilize more fully the leadership of professional educators in setting and implementing priorities. Whether enough educators are willing to subordinate their vested interests in particular departments, disciplines, projects, and institutions to place the common or national interest paramount remains to be seen. T. R. McConnell's view is that interinstitutional coordination is effective only when compulsory. And I agree that politically prompted schemes of mandatory coordination are pushing educators into thinking more realistically about the give-and-take of interinstitutional cooperation.

As was shown at the American Council on Education's most recent annual meeting, traditional forms of institutional autonomy are being displaced by emerging patterns which emphasize interdependence rather than independence in the expansion and improvement of colleges and universities. Consortia and the statewide and regional systems are evidences of a new era in the governance of higher education and reflect an inescapable need to think beyond the confines of a single campus in allocating priorities of educational effort.

The growth of federal aid to higher education in the fifty states has also led to the necessity for the establishment of central agencies, such as commissions, to determine institutional and program priorities. Although the academic community at large still uses divergent approaches to Congress, the American Council on Education is endeavoring to develop a more unified front, and each year it formulates and distributes widely a statement of program priorities. Neither the Council nor any other single agency can claim to be the one voice speaking for all of higher education, of course, but I am hopeful that we can reduce the confusion of voices being heard in Washington and reach more agreement about how the pressures on higher education can be channeled constructively.

One of our current difficulties, it seems to me, is a reluctance in educational circles to face up to the need for a more logical division of labor among institutions to counteract indiscriminate local responses to pressures for proliferation. Despite our lip service to diversity and pluralism, it looks at times as if we were trying to homogenize higher education. One manifestation of this is the "university syndrome" which in effect means that a single institutional model is imitated so indiscriminately that many campuses begin to lose their unique character and purpose. I would not argue that uniformization in higher education is invariably bad, but I do contend that variety of form and function is useful and should be maintained. Junior or community colleges, for example, can hardly serve their distinctive purposes if appreciable numbers of them yield to pressures to become higher level institutions. Liberal arts colleges, technical institutes, and other distinctive kinds of higher learning centers also have important functions which may be submerged if too many of them are transmogrified into so-called universities in response to local and popular pressures.

The pressure for funds also is tending to homogenize the support and control of our institutions as more and more public institutions seek to augment their budgets from private sources and more and more independent institutions rely increasingly on tax support. There are advantages to any institution in varied support, of course, but if forms of support and control become too mixed everywhere then the duality of American higher education may be lost.

In short, a unified system of higher education should also be diversified, with each type of institution playing a distinctive role in the whole division of labor, and each having a unique character. All colleges and universities may share in varying degrees the collective functions of teaching, research, and public service, but every place needs its own priorities. Our common ends may be almost infinite, yet the local means to pursue them are always finite. Even a Harvard or a California has to make decisions about the kind of clientele it wishes to serve, the caliber of faculty it wants to maintain, and the range of programs it will or will not carry forward. Where resources are more limited, operations should be within more restricted ambits, with no institution undertaking more than it can do well.

Inasmuch as institutional mistakes in determining priorities stem more commonly from overweening than from modest ambitions, many campuses would benefit from more insistence on adequacy and less rhetoric about excellence, more underpinning for basic programs and less dissipation of resources in a multitude of projects, more attention to strengthening the citadel of higher learning and fewer sorties into the countryside.

All of this may seem unduly conservative, but in my judgment the first order of business for administrators, faculty, and students alike is to foster the best possible campus environment for learning. Commenting on some current aspects of student behavior, Sidney Hook recently noted:

They cannot be encouraged too much to broaden their intellectual interests, and they certainly must not be discouraged from giving expression to their generous enthusiasms for civil rights, for human welfare, for peace with freedom. But good works off campus cannot be a substitute for good work on campus. Ultimately, the good causes our society always needs have a better chance of triumphing if their servitors equip themselves with the best education our colleges and universities can give them.[1]

1. *New York Times*, Jan. 3, 1965, p. 18.

Our primary obligation to students in residence implies a top priority for the teaching function. There is a danger in many places that the student, and particularly the undergraduate, may become the "forgotten man" as our institutions become increasingly involved in such off-campus concerns as aiding various levels of government with political problems, meeting miscellaneous demands for continuing education, lending staff personnel to the developing nations, and so on. These and many other endeavors have strong claims for academic attention, but in my opinion never to the extent that basic on-campus obligations come to be neglected. Further, because of our reluctance in academic circles ever to drop anything or anybody—from an unneeded course to an unwanted professor—some of our priority problems are self-made.

Research should have the next priority in many, but by no means all, institutions. In the foreseeable future our nation can fully support probably no more than forty or fifty really distinguished, research-oriented universities. Such centers should be more numerous and more widely dispersed than at present, but it is not only wasteful but also futile to think that every locality should aspire to having one or more. Although research of the kind that contributes to the advancement of knowledge should be a major emphasis in perhaps two hundred of our institutions, I believe that on most campuses it is sufficient to expect the average faculty member to keep abreast of his field.

Because real creativity in research is a very scarce talent, I think that most faculty persons would benefit themselves and their institutions more by devoting greater effort to the improvement of teaching. Contrary to the publish-or-perish myth that is much talked about of late, in all except a few leading institutions less than 10 percent of the faculty accounts for 90 percent or more of all published research. My recommendation would be that we reduce the strain on the majority, trim the output of needless publication, and upgrade the quality of instruction by a more realistic adjustment of the talents available.

Insofar as research involves the production of new knowledge of theoretical or practical significance rather than keeping oneself well-informed about a field, however, it does entail an institutional commitment of time and money as well as talent. It therefore follows that many kinds of research cannot be conducted by the faculty in their spare time with the same libraries and laboratories they use for undergraduate teaching.

For the institution with a heavy commitment to research, there are many kinds of policy questions to be answered. Who should make the decisions about the kinds of inquiry to be undertaken? What criteria should be used in selecting or rejecting proposals? Is the distinction between basic and applied research meaningless, and, if not, does an academic institution abuse its societal role by engaging in development projects? Does the individual researcher owe his first loyalty to his college or university, to his discipline, or to the funding agency? To what extent should the availability of funds determine the directions of research? In answering these questions, it seems obvious that the institution with no priorities of its own will be the place where outside pipers will call its tune.

Although I assign a third-rank priority to what is usually called "public service," I would remind you that teaching and research are themselves public services of indispensable importance to the larger society.

Those miscellaneous other outside involvements that we have come to designate as public service are now considered to be legitimate claimants for faculty and staff attention. Beginning with the president, public service demands on him are often so numerous and so pressing that he functions only residually as an educational leader on his own campus. Other staff persons and many faculty members are also likely to be drawn into a gamut of peripheral service activities having to do with everything from the local chamber of commerce to the most distant foreign country. Indeed, if all the outside demands were met—and few of them can be readily brushed aside as unworthy—nobody would be left on many campuses except students and custodial workers.

To my way of thinking, every institution needs to engage continuously in a reassessment of its ends and means. It must ask itself such questions as these: Is this service important or merely urgent? Would it strengthen or weaken activities with higher priorities? Can another agency do it just as well, or better? In some instances a new project may be of special interest to, say, the bursar's office or the public relations bureau, but we keep telling ourselves and others that capable academic personnel are in short supply. If this be true, then there ought to be devil's advocates in all institutions to deal with the proliferation of services.

In conclusion, I realize that at times I may have seemed to reflect the conscience of an educational conservative. If so, this has not been my intention, for I am a staunch believer in an enlarged and enhanced role for higher education as a prime mover toward the Great Society. As someone has aptly said, colleges and universities are the engines of modern civilization. I am confident that we can continue to step up their power and increase their load capacity. If we are to make them the main vehicles of social progress, however, I urge their users to know where they want to go and to choose main roads rather than byways to get there.

Part Five

THE UNIVERSITY—
ITS NATURE AND NURTURE

Originally written for publication as a journal article in 1961, this analysis of the human organization of the university concerns itself with three major sources of the kinds of conflict found in faculty-administrative relationships.

The University
as a Social Organization

O
NE DOES NOT NEED to be a philosopher to be aware that human existence is characterized by struggle. Men not only struggle against adverse natural circumstances but also against one another. It is this latter kind of struggle that is a major preoccupation of many social scientists. In particular, sociologists have long shown an interest in those forms of behavior they call "disjunctive social processes." Despite earlier notions about the pathological or abnormal character of such manifestations, it is now rather generally accepted that competition and conflict no less than accommodation and cooperation are inherent in human association. Certain of their forms vary in time and space whereas others remain relatively unchanged. Thus, feuds, lynchings, and strikes accompanied by violence have virtually disappeared, even though other forms of personal, ethnic, and economic conflict have taken their places.

Sociological inquiry has dealt in large part with those open and readily discernible disjunctions which from time to time appear to threaten the societal equilibrium. Large-scale and intense forms of competition, inter- rather than intra-group conflict, and overt instances of hostility have afforded ready-made problems for research. From such studies has emerged an unwarranted assumption by some that competition and conflict are invariably related to such factors as class differences, cultural disparities, economic antagonisms, ideological antitheses, and other conventional bases of social differentiation. There has been much less research into the relatively subtler and more muted forms of disjunction occurring within relatively homogeneous groupings, and thus there are correspondingly fewer assumptions about the sources of tension and hostility and the origins of competition and conflict in this kind of milieu.

Approximating
the Ideal Type

One example of this sort of milieu is a college or university. A university is, in theory, an intellectual community in which hostility and conflict are at a minimum. The actual state of affairs, as any knowing observer can report, is usually somewhat different. In my own experience with a wide variety of educational institutions, the only situation I have encountered which approximates the ideal type is neither a college nor a university. It is the Center for Advanced Study in the Behavioral Sciences, near Stanford, California. As many scholars and scientists are aware, the Center was established by a private foundation so that a hand-picked group of forty to fifty outstanding behavioral scientists could get away each year from the impediments to higher learning which often beset scholars and scientists in even our best colleges and universities. Thus far the experimental program at the Center has proved to be highly successful in providing an environment more conducive to productive scholarship and individual satisfactions than that in which the fellows normally function.

A prime source of satisfaction provided by the Center to members of the community is the virtually unstructured nature of the situation. There is no hierarchy of any kind; authority—except that of the sought-out expert or specialist—is completely lacking; and administration, insofar as it affects the members in any way except to find solutions for the minor and usually personal problems they bring to it, is at a minimum. There are no academic divisions of labor in the form of departments or divisions, no classes to be met, no committee assignments, no scheduled activities in which anybody is required to participate. The Center gives each fellow a stipend to match his regular salary, and provides him with an office, library facilities, and some research assistance. Almost without exception, according to my information, the participants feel that they are helping to accomplish the main purpose of the Center by contributing more to the development of behavioral science than they could in their usual settings.

The Center has characteristics that may help explain the absence of either individual or group tension. The fellows have only one responsibility, instead of several. Most of them are highly motivated and fully capable of discharging this responsibility. Their status—and that of their families—in and about the Center is relatively unimportant because it is temporary. The whole operation is on such a limited scale that bureaucracy is almost altogether unnecessary, and with the membership changing each year there is no opportunity for continuing superordination and subordination to develop. Moreover, there are no outsiders to be kept satisfied with the performance of the Center.

Inevitability of Conflict

An unanswered question I have about the value of the Center experience is the extent to which its former members may find difficulty in readjusting to college and university environments. Some may feel impelled to reshape the conventional academic community in accordance with a new focus of expectations, and perhaps this is desirable, although in most institutions it is obviously not possible. Despite the credo of academic freedom and the fact that professors enjoy a larger amount of occupational latitude than do the employees of other organizations, institutions of higher education necessarily must have definitely established and enforced lines of authority and responsibility. This being so, it is inevitable that conflict arises.

How does conflict manifest itself? Insofar as faculty-administrative relations are concerned, it ranges from mild expressions of annoyance, dissatisfaction, and distrust to a continuous cold war which at times may break out into the open as a pitched battle, with the faculty on one side of a dispute and the administration on the other. The absence of evidences of conflict does not mean, of course, that the two parties must see eye to eye on all issues and form a mutual admiration society. Disagreements are not only to be expected in a normal situation, but are also desirable even in an idealized situation. The conflict of persons, in other words, should not be confused with the competition of ideas.

One commentator, Harold W. Stoke, has asked:

How much of all this conflict is inevitable and how much avoidable? How much is inherent in the nature of organization itself—the necessity for superiority and subordination, division of labor, the disabilities of sheer size? How much is due to problems of personality, to ineptness, to inexperience, to faulty organization? What steps can be taken to reduce strain? In what specific fields does it most frequently arise—financial, public relations, personnel, educational philosophy and conviction? Perhaps the subject is worth more concentrated attention than it has received. (Unpublished manuscript.)

In answer to Dr. Stoke, it may be noted that, whereas colleges and universities are characterized by the conjunctive social processes of accommodation and cooperation, the disjunctive processes of competition and conflict are ubiquitous. In human affairs, these latter processes occur when some persons think that other persons hinder, block, or otherwise impede the realization of their desires, and a state of tension typically results. When competition ceases to be impersonal, it shades over into conflict in activity directed toward ends not easily achieved. Thus the clashing of interests may turn participants into adversaries and activity may assume the form of a combat. In collision, energy or activity is largely deflected toward weakening or even eliminating the opposition. This is why, of course, actions leading to the dismissal or attempted dismissal of academic personnel, either faculty or administrative, are often the culminating events which attract the most outside attention to serious intramural conflict.

It is of no particular value to list here the familiar symptoms or evidences of conflict. Perhaps we should expect what is referred to in the army as a "normal level of griping." Both casual observation and careful surveys confirm the impression that almost everywhere faculties are restive about low salaries, heavy teaching loads, lack of research and secretarial assistance, burdensome committee work, inadequate office space and laboratory facilities, faulty promotion policies, administrative arbitrariness or vacillation.

Professors, in brief, do not differ materially from others in desiring higher pay, shorter hours, more job security, speedier promotion—and, in general, more satisfactory working conditions. Furthermore, a vague sense of frustration about these matters can be given a more satisfactory emotional focus when blame is attached to concrete entities such as administrative officers.

Although nobody seems to bother very much about whether administrators themselves are restive concerning their working conditions and faculties, they too have their chronic complaints. Their accountability is spread more widely than that of the faculty, however, and hence the causes of their tension are more diffuse and perhaps less likely to be rationalized in terms of faculty provocations. Like the ancient deity Janus, they must always look in different directions for hazards in the offing, but unlike him, they are endowed with neither immortality nor omnipotence. Vicariously, at least, most of the frustrations of the faculty are ipso facto the administrators' own frustrations, plus the pressure of a widely held sentiment that it is their responsibility, regardless of authority or means at hand, to do something about alleviating faculty frustrations. It is no wonder then that some administrators except for the incurable optimists become calloused by conflict or else reduced to a constant state of tension.

Most administrators recognize that they earn their pay mainly in trying to solve problems stemming from and created by other persons. Some find this exciting, others overwhelming. Here I am reminded that not long ago I inquired of an acquaintance about a certain administrative officer in his relatively new post. "Oh," he said, "haven't you heard? He got fed up with working on other people's problems and went back to teaching, where he could pick his own problems." When I related this to another person who also knew the former administrator, he added, "What he meant was that it is more fun just to be a problem."

It seems reasonable to assume that tensions and conflicts are to some extent inevitable in any large and complex social organization. Their most common manifestations often take the form of minor disjunctions which neither undermine the structure nor seriously interfere with the functioning of an institution of higher learning. Academic life would be pleasanter without them, but despite the current fetish being made of adjustment and getting along, few persons would contend that the main criterion of successful functioning for a college or university should be the absence of frictions or that its main purpose should be to afford contentment to those in its employ.

Sources
of Disjunction

Our real concern, therefore, should be with faculty-administrative disjunctions that are readily avoidable, especially those that seriously impede the achievement of institutional goals. To avoid or at least minimize the severe kinds of hostility and conflict, we must first locate their causes. These, it seems to me, necessarily must be centered in the following: attitudes or values, persons, or the structure itself.

Beginning with attitudes or values, the broadly accepted ends of institutions of higher learning are to conserve, diffuse, and advance learning. Honest differences of opinion may turn into conflict, however, in the specification of this objective. Without attempting to establish any order or importance or go into any details, I shall simply list some of the familiar issues that frequently precipitate divisive alignments.

Long-range objectives. Several dichotomies are apparent, such as that between the belief that a large institution, particularly a state university, has an obligation to "be all things to all men," and the view that it should confine itself to traditional aims. The idea of regarding all aims as being of equal importance frequently imposes the opinion that realism demands an assignment of priorities. The leadership concept may be aligned against the response-to-needs concept; diffused aims, such as "the pursuit of truth," may be in opposition to adherence to clearly specific objectives. One may find a conflict between overall objectives and departmental or individual ambitions. Finally, division is sometimes created when the relative emphases on teaching, research, and public service are considered.

Allocation of means. Several questions are frequently raised here, such as who shall do the allocating, and through what procedures should it be done? The bases of allocation are also often causes for division. For instance, such diverse criteria as need, merit, the "squeaking wheel principle," or publicity value may be championed. The role of outside pressure may figure prominently on top of all these considerations.

The curriculum. Liberal and general education may be opposed to vocationalism and specialization. Vested interest in the status quo will appear in contrast to recognized needs for curricular modifications. (As someone has said, changing the curriculum entails all the physical and psychological difficulties of moving a cemetery.)

Organization. There is also a tendency to make a fetish of democracy and freedom and to proliferate rules and regulations to the point that freedom to act becomes hamstrung. There is sometimes confusion between decisions having to do with professional authority and those relating to administrative responsibility. The overt recognition of the necessity for a division of labor is at times vitiated by the covert belief that everybody should try to get in the act.

Members of the organization. Here one finds the academic tradition of a "body of equals" in contrast with sharp disparities in individual worth to the institution. The individual desires for more certainty, security, and participation in important institutional decisions may conflict with the dislike for red tape, inflexibility, and the distractions of outside concerns.

These and many other issues make it obvious that colleges and universities are usually in a state of disequilibrium about intermediate ends as well as ways and means. Although there may be a consensus regarding ultimate objectives, there is no unitary output, as is normally the case with a business corporation, and no annual balance sheet in simple form against which endeavor may be objectively appraised. Stockholders are nonexistent in academic enterprise, and the board of directors or regents typically leave to the faculty and administration the settlement of most disagreements of the kind mentioned. As will be noted presently, there are usually structural mechanisms for the handling of differences and disputes over matters regarded as important, and if these are carefully thought out and well established, more light than heat will result. Sometimes, however, the ground rules are not adequate, and even when they are there may be faculty and administrative participants whose personalities and behavior are sources of conflict. To put it another way, there often are a certain number of "problem people" around, whose attitudes and actions interfere with the harmonious and effective functioning of the institution.

Problem People

Here the observation should be made that those persons who never cause any trouble may likewise be those who contribute very little to the ongoing purposes of a college or university. Henry Wriston has noted that "far greater errors have resulted from timidity, indecision, and inaction than from the patently tyrannous misbehavior of a few heads of institutions." I would add also that in terms of effective institutional functioning, the real "problem people" on most faculties are not the obstructionists but the mediocrities. As is the case with popular and not especially competent administrators, these individuals are often very likeable personalities, and this is precisely the reason nobody ever had the courage to get rid of them. Our immediate concern, however, is not with the miscellaneous shortcomings of faculty members and administrative officers, but only with those objectionable types who, as Donald C. Stone has indicated, "endeavor to thwart the legitimate function of other persons and groups . . . sow dissension and controversy, and concentrate on issues which are divisive."

Because of faulty initial selection, absence of an "up or out" policy of retention, procrastination or buckpassing in the matter of unpleasant decisions, and an obsession with the individual prerogatives rather than the institutional consequences of tenure, almost every college and university has on its faculty some persons whose actions foment conflict. The damage they can do depends on a number of factors, such as the kind and size of the institution, faculty and administrative attitudes toward their behavior, and the stability of the structure. From an administrative point of view, I will classify some of the kinds of individuals commonly found on faculties.

Fundamentally disordered personalities. Any sizable enterprise is likely to have in its membership some maladjusted individuals who simply cannot function amicably and effectively in any kind of normal environment. Since a college or university chooses its professional employees largely on the basis of technical competence and often pays scant attention to personality traits, it is perhaps to be expected that there is sometimes a fairly high proportion of screwballs. Both the system of tenure and the respect accorded the independent spirit in academic circles, furthermore, result in a greater measure of tolerance for difficult persons than would be found in almost any comparable social system.

The frustrated and disgruntled. Every employing organization of any size and complexity will likewise have some members who place a higher value on their services than do those who must evaluate them. Frustration in turn may lead to disgruntled attitudes and behavior toward those who exercise these judgments. Human nature being what it is, there is a tendency to place the blame on flaws in the structure and on shortcomings of those most directly responsible for it, administrators. Whatever energies may initially have been channeled into teaching and research often become heavily diverted into schemes of protest and other efforts to redefine the situation more to the disgruntled individual's liking. In short, by his own consistently antagonistic activities, the faculty person in question comes to be known to the administration and to many of his colleagues as a "sorehead" or "troublemaker."

The misfits. Faculty misfits may be defined as those who insist on playing roles other than the ones in which they are cast as teachers, scholars, or scientists. They are typically less interested in the pursuit of truth than in missionary activity, partisanship, and the promotion of various causes. Frequently combining emotional fervor with a tendency toward exhibitionism, they regard the classroom and the faculty meeting less as places to solve problems and examine different points of view than as sounding boards for a particular gospel. Regardless of the sincerity of their motives, the net effect of their actions is often to involve the institution in controversies which seriously impede its support and forward movement. Sometimes, of course, as one commentator has put it, they are really carrying batons under their coats and are waiting hopefully to assume direction of the organization itself.

Although some of the deviant types enclaved in the ranks of

the faculty would get short shrift in administrative roles, these latter posts also produce their own special varieties of miscreants. Indeed, I think it can be fairly said that whenever a serious conflict rends a college or university, the administration is necessarily more at fault than any person or group of persons on the faculty. I reason that one of the primary obligations of top administration is to resolve conflict, and hence any continuing and deep conflict is prima facie evidence of administrative ineptness. My point is not that the administration should yield to the faculty in a dispute over principles or other matters, but merely that it is the duty of administration to keep impasses from becoming imbedded as barriers to change.

In view of the extremely diffuse responsibilities of most key positions in academic administration, the persons who occupy them are ordinarily chosen with at least as much of an eye to their personal characteristics as to their technical qualifications. Furthermore, a variety of different individuals and groups normally participate in the selection process. For these reasons, administrative posts are seldom occupied by near-psychotics, misanthropes, soreheads, and other types who are prone by disposition to be troublemakers. One of the difficulties in picking the right person for key administrative posts, however, is that the inexperienced appointee always involves a situational risk. Professors presumably acquire tenure only after they have demonstrated their worth in the lower ranks by performance at essentially the same kinds of tasks. Deans and presidents, on the other hand, are often lifted from virtually unrelated assignments into totally new and different responsibilities.

None is ever drafted against his will, to be sure, and most have supposedly demonstrated some aptitude for educational leadership. But few people, including those who name administrators, realize that to move from a professorship to a presidency is to change occupation, as someone has aptly said. It is therefore inevitable that some errors should be made, and a mistake on this level is by definition a serious mistake. The appointee may discover what he thought was a leadership role is in large part a sort of brokerage function, or that he cannot avoid spending a good part of his time acting merely as a shock absorber or buffer.

Subjected as he may be to pressures from all directions and

often from opposite directions, the administrative officer may readily fail to develop as a real leader or may deteriorate into a buck-passer, or weaseler. In so doing, he inadvertently gives rise to situations where conflict and tension may become rife. This same thing holds when he conceives of himself primarily as an office-holder who performs ritualistic and routine functions. At the other extreme is the martinet or authoritarian who conceives his job as that of running the institution in the same way that the owner of a small business may operate when he is the entire management and everybody else is merely a salaried or wage-earning employee. Although the "boss" is a vanishing phenomenon in all forms of corporate enterprise today, he still persists strongly enough as a mental image to cause faculties to keep him in mind in drawing up their codes of ethics and articles of government. Properly sensitized administrators, accordingly, need always to consult with the faculty if they are to avoid giving credence to the widely held belief that they and their kind are motivated by a "Jehovah complex" in "doing God's will."

Structural
Shortcomings

Even with the right attitudes or values and with capable persons in the faculty and administration to carry them out, an institution may still flounder for want of proper social organization. Although there is admittedly no one form of organization equally well suited to all educational needs, surprisingly many existing structures fall short of meeting basic requirements for smooth and effective functioning. These are some of the more prevalent shortcomings:

Gaps between responsibility and authority. One difficulty of the typical college or university as a form of social organization is that certain responsibilities may be diffused throughout the entire system to the extent that accountability gets lost. Correspondingly, authority to see that particular tasks get performed may turn into a kind of academic shell game. As Robert Hutchins has pointed out, an institution has to decide "whether it wishes to be managed by an administrator or ornamented by an officeholder."

Reluctant to make hard (unpopular but necessary) decisions

themselves, faculty committees, departmental chairmen, and deans may pass matters of this sort up to the president's office. Desiring to avoid being unpopular himself, the president sometimes passes such matters down the line or else tries to formulate blanket rules and regulations to avoid the exercise of individual discretion. In contrast to the army, there is nobody on the academic scene who issues orders and then sees that they are carried out. If one were seeking an analogy to academic processes of government in some colleges and universities, perhaps the nearest thing would be a perpetual debating society. Such goings-on are enjoyed thoroughly by academic windbags and parliamentarians, of course, but they are extremely frustrating to the majority who would prefer to move ahead with the real business of higher education.

Ambiguities in the division of labor. Many academicians strongly feel that everybody on the faculty is entitled to have a hand in all important policy matters, so that there is a sentiment favoring committee management, innumerable group meetings, and other time-consuming procedures on the grounds that they are democratic. One difficulty with this mode of organization is that faculty representatives are accustomed to thinking in terms of departmental and other specialized interests, whereas many of the problems to be solved require an institutionwide perspective.

Furthermore, as someone has noted, there are structural requirements of efficient bureaucratic organization which probably set sharp limits to the amount of feasible decentralization and spreading of control. Regardless of ritual and precedent, inherent conservatism and inertia, there is on occasion a need to get things done promptly, so that some centralized authority has to override the vested interests of particular individuals and compartmentalized groups. Confusion is compounded when many faculty members are administrative officers, and vice versa, and if lines cannot be clearly drawn between what is or is not properly a matter for administrative action. Such ambiguities and uncertainties necessarily result in varying amounts of tension among participants as well as nonparticipants.

Categorization of members. Even though academicians are professional men and women enjoying a high degree of independence as specialists per se, they function within an institutional framework that evaluates, ranks, and rewards them according to their presumed value to the organization. The whole process is so complex that it is inevitably a source of misunderstanding, and the results are unavoidably a further source of real or alleged grievance to some individuals. All of this runs counter to the "body of equals" tradition, but apparently there is no organizational substitute for it not only as an incentive device, but also as a means for ordering the allocation of limited ends. In contrasting the flat and hierarchical patterns, there is some experimental evidence to indicate that in the former variety, members of the organization may be happier but less efficient whereas in the latter they will be more efficient but not as happy. In any event, this structural aspect of the college or university seems to be a source of considerable tension and conflict.

Faulty communication mechanisms. Many faculty-administrative conflicts have their origin in misinformation, partial information, or lack of information on both sides. Thus, the manner in which a decision is reached or an action accomplished is often of critical importance in gaining full acceptance and implementation. Here certainly is one area in which improvement can be made.

In conclusion, I want to issue a reminder that my focus on the problem of faculty-administrative relations has necessarily emphasized disjunctive rather than conjunctive processes and weak rather than strong points. The longevity of most colleges and universities is prima facie evidence of their successful functioning as social organizations. Even though our colleges and universities exhibit many shortcomings and imperfections, most persons who have chosen the academic profession regard their environment as the one they prefer to all others. As yet the college or university as a form of social organization has not been subjected to the same intensive analysis and study that have been brought to bear on various forms of business and industrial enterprise in an effort to improve the morale and working efficiency of employees. My suggestion to social scientists interested in participant-observer studies, occupational sociology, and empirical inquiry into the problems of social organization is that they need not roam from their own locale to cultivate a fertile field of investigation.

Who decides what in higher education depends heavily on the nature of institutional autonomy. My commentary here combines a paper I gave on the Berkeley campus in July 1963 with one I gave at an educational conference held at Allerton House (University of Illinois) in November 1967.

Institutional Autonomy

A<small>LTHOUGH MANY</small> academicians like to think of a Golden Age when the higher learning meandered with no outside interference, W. H. Cowley has shown the mythical nature of this view. College and university professors, he asserts, have seldom—if ever—managed their own affairs unchecked by any external constraints, and one would be hard put to find a single example in the Middle Ages or later of a completely "free republic of scholars." That most venerable prototype, the University of Bologna, for instance, was originally run by the students themselves, who hired and fired the rector and the teaching staff until control gradually shifted to the civil government. Another frequently mentioned institution, the University of Paris, was really under the authority of the Church.[1]

Contrary to the notions of some persons, moreover, the lay board of trustees is not an American invention. It came to this country by way of Scotland and Ireland, where it had been adopted

1. See Cowley, "Some Myths About Professors, Presidents, and Trustees," *Teachers College Record*, November 1962, pp. 164–68.

232

from Holland and Switzerland. Cowley further comments that from the beginnings of American higher learning most institutions have had lay governing boards, and he observes too the long-established tradition of an academic president.

The predominantly lay boards and appointive executive officers have in general made institutions more responsive to the public interest and have tended in the main to render colleges and universities more rather than less accountable to society at large. Virtually all American institutions of higher education are governmentally chartered, tax-exempt, and nonprofit; these facts argue strongly that our colleges and universities exist to serve the common welfare rather than for the sole or even primary benefit of students, professors, or administrators. Furthermore, the full control of a profession or occupation by those who practice it directly—be they teachers, lawyers, merchants, clergymen, or civil servants—is syndicalism rather than democracy.

Just as some academicians might prefer syndicalism, others would do away with all controls. Robert Hutchins once quipped that professors really prefer anarchy to any form of academic government. More recently, Paul Goodman and others have attacked administrative and outside restraints of any kind, with the claim that they are "excrescences that have swamped our community of scholars."

Despite inside and outside constraints, however, faculty persons at most institutions have enjoyed and continue to enjoy a large measure of freedom to interpret, disseminate, and originate knowledge. Their custodianship of higher learning is indeed a critical one, and their influence on the culture and society can be far-reaching. The environment in which they go about their daily tasks must be surrounded, accordingly, by many safeguards to insulate it against improper outside pressures. Because professors and the institutions in which they work are presumably committed to the pursuit of truth and the transmission of knowledge, academic freedom is a functional necessity rather than a traditional prerogative of their guild.

Insofar as the individual professor is concerned, the 1940 *Statement of Principles on Academic Freedom and Tenure* of the Association of American Colleges and the American Association of

University Professors sets forth a widely accepted norm. Its pertinent parts read as follows:

(*a*) The teacher is entitled to full freedom in research and in the publication of the results, subject to the adequate performance of his other academic duties; but research for pecuniary return should be based upon an understanding with the authorities of the institution.

(*b*) The teacher is entitled to freedom in the classroom in discussing his subject, but he should be careful not to introduce into his teaching controversial matter which has no relation to his subject. Limitations of academic freedom because of religious or other aims of the institution should be clearly stated in writing at the time of the appointment.

(*c*) The college or university teacher is a citizen, a member of a learned profession, and an officer of an educational institution. When he speaks or writes as a citizen, he should be free from institutional censorship or discipline, but his special position in the community imposes special obligations. As a man of learning and an educational officer, he should remember that the public may judge his profession and his institution by his utterances. Hence he should at all times be accurate, should exercise appropriate restraint, should show respect for the opinions of others, and should make every effort to indicate that he is not an institutional spokesman.

Insofar as the individual institution is concerned, there is unfortunately no generally accepted counterpart of the statement just quoted, even though it is recognized in most circles that a college or university must also be reasonably free and independent if it is to flourish as a disinterested center of teaching and research. One evidence of this is that trustees are seldom popularly elected, and, when chosen, usually serve for an extended period. Similarly, direct democracy is rarely the mechanism used for choosing presidents, deans, and other educational leaders, or for removing them from office. Professors, in turn, do not serve at the pleasure of their students, even though classroom reactions to teaching may be an important component in the judgment of their worth to an institution.

Institutions of higher learning, in short, must have leeway to rise above and go beyond immediately felt needs in their pursuit of knowledge as an end in itself. Without such freedom, their impressive accomplishments in the arts, humanities, and sciences would soon be matters of past history.

Even so, the contemporary college or university has a closer similarity to the community at large than it does to the cloister. To survive and be significant, it must be responsive to the world around it. In terms of its own objectives, it may respond selectively to the claims pressed forward, but it cannot be entirely aloof. Although academics may disdain the marketplace, their ethos cannot ignore the concerns of the outside world.

Differing Ideas of Autonomy

Because of the intricate and changing relations between most campuses and the larger community, it becomes understandable why there is no normative statement about institutional autonomy that corresponds to the 1940 *Statement of Principles* I have quoted. As Sir Eric Ashby has noted, the main argument for institutional autonomy, like the case for academic freedom, should not be a querulous appeal to tradition and privilege, but the pragmatic one. An educational system, "like an airline, is a highly technical organization," and those who know best must be in charge of actual operations.

In his book, *Universities: British, Indian, African,* Sir Eric sets forth what he considers to be the essential ingredients of institutional autonomy: (1) freedom to select students and staff and to determine the conditions under which they remain; (2) freedom to set standards and to decide to whom degrees should be awarded; (3) freedom to design the curriculum, recognizing, of course, constraints from professional bodies; (4) once having obtained external support, freedom to allocate it without further inspection; (5) and finally, the right to require nonacademics participating in governance to identify with the university and not to act as representatives of outside interests, and also to delegate all academic decisions to the academics themselves.

Prior to the publication of this statement, I was in a seminar with Sir Eric when he referred to these "essential ingredients." As I listened to him, it crossed my mind that some of the best-known American institutions do not meet all of these specifications. The University of California, for example, under the division of labor established by the California Coordinating Council, may admit no California students except those in the top eighth of their high school graduating classes. State colleges within that same system do not have complete latitude to design their own curricula and must confine themselves within limits that are centrally determined. Throughout the country, moreover, publicly supported colleges and universities lack full authority to decide internally how their funds will be allocated; and all institutions receiving federal funds must open their accounts to governmental inspection. Finally, there are lay trustees who regard themselves as primarily obligated to interests outside the institutions of their affiliation, as may be witnessed in this 1967 statement by the regent of a Western state university: "It is not only within the powers granted to the regents but it is their duty to grant or deny tenure or promotion to faculty members as they believe it is to the best interest of the university, even if such action is contrary to the recommendations of the deans and the administration. To do otherwise would admit being a rubber-stamp board, to which I will not be a party."

The foregoing examples make it apparent that we have no universally accepted norms of institutional autonomy, and hence that we lack precise guidelines to differentiate between proper and improper constraints. In extreme cases, of course, it is easy to recognize that an individual or a group is improperly impinging upon the rights of a college or university and damaging its integrity, but commonplace occurrences suggest some questions about which there is no consensus.

Let me illustrate. Is it proper for a state legislature to decree that all state-supported institutions must require a year of American history for the bachelor's degree? Should a professional association be allowed to determine the program of courses required for accreditation? How much voice should alumni have in athletic policies? Is it legitimate for local business and industry to exert strong pressures for vocational programs? Do philanthropic foundations interfere with institutional autonomy when they support only those projects that are in accord with foundation preferences? Is it improper for a legislative body or an influential group of constituents to "punish" a college or university through reduced appropriations or withheld support?

Outside
Influences

Like the debutante's father who is fearful that young men may make passes at his daughter but is even more fearful that none will want to, every institution desires the interest and attention of its constituents without their interference. This delicate equilibrium, of course, is not easy to achieve. The varied constituencies all have their special interests and favored pressure points. They make themselves felt in ways that range along a continuum from hindrance to assistance, and no campus survives in either complete harmony or discord with its wider environment.

Scholarly societies and professional associations intrude on local faculty authority over the curriculum. Accrediting associations set minimum standards. Of late, the courts too have been acting in matters of student discipline, professorial grading practices, employment policies, and other situations long regarded as strictly internal concerns. Clark Kerr lists additional forces of influence:

> When "the borders of the campus are the boundaries of our state," the lines dividing what is internal from what is external become quite blurred; taking the campus to the state brings the state to the campus. In the so-called "private" universities, alumni, donors, foundations, the federal agencies, the professional and business communities bulk large among the semi-external influences; and in the so-called "public" universities, the agricultural, trade union and public school communities are likely to be added to the list, and also a more searching press. The multiversity has many "publics" with many interests; and by the very nature of the multiversity many of these interests are quite legitimate and others are quite frivolous.[2]

Another leading critic of American higher education, Jacques Barzun, contends that it is just as important for a college or university to consider what it should not do as what it should do. In his view, a university should not allow itself to be diverted or distracted from its traditional purpose (the removal of ignorance) by outside demands. He protests the bombardment of outside demands since World War II, with mounting requests upon faculty

2. *The Uses of the University* (Cambridge, Mass.: Harvard University Press, 1963), p. 27.

and staff "to drop what they are doing and to go some place which is not related to their task . . ." to help world peace or social welfare or local culture, "by providing the means, the place and the talent for some worthy cause—an exchange program, a clinic, a survey, a world conference on fingernail biting." In Barzun's opinion, yielding to these claims, regardless of their seeming urgency, will fragment and ultimately destroy an institution.[3]

In view of higher education's increasing importance to society, it seems to me that the diminution of institutional autonomy is more likely to come from yielding to these miscellaneous importunings than from being overwhelmed by the crude force of open interference. If a college or university permits itself to become a kind of supermarket trying to please all possible customers, or a mere service station catering to every passerby, it can hardly expect to maintain even the fiction of autonomy.

In our pluralistic society there is no question about the need for many kinds of institutions, and for a wide range of purposes in those which are large and complex. The demands we confront, however, increase rather than decrease the urgency of making rational decisions about who should undertake what responsibilities in our vast collective endeavor. We live in a highly interdependent era when we can no longer afford to operate with anachronistic ideas of institutional autonomy. Educational leaders can put their time to better use by being realistic about the unavoidable involvements of their institutions than by rhetorical defenses of fading ivory tower images. In my judgment, we must soon stop talking and acting as if our separated colleges and universities were islands or enclaves and face up to the inevitabilities of more coordination. Our only real choice is whether we shall do this ourselves through cooperation and joint enterprise, or wait for others to do it for us.

One of the facts of modern life we must accept is that both private and public institutions of higher education are being moved more and more into the public domain both because of the undeniable claims of the larger society and because of the growing involvement of all levels of government with higher education.

3. "What Is a University?" *College and University Journal*, Fall 1962, pp. 10–14.

Professional educators no less than politicians and bureaucrats should play important decision-making roles in the changing set of relations.

In 1957 the Fund for the Advancement of Education underwrote an inquiry which resulted in the book, *The Campus and the State*. This inquiry, it was hoped, would lead to improved relationships under which the essential freedom of each institution would be fully protected while the legitimate fiscal, management, and program interests of state government would be equally safeguarded. The study pointed out that excessive bureaucratic controls and all-embracing supervision are sure recipes for mediocrity in higher education. It also stressed that institutions themselves could do more in the future than they have in the past to enhance their reputations for efficiency and sound management.

Expanding relations between higher education and the federal government have likewise been a subject of inquiry during recent years. We are rather belatedly recognizing some of the implications of this growing involvement. As Babbidge and Rosenzweig have expressed it, the heart of the problem here is often that of indirection rather than direction, and lack of control rather than control.[4] The *Educational Record* in 1963 reported the results of a Carnegie Foundation sponsored inquiry into the impact of federal programs on twenty-six different campuses, as viewed by the institutions themselves.[5] In general, these self-studies report many more good than bad effects of participation. They point to enlarged and improved research programs, faculty benefits, graduate student assistance, plant and equipment gains. They view with deep concern, however, the imbalance created in favor of science departments, the diversion of institutional funds for matching purposes, the neglect of teaching, and the inroads on an institution's traditional areas of decision making.

Problems arising from the mutual relations of higher education and government illustrate some of the concerns requiring our attention. Others could be mentioned—business and industry and many

4. Homer D. Babbidge, Jr., and Robert M. Rosenzweig, *The Federal Interest in Higher Education* (New York, McGraw-Hill Book Co., 1962).

5. "Twenty-six Campuses and the Federal Government," *Educational Record*, April 1963, pp. 95–136.

other interest groups which have a stake in educational decisions and actions. Within and among institutions and between them and virtually all sectors of the larger society, there is a pressing need for improved mechanisms of communication, deliberation, and action.

However paradoxical it may seem, as a college or university grows in influence and power, it becomes caught in an enlarged web of relationships. Inherent in this involvement is the potential of compromised integrity and independence, so that closer surveillance and tighter internal organization are required as countervailing elements to offset centrifugal forces from extramural sources.

Checkpoints
for Institutional Autonomy

Although some of the literature on academic freedom leaves the impression that the ideal collegiate environment is one where outside constraints are at a minimum, from the point of view of the general welfare this is not the case. Colleges and universities must maintain their identity to survive and their integrity to be worthy of survival, of course, but they also have other important purposes.

At present, unfortunately, there is comparatively little systematic knowledge of theoretical significance about the complex interrelations of colleges and universities and their environments. We know that community junior colleges tend to be more closely related to social forces at work in their immediate locales than are institutions with more dispersed constituencies. A well-endowed and long-established private university is likely to be in a better position to resist encroachments than is an impoverished college with a vacillating past and an uncertain future. A cosmopolitan environment is perhaps more conducive to institutional autonomy than a provincial one. Diversified financial support is commonly considered preferable to reliance on a single source of funds. Members of the academic profession attach considerable importance to tenure rules as protections against outside interference. One of the traditional functions of boards of trustees is to shield their institutions from undue outside intrusions.

We are aware that still other factors need to be taken into account. Our real difficulty is that we lack the objective knowledge of causal relations needed to make well-informed decisions. Faculty persons are in the main oriented toward the problems of disciplines and programs rather than structural and functional problems of the institutions employing them. Administrative officers, in turn, are likely to be immersed in quite specialized aspects of college and university operations or with the ad hoc daily perplexities of keeping their institutions afloat and moving—and, at times, without enough regard for where they may be headed. As a consequence, not enough attention is paid to some of higher education's most important issues.

In this changing climate, it seems to me that educational leaders need to reassess the whole matter of institutional autonomy, put rhetoric aside, and take a hard look at the concessions to be made and the claims to be stoutly maintained. I have no bill of particulars to offer, and doubt that one equally suited to the purposes of all institutions could be drawn, but I am prepared to suggest a set of checkpoints regarding the minimum autonomy required by every college or university if it is to remain viable as an institution of higher learning. These checkpoints would be as follows:

1. Every academic community must be able to exercise the functionally necessary control of its membership of faculty, staff, and students. Although public policy may legitimately influence this membership, outside agencies should not be permitted to dictate the entry, retention, or exit of particular individuals.

2. Consistent with the requirements of accrediting associations and recognized professional groups, each institution should be responsible for maintaining its own academic standards. With regard to other internal standards, to quote a decision of the California Supreme Court, "[The] University, as an academic community, can formulate its own standards, rewards, and punishments to achieve its educational objectives. . . . Thus, except for the applicable constitutional limitations, the relationship between appropriate University rules and laws of the outside community is entirely coincidental."

3. Conceding the right and the power of outside agencies to grant or withhold funds, and to influence their allocation, no insti-

tution should be deprived of the kinds of discretion required for their most effective internal utilization.

4. A sufficient degree of autonomy must be maintained for the institution's trustees, administrators, faculty, and students to exercise distinctive rights and shared responsibilities. Such rights and responsibilities should be respected both internally and externally.

5. In the realm of ideas, colleges and universities must be accorded the functional freedoms necessary for intellectual enterprise.

You will note that my itemization is less inclusive than the Ashby list of "essential ingredients" cited earlier, and is admittedly minimal rather than optimal. In view of the erosions of institutional autonomy that are becoming widespread in this nation, however, it is high time for educational leaders everywhere to reach some basic understanding and to alert the general public about what can and what cannot be permitted if American colleges and universities are to maintain the integrity necessary for them to continue to serve society's best interests.

In May and June of 1965 I gave variations of "Whose Universities?" as commencement addresses at the Louisiana State University in New Orleans and at the University of Tennessee in Knoxville. My main intent on each occasion was to direct critical attention toward the need for a sensible division of labor in the contemporary American university.

Whose Universities?

A<small>N ASPECT</small> of higher education much in the public mind of late is often simply put as the question, Who runs our universities? The governance of higher education, like the conduct of foreign policy or the handling of civil rights, readily becomes a public policy issue that brings forth arguments from a good many self-appointed authorities. Some persons in academic circles, for example, like to entertain the notion that universities originally ran themselves. A few students at Berkeley and elsewhere seem to advocate returning to the earlier prototype, but as yet I have not heard any expressions of enthusiasm for the idea from trustees, administrators, and the general public. However this may be, current student unrest and the apparent desires of some students and faculty members to revolutionize things, both on their own campuses and away from them, are so manifest that laymen are becoming confused about who is supposed to do what in the realm of higher education.

Although the histories of some colleges and universities might lead one to conclude that institutions of higher education are almost invariably carefully planned and articulated enterprises, the facts in some situations, unfortunately, have been quite different. Some were mistakes at the start, and others have little excuse for continuing their existence. Even more surprising, perhaps, is our tolerance of a few fraudulent institutions. We have learned—from hard experience—that developing and maintaining places of genuine significance is no easy undertaking.

Really meaningful higher education today is a complex and expensive undertaking. A new junior college may call for an investment of several million dollars, and a new medical school may require a minimum outlay of at least twenty-five million dollars. Few individuals and private groups can command funds of this magnitude, and it is not surprising that higher education has been moving steadily into the public domain. Furthermore, the support and operation of viable colleges and universities are by no means the simplified matters that some of their critics would have us believe. Cooperation and coordination among many diverse interests are a precondition for a successful enterprise, and there must be some basic understanding about a reasonable division of labor in the achievement of common objectives. Little wonder, then, that it is easier to criticize existing institutions than it is to establish and maintain new ones.

To begin with, a modern university must have a sizable constituency. At one time a handful of teachers and learners could band together and maintain any kind of academic community the surrounding society was willing to tolerate. Today few students and even fewer faculty would be willing to take the vows of poverty required to maintain such an enclave. Moreover, they would not be able to marshal the financial support necessary to maintain adequate libraries, laboratories, and other essentials for contemporary teaching and research. Not only is the university an indispensable institution for contemporary society, but also broad-based support of the society is essential for the university.

It is a truism to say that state universities were created to serve the educational needs of their states. It is also a mistake to regard these institutions as state agencies differing in no significant way from highway departments, welfare bureaus, and other governmental operations. Legislatures have the authority to provide or withhold funds for teaching, research, and public service, but the advancement of learning is impeded rather than aided when legislatures try to determine what should be taught, how research should be conducted, or how the public must be served. Like independently controlled institutions, state universities can serve their constituents best when they are assured the academic freedom necessary to their missions as sponsors of unhampered inquiry. In short, whereas centers of learning may decay from being too isolated from the surrounding society, they also may deteriorate from being insufficiently insulated against its direct pressures.

Trustees;
Administrators; Faculty

Standing between the outside world and universities are those appointive or elective groups of laymen variously termed trustees, regents, or governing boards. They have the duty of representing the interests of the public at large to the academic community, and vice versa. They possess the legal prerogative to run our universities, but most of them sense the folly of trying to exercise it. The most effective governing boards confine their efforts largely to basic policy questions and other areas where their influence can be most useful in maintaining and improving their institutions, and actually do very little direct governing. Even though boards are not invariably clear about their basic functions, by and large, it seems to me that lay trustees are underutilized as a source of strength in the progress as well as the stability of American institutions of higher education. Many of them give unstintingly of their time and energy, and not a few contribute substantially from their personal means to the institutions they serve without compensation; more of them need to be drawn into the university's most basic concerns.

Of the many decisions a governing board may make from time to time, one of the most crucial is choosing its chief executive officer. The president must be a capable executive for the trustees; he must also be an understanding spokesman and leader for his colleagues in administration, for the faculty, the students, and, on occasion, the alumni and other groups. If the president is to be an effective administrator, he must delegate large measures of authority and responsibility to the deans and to the faculty; if he is to be a courageous leader, however, on some occasions there are no substitutes for his own firm decisions and actions.

A recent American Council on Education inquiry revealed that most academicians would prefer to spend more time on research and writing at the expense of a reduction in their undergraduate teaching and in their administrative duties. It is therefore paradoxical that many faculty members complain of complex universities being overadministered by professionals at the same time they wish to minimize their own participation. With many professors unwilling to administer and students incapable of doing so, everybody would fare better—at least on some campuses—if there were less grousing about *the* administration (always referred to as "they" when things are not going well) and greater acknowledgment that administrative officers are more useful than the academic anarchists would have us believe.

Turning now to the faculty, the familiar cliché is that they are "the heart of the institution," and indeed they are—even in our multiversities, which are supposed to be heartless. Since other kinds of organizations may have trustees, administrators, and even students, professors constitute the unique genus in the groves of academe. Professors preside over the curriculum. They exercise individual judgments about which persons may become teachers, accountants, doctors, lawyers, scientists, and what not. In addition to passing critical judgments on students, they initiate appraisals of one another to help determine which of their colleagues will be promoted, held back, or dismissed. In brief, professors have a good deal to do with making and implementing university policy—despite their professed distaste for administration.

During the last decade or two, many university professors have likewise become heavily involved in research and public service. In response to pressures from business, industry, and government, they are more frequently in their laboratories, secluded in their offices, or even away from the campus altogether for considerable amounts of time. Thus, one hears complaints about the neglect of undergraduate teaching and the divided loyalties of faculty persons between their local duties and their outside assignments.

In view of the rapidly enlarged size and greatly increased complexity of many universities, disjunctions are to be expected. Gone forever are the days when campuses were retreats for those who merely wanted a quiet life. Institutions of higher education in general and universities in particular are now deeply involved in the most basic problems of our era. Classrooms, libraries, and laboratories are now occupied from early morning until well into the night, and the long summer vacation when operations ceased altogether has become a memory.

The Place of the Student

Reflecting many of the conditions of modern life, the university is inevitably a locus of keen and sometimes fierce competition. The spirit of a homogeneous community has in many places given way to the depersonalization of a heterogeneous society. Although correlations between the size of an academic community and the satisfactions or dissatisfactions of its members remain to be demonstrated, the wave of student disquiet all over the country is undoubtedly related to these environmental changes.

We have all read and heard a great deal about the Free Speech Movement at Berkeley. I have seen dozens of news stories, editorials, and magazine articles, and have heard firsthand accounts from President Kerr, former Chancellor Strong, and numerous other persons closely involved. The explanations of why these unfortunate events occurred are even more varied, I can assure you, than the accounts of what happened. Campus troubles elsewhere of late have also been publicized. The protest at Yale in which students objected to the decision not to grant tenure to an associate professor they liked was widely reported. There were the "perform or perish" demonstrations against the denial of tenure to a music professor at Brooklyn and the protests at St. John's in which five hundred students attacked the university's "reactionary paternalism" and "low" faculty salaries. At the University of Kansas 110 students were suspended and arrested after a sit-in protesting alleged racial discrimination. Students and faculty joined at the New York City Community College to demonstrate against "intolerable conditions" in an ancient building which houses an annex of that institution. At Fairleigh Dickinson, fifteen hundred students, in shifts of thirty-five an hour, staged a picket operation as "an expression of general student discontent." I could add to the list, but let me conclude with the report I heard recently from a friend who heads one of our best-known liberal arts colleges. He said the editor of their student newspaper had just resigned in protest over the tranquil conditions prevailing on that campus!

The problems behind these episodes have ranged from freedom of speech and political action to complaints about library hours and dormitory rules. The issues have been economic, social, ethical, legal, philosophical, administrative, and occasionally, educational. Some of the protests have been deeply felt and responsible attempts to express legitimate points of view. Others have been unruly expressions of ill-defined dissatisfaction and general antagonisms regarding matters having little—if anything—to do with the campus itself.

A decade ago the American Council on Education conducted a study reported in *The Student's Role in College Policy Making*, where it was stated that "Student participation in the making of college and university policy is an accepted fact on some campuses, an unrealistic proposition on others, but on many others a subject of serious study and discussion." Even before the first incident at Berkeley last year, we decided at the Council that the time was at hand for a close look at the changing role of the student in American higher education, and this will be the topic of our annual meeting this fall in Washington.

Meantime, in colleges and universities all over the nation we need to re-examine the rights and responsibilities of trustees, administrative officers, faculty, and students. During recent years faculties almost everywhere have gained immensely in their rights and privileges, and justly so, but perhaps the time is overdue for some of our institutional faculties to codify the responsibilities they should assume to go along with their freedom and influence. Also, we need to get a dialogue under way about the freedom being claimed by and in some instances extended to students. What are their corollary responsibilities? Should they, for example, have the same rights and obligations as citizens outside the university?

Even if one assumes the narrow view that the only right a student is entitled to is the freedom to learn as much as he can while enrolled, this alone would appear to entitle him to express himself regarding the learning and living opportunities provided by the institution of his choice. Let me illustrate. Professors grade student learning; I see no really valid reason for denying students the right to grade faculty teaching. If done in a careful way, then it might have very beneficial effects on both learners and teachers. I believe that students also are entitled to be heard about the rules and regulations pertaining to their behavior, but not to be the final arbiters—as some collegians are now demanding—in such matters. I have little sympathy, for example, with those students who feel their freedom encroached upon because university dormitories are operated differently from commercial hotels or motels.

A recently issued *Bulletin* of the International Association of Universities has the title, "Some Basic Problems that Confront Universities in All Parts of the World." One of the fourteen basic problems raised is "The Place of the Student in University Life," which is stated as follows:

What is the place of the student in the corporate life of a unversity? Is he raw material to be fitted into the conveyor belt of the academic curriculum and, when satisfactorily educated, to be given a degree, although during all his years at the university he has played no lively and active part either in its government or in association with the members of the teaching staff? Is he a colleague of the faculty, to be considered as an equal, if younger, member of the community, as used to be the pattern in the colleges of Oxford and Cambridge? Is he, in fact, the boss of the institution (as sometimes happens in South American universities) where the students, constitutionally or unconstitutionally, exercise a veto upon the appointment of rectors and senior university officials, not infrequently dis-organize the operations of the whole institution, and sometimes embroil the university in politics by their demonstrations and strikes?

There are no simple or easy answers to these questions. Between the extremes of the student as an assembly line product and the student as the arbiter of academic enterprise, there may be many workable forms of relationship between the individual and the institution. Existing forms are often quite imperfect, of course, and many of our procedures undoubtedly need restructuring to improve communication and participation.

Where reform is needed, I hope that we can proceed through

persuasion rather than force and that all parties concerned will view themselves as partners rather than adversaries. I believe that change can be accomplished more effectively through orderly procedures than through explosive demonstrations and other extremes of action and reaction. In my judgment, the quality of university education in the United States will be undermined and the public benefits of our institutions diminished if we permit our campuses to become centers of dissension and continuous embroilment.

A university is, in one of its basic functions, a testing ground for ideas. It is not an authoritarian institution where behavior is expected to take the form of command and obedience. The competition of ideas on the campus necessarily produces tensions and countervailing forces, and this is a sign of intellectual vitality as contrasted to the placidity of stagnation. Nevertheless, competition must not be allowed to degenerate into the kind of conflict that destroys academic freedom itself.

In addition to needing freedom, so as to nourish criticism of society, the university also must have discipline and order, so as to foster respect for law. For the students, it is intended to be neither a country club nor a perpetual debating society, but a place where they can acquire the intellectual foundation for a more satisfying, more productive place in the larger community. This objective implies the observance of good manners and social decencies, together with the development of a well-trained mind. Some of today's students with their "dirty sneakers, unkempt hair, dreary folk songs of the social struggle, and semi-barbarian speech and manners" (to use Mortimer Smith's phrases) convey just as false an image of the university as did yesterday's stereotyped generation of contented playboys. The typical university student today is represented by neither of these images.

Fortunately for our nation as well as for higher education, the public has a very favorable image of the modern American university. It is rightly regarded, I believe, as one of the wellsprings of our civilization. We can keep it this way if responsibilities are kept in balance with privileges, and if everybody concerned will think about duties alongside rights. We must all remember, furthermore, that every university is much more in the public view than it once was. Its traditional immunity from undue outside inter-ference implies a capacity for self-regulation and self-renewal, and to protect this autonomy all of us who really care must see that its integrity is preserved.

The task of maintaining and improving higher education will not accomplish itself. Those individuals who are now being gradu-ated have a continuing obligation to give their university in par-ticular and higher education in general informed and active support. What happens *in* our colleges and universities may be of most immediate import for trustees, administrators, teachers, and students, but what happens *to* them is an outcome in which every member of our society has a stake.

My commencement address at Michigan State University on March 10, 1968, was a turn-around of the title Clark Kerr used for his much-quoted book, The Uses of the University. *Four current misconceptions of the university are analyzed, with suggestions for changing them.*

The Abuses of the University

ALMOST FIVE YEARS have gone by since the publication of Clark Kerr's provocative book, *The Uses of the University.* His foreword stated that he was not mainly concerned with the *misuses* of the university, and that his title implied "a generally optimistic tone." Although my remarks are not intended as generally pessimistic, I believe that disturbing occurrences since 1963 are alarming enough to warrant our attention to "The Abuses of the University." All of us are concerned not only with what happens within and around the nation's campuses, but also with what may happen *to* our institutions of higher learning.

Let me begin by expressing confidence in the viability of American higher education. Our belief in the importance of colleges and universities is witnessed in our establishment and maintenance of more than twenty-three hundred such institutions. Nine antedate the founding of our nation and, compared to other social agencies, institutions of higher education are remarkably tough and durable organisms. Even so, they can wither away for want of understanding or support, or we can so maim their structures and functions as to render them incapable of serving their basic purposes. Their structures and functions have been evolved over a long period of time, and it is doubtful that their purposes are going to be changed overnight as a consequence of either committee recommendations or activist onslaughts. Caryl Haskins, president of the Carnegie Institution of Washington, recently cautioned that, in social as in biological evolution, there is a limit to the rate at which change can take place. To be successful, innovations must not be severely disorienting. "As in biological evolution, effective social evolution must be at once radical and conservative, freely embracing the new, yet scrupulously preserving basic and well-tested elements that have had a high survival value in the past and which remain relevant to the present."

There is nothing immutable or inalienable about the ways in which contemporary universities are organized and operated. They have changed with the passage of time; they are the way they are today, not because of any conspiracy of governing boards, administrators, or faculties, but because of their response to the logic of history and through their interplay with other parts of society. As a Canadian educator, J. E. Hodgetts, describes the matter, there is no need to conjure up "false dragons" to explain their shortcomings or to forget that at times "the unripe better is the enemy of the ripening good." To maintain their integrity as centers of higher learning, colleges and universities must manifest some continuity with the past and must be able to resist both inside and outside pressures that would distort their basic objectives and perhaps even destroy their greatest social utility.

In my consideration of the abuses to which our institutions seem to be increasingly exposed, I am not impugning the motives of all advocates of innovation. The well-intentioned friends of higher education vastly outnumber its avowed enemies, but, to draw from Louis Wright's salty comments in his last report from the Folger Library, shenanigans do get perpetrated in the name of "freedom of expression," and its more dim-witted defenders are sometimes unaware that they may be countenancing "the techniques of Ku Kluxers and Brown Shirts" on and around their campuses. This being so, I believe that all of us become a party to mayhem on the body of the university if we stand by as passive witnesses to its mutilation.

What I shall stress here is not a defense of the status quo in American higher education but, rather, is an attack on those abuses that in my judgment will denigrate the integrity and effectiveness of our universities if we do not speak out against them and take strong counteractions. To act intelligently, we must begin by identifying and uprooting erroneous ideas about what an institution of higher education is supposed to be and do. Although I am no longer in the thick of the campus fray, I have gone through a variety of experiences as student, teacher, administrator, and trustee of more than a dozen different institutions. I hope to speak to you as a voice that represents both sympathy and detachment. In any event, you are a captive audience, and you have no option but to hear me out, as I set forth my personal views about four current misconceptions of the university and what to do about them.

1. *The university as a microcosm.* The notion that the campus should replicate in miniature the larger community is not the worst current misconception, but it is a common one. Merrimon Cuninggim has pointed out, in a recent and as yet unpublished paper, "the university at its best is not merely a human community, it is a humane community." It differs from other types of human communities because of its focus on gaining, sharing, and using knowledge. Even though actual institutions may fall short of the prototype, they are committed to the pursuit of truth and the dissemination of knowledge. This commitment in turn implies a measure of insulation from mundane affairs, a due regard for history and timelessness as well as for the here and now, and the right to criticize as well as serve the society that supports them. In the larger structure of the whole social system, the university is intended to be the mansion of the intellect and not a sheltered roosting place or a staging area for partisan political forces.

Members of the academic community, whether students, professors, administrators, or trustees, are involved, of course, in many of the affairs of the outside world, and much that goes on intramurally is highly relevant extramurally. The university is a special-purpose, rather than a general-purpose, community, however, and it should not be expected to express all the varied desires of its human components.

The relevance of what it tries to do is not necessarily tested by a direct and immediate relation to the burning civic issues of the day. To be viable, a university must be contemporaneous, but in its functioning as a main vehicle of civilization a major aim must also be that of transmitting the best that has been thought and said in the past. The preoccupations of the university not only transcend the immediacies of time but also those of space, for, as the generic name of the institution implies, many of its concerns are universal rather than provincial. Although its student members enjoy considerable freedom in choosing what they will study and in determining how they will use their extracurricular time, they should not have the illusion that the university is intended to resemble either a supermarket or a boutique. It is likewise preposterous to contend that each student generation can devise anew its own curriculum or construct its own ground rules for the advancement of learning.

In view of the generally messy conditions prevailing in politics at home and abroad, I am at loss to understand why some persons feel that university affairs are best conducted by all members of the academic community on a one-man, one-vote basis. It is interesting to speculate what would happen to the faculty if, like political officeholders, they were hired and fired by vote of their principal constituents, the students. It is also interesting to ponder what the curriculum might be if some academic equivalent of partisan politics were used to determine course offerings.

I could continue possible permutations and combinations that might stem from implementing erroneous notions about the university as a social microcosm. The point to emphasize here, however, is that if the university were not a special-purpose institution it really would have no excuse for being, and I suspect that most taxpayers and other benefactors would agree. Furthermore, we should keep in mind that a social price exacted for the autonomy accorded such an institution is the requirement that it conduct its proper affairs in an orderly and productive way, with a reasonable expectation of ultimate payoff for society's investment. In this vein, the highest court in California ruled, in 1967, on a case originating in Berkeley that "[The] University, as an academic community, can formulate its own standards, rewards, and punishments. ... Thus, *in an academic community, greater freedoms and greater restrictions may prevail than in society at large,* and the subtle fixing of these limits should, in large measure, be left to the educational institution itself."

For the university to maintain its autonomy and distinctiveness as a place where the pursuit of truth and the advancement of learning have traditionally been shielded from outside intrusions, its members not only must have high standards of conduct but also must live up to them. When they fail to do so, and deviant behavior takes such extreme forms that the police and the courts are required to maintain order and settle disputes, then autonomy is already giving way to heteronomy—and the university is indeed becoming a microcosm.

2. *The university as a welfare agency.* However erroneously, formal education is regarded increasingly as a panacea for most of our social and economic ills. It is in some respects unfortunate, therefore, that education is not a commodity to be bought and sold, or even given away. In a welfare state we have moved very commendably in the direction of equalizing educational opportunity, but there is nothing we can do about equalizing innate capacities for learning, and we are finding out that even the desires for learning are affected by some circumstances entirely outside the educational community.

Accordingly, it strikes me that it is necessary to safeguard our institutions against all sorts of popular misconceptions about their potentials as reform agencies for offsetting inadequacies and failures that are traceable to other sources. Yet not only are colleges and universities expected to transform young persons in attendance, but they are also being asked to play key roles in uplifting the population at large. Whether it be the elimination of poverty and criminality, the reduction of unemployment, the improvement of cities, the uplift of morals, or the placement of men on the moon, institutions of higher education are being drawn into a welter of problems.

Oblivious to Sidney Hook's dictum several years ago that "good works off campus cannot be a substitute for good works on campus," many students are being distracted from their primary obligation by outside interests. The outside involvements of professors are likewise causing increasing numbers of them to be charged with neglect of teaching. Administrative officers, too, find it difficult to resist a fragmentation of their time and energy. While acknowledging many new obligations and opportunities for the university to be of wider service, we must be wary of letting any institution be pulled apart in the futile endeavor of trying to please everybody. Even our most affluent universities have limited resources, and they cannot simultaneously orient themselves to every conceivable discipline, much less to every possible mission. We do not give credit courses in every subject that interests some students or professors, and we cannot reasonably expect campus attention to be equally directed to all social problems.

If we thrust universities into areas that are alien to their missions or if we burden them down with responsibilities more logically belonging to other agencies, we can readily distort their basic purposes and splinter their effectiveness. In serving society, colleges and universities must not become subservient to it. Their highest utility is in their distinctive functions, and if they become unduly enmeshed as agencies of social welfare, these functions will be eroded. We must be on guard, therefore, against the inadvertent kind of distortion which attenuates core purposes in a vast disarray of welfare services.

3. *The university as a retreat.* Just as it is an illusion to expect too much from the university as a special community, so is it a delusion to hold that its members may enjoy life in a kind of secular sanctuary where they have many rights but few duties. Perhaps I am too far beyond thirty to understand and appreciate the changed facts of academic life, but I confess dismay over a currently circulated pronouncement on student rights and freedoms that has virtually nothing to say about duties and responsibilities. Also, it troubles me to see faculty members share in the ethos of mounting permissiveness to the extent that they stand passively by while some of our campuses are rife with disorder and violence.

To paraphrase some thoughts of other concerned educators, I think we do ourselves and our institutions injury when we make private will into a sufficient justification for almost any act, when we regard individuals entirely as ends in themselves, and when we yield to the opinion that the whims of individual members of the academic community should be made into university mandates.

Living as I do in the Georgetown section and working in the Dupont Circle area of the nation's capital, I have grown accustomed to looking at the wildest varieties of hippies and flower children, but I share Joseph Wood Krutch's view that they are certainly exercising the prerogative of coming "as near as our society permits to freedom from moral imperative and the obligation to be socially useful." Campus environments, I submit, have not been carefully cultivated all these years as hideaways where everybody should be permitted to "turn on" in his own way!

Since I favor upholding the university as a place to further higher learning rather than as a haven in which to further student contentment and staff tranquillity, I admit to being disturbed by a spreading permissiveness. For example, I have the old-fashioned notion that dormitories are not supposed to cater to the kind of "togetherness" provided by motels. I do not find myself attuned to the trend toward pass-fail marking in all courses, or to the notion that the ideal faculty teaching load is no courses at all. I do not see the pertinence of easy self-expression and life-adjustment substituting for courses in mathematics, science, and a whole range of other rigorous disciplines. Egalitarian proposals to junk credit hours and standards of accreditation suggest effects on later professional performance that I would not want as a doctor's patient or a lawyer's client.

In brief, I still hold that colleges and universities are the principal trustees of civilization, and that they cannot maintain this role and be environments where individuals are exempt from the consequence of their own action or inaction. Like George Kennan, I am distrustful of simply letting persons be guided by "inner voices," and of supporting our institutions of higher education as sanctuaries for the estranged, havens for the escapists, or refuges for those who disavow widely accepted and legitimized standards of aspiration and accomplishment.

4. *The university as an arena.* Although the transmogrified university might retain some of its basic identity in spite of the

debasements resulting from misconceptions I have mentioned up to this point, I doubt that it can survive if it is turned into a battleground or an arena. The arena, as you know, was originally a place where lions devoured unarmed Christians and gladiators fought to kill. Civilized society no longer permits this kind of bestiality, yet the campus has witnessed scenes of violence where the majority of the members of the academic community have been bemused spectators while defenders of the institution were in effect mauled and sometimes chewed to pieces by rapacious nihilists.

You share my alarm also, I trust, over the growing evidences that some members of academic communities are lining up as adversaries determined to impose their own wills on others through collective bargaining, power groupings, organized disruptions and obstructions, not to mention other tactics hitherto alien to the collegiate environment. Their proclaimed grievances range from complaints about local situations to protests about racial injustice and the war in Vietnam.

The National Student Association reports that, during only two months last year, 477 students were arrested and 1,728 faced disciplinary action as the result of demonstrations. To be sure, just 62 of our 2,300 campuses experienced such episodes and only 14,564 students—about two-tenths of 1 per cent of the 6,964,000 enrolled everywhere—had any involvement, but I still think that all of us should be concerned. "Happenings" in such places as Berkeley, San Francisco State, Madison, Iowa City, Cambridge, and other locales are danger signals not to be ignored. If you are inclined to brush aside the talk that some of the activists have a program and a national network, read the manifestos of the Students for a Democratic Society or follow the actions of the Carmichaels who gives cues to the Student Nonviolent Coordinating Committee.

Under Newton's third law of motion, however, for every action there is an equal and opposite reaction, and it is beginning to look as if this law applies to abuses of the university. On my desk in Washington I have a growing stack of cogent declarations from embattled presidents and chancellors—some of whom are speaking out singly, and some in unison. There are also similar documents from trustees, and—I am especially pleased to observe— one from the American Association of University Professors. Even though it is unfortunate that so much time should have to be diverted from the main business of academia and given to riot prevention, it is gratifying to me to see that a stout defense of orderly governance is developing.

I am disturbed, on the other hand, by some tendencies analyzed in James A. Perkins' paper, *The University and Due Process*:

> If we are not to be legislated into total paralysis, there is nothing for it but that each of us goes to work to put the pieces of the community together again. Students and administrators will have to stop regarding each other as implacable enemies. For students this will mean a recognition that they can't have it both ways: they can't ask for full participation in a community that they are systematically proceeding to destroy. And before students leap too quickly into the arms of civil law, they should be reminded that they will have to live with all the law, not just the parts they like. In such quasi-political matters as the draft, pornography, and discrimination, students may be subject to laws they don't like at all. He who appeals to the law for protection must be prepared to obey it.

> For administrators it will mean a very hard look at all the rules and procedures by which their institutions live; quite possibly, it will also mean limbering up some very stiff attitudes about the role of students in academic affairs. And for faculty it will mean not only that they take the time to act as arbiters and to provide the balancing force, but that they reorder their work and give campus affairs a higher priority. A community of any kind is strong only to the extent that its members make the effort required to sustain and nourish it. We must all be willing to make the effort.

Should members of the academic community prove unable or unwilling to put their own houses in order and get on with the central enterprise, we can be certain that others will take over the controls, with students, faculty, administrators, and perhaps trustees all paying dearly for our failure to correct derelictions. I need not detail for you any of the outside controls that are already in the making here and there, or the possible recriminations in reduced financial support, political interferences, and other consequences we may prefer not to think about.

Our real challenge is to meld continuity and change in ways that bring about improvement, and I am confident that we can counter the abuses of the university and at the same time enhance its uses.

Visiting lecturers are invited annually for the Mont-
gomery Lecture Series at the University of Nebraska in
Lincoln. In May of 1968 when I gave these two lectures
there, I attempted to summarize, analyze, and evaluate
basic changes taking place or contemplated in the
governance of many colleges and universities.

Changing University Governance

IN THIS ERA of rapid change and rising egalitarianism, it is not surprising that traditional
modes of college and university governance are under fire. What
happens in and to the nation's institutions has come to concern
growing numbers of persons and so little wonder that more voices
want to be heard. Centers of higher learning, not being proprietary,
belong to nobody in particular, yet almost everybody these days
seems to be pressing forward with special claims. From within, the
disorder fomented by extremist demands has completely disrupted
some campuses. From without, a mounting public reaction to campus disorders further threatens time-honored forms of institutional
governance.

Although modes of institutional governance have long been
subject to debate in academic circles, colleges and universities all
over the country are now manifesting a deeper interest. Some have
named task forces to make studies and recommendations; others
have already proposed or made drastic changes. Stanford University
has added students as voting members of academic council committees and will also have three students as nonvoting participants at

261

meetings of its trustees. Maryville College in Tennessee has formed an all-college council of six students, six faculty members, and six administrative officers. The state of Kentucky has made the student government presidents from the six state-supported institutions nonvoting members of their governing boards. At the State University of New York at Binghamton, a new community government scheme entails a membership ratio of five faculty members to three students to two administrators. At many other institutions joint committees are considering reforms and making recommendations. To get judgments on a proposal for restructuring its governance, Columbia University recently circulated a ballot to nearly twenty-three thousand students and faculty, and 8,420 actually voted. In brief, reforming university governance is a major preoccupation on many campuses.

Much of this activity is, of course, long overdue. Before an institution plunges into radical reorganization, however, some basic questions need to be answered: Who *now* decides what? Which facets of governance are sources of dissatisfaction, and for whom? What changes are being proposed, and why? How can their feasibility and desirability be assessed? What are the implications of proposed changes?

It is my guess that on the average campus few persons can answer knowledgeably even this first question. If anybody has ever made a thoroughgoing empirical study of how decisions are now reached on a single American college or university campus, I am unaware of it. To be sure, there is an extensive body of rhetorical literature on collegiate governance, and there is certainly no shortage of self-presumed experts. As a former colleague recently noted with some irony, the top administrator "who once thought he knew something about the conduct of academic affairs is now a wiser but sadder man. For if he has learned anything in the past five years it is that everyone else is more expert than he."[1]

Present Status

Modifying the machinery of academic governance at any institution should involve at least a rudimentary understanding of exist-

---

1. David C. Knapp, "Management: Intruder in the Academic Dust," *Educational Record*, Winter 1969, p. 55.

ing mechanisms, how they came to be, and how they function. It is highly relevant to know who now makes what decisions, and under what circumstances, before questions are formulated about who ought to decide what under changed arrangements. Another requisite in most institutions is a realistic view about the extent to which the institution will be granted unlimited autonomy to make any, let alone all, decisions affecting its welfare. The limits on autonomy are well illustrated by some of the external controls already imposed upon many institutions.

In the manner of autonomy, or self-governance, probably no generalizations apply equally to all places. In the main, junior colleges, former teachers colleges, and church-related institutions exercise greater autonomy than they did a generation or so ago. Many junior and community colleges are out from under the regimentation of public school system controls; teachers colleges have not only changed their names but also have moved away from authoritarianism; and church-related institutions are less dominated by religious bodies. In nearly all institutions, students and faculty are less submissive to regulations of their behavior. The force of tradition has weakened, and the demand for conformity has correspondingly diminished. Students and professors are more mobile and less tied to a particular campus. These and other circumstances are symbolic of significant gains here and there in institutional as well as individual freedom.

These gains, however, are offset by some losses. In nearly all states the uncontrolled and unplanned diversity of public institutions, resulting from local autonomy in decision making, has already been swept away. Policy decisions about size, governance, programs, facilities, faculty and staff components, student clientele, and budget are less and less matters for internal resolution. Drastic curtailments of autonomous actions have taken place and are still occurring. Behind these changes lies an intensified public, and hence political, concern with the greatly increased cost, complexity, and importance of higher education. Gaining ascendancy is the view that a rational interdependence of institutions is perhaps just as essential as a proper regard for their independence.

In this same vein, only a few states are now without a formal coordinating board or agency for public higher education. In most states the sentiment prevails that higher education has become too crucial to the general welfare for its development to be left entirely to the individual institution or in local hands. Unilateral approaches and piecemeal actions are seen as unsatisfactory ways to solve widespread problems. In brief, even though students and faculty may be participating more widely in decision making within the institution, the current tendency toward collectivism has caused more and more decisions and actions affecting the present and future of higher education to be transferred from the private to the public arena and from the local to the state or national level.

This trend toward limiting institutional independence is by no means confined entirely to the public sector of higher education, however. For a number of years decisions made by the legislative and executive branches of the federal government have tended to reduce the autonomy of institutions by increasing their *outer* direction at the cost of their *inner* direction. A well-known medical dean in a private university has remarked that decisions within his bailiwick control only $200,000 of his $8 million budget; the remainder is controlled largely by decisions in the nation's capital. And although we often think of Harvard as a model of independence, a noted political science professor there has expressed amazement at how little control even Harvard now has over Harvard.

Let me stress that these changes are not to be attributed to any ulterior or sinister motives anywhere. Most of the erosion of institutional autonomy or independence has taken place so gradually or so indirectly that awareness of what has happened occurs well after the fact. Moreover, most of the pieces of autonomy have been traded off for substantial material benefits.

To minimize erosion of institutional autonomy, one educator has urged that every institution have a clear set of goals, a strategy to follow, the resources to monitor itself, and leadership strong and sensitive enough to ensure that goals are the touchstone of every action. This admonition comes at a time when there is a tendency on many campuses to undermine legitimate local authority rather than strengthen it. Most trustees and presidents have long since abandoned in fact, if not in law, any pretensions to absolute power. What completely eludes me is the reasons student activists and faculty militants find for conjuring them up as authoritarian devils responsible for all the shortcomings of academic governance.

Although its practitioners have long accepted the wry definition of academic administration as the "roughest profession," it is currently denigrated in ways that bode ill for the future of our institutions. By way of example I quote what a rather hysterical student said to an eastern university president in an open meeting: "This university is faculty and students and we need you for only one thing—to get money. You and the deans should have no say in education. You administrators get in the way." This naïve view is widely shared, and most unfortunately, by many persons who should know better. Paul Goodman has advocated getting rid of all external control. Presumably advocating syndicalism, J. Kenneth Galbraith has said that "the faculty now governs and only the faculty can govern" what he calls "the mature university." Although he largely ignores the functions of administrators and relegates trustees to merely ceremonial roles, he concedes that it might be helpful for professors to bring students and alumni into an alliance with them.

Such misconceptions of the divisions of responsibility and authority required to operate and maintain viable universities increase the difficulties, of course, of persuading able men and women to accept responsible leadership positions. And once they are in office, the spread of negative attitudes makes the performance of their duties even more difficult. If the multiversity is not to degenerate into what might be called a "nonuniversity," it seems self-evident that somebody has to reconcile competing purposes, adjudicate conflicting claims, and try to coordinate the complex enterprise. In conflict-prone institutions, as modern universities frequently are, strong leadership is more needed than ever before.

Even so, university presidents are being subjected to more and more exasperations, as noted in the comments of a Canadian university president who recently resigned:

As at present conceived the presidency is a burden because the university does not really know its own mind. The president is the chief executive officer of the university, and not simply of the board of governors, as is sometimes wrongly stated.... Now an executive officer must know what, rather than whom, to execute. He must work from a body of agreed policy. Clearly he must also be allowed certain prerogatives, and certain powers of initiative....

It is my suggestion that neither policy nor prerogatives have in fact been agreed on by the academic profession. The president hence works in an exasperating vacuum. The point, in my view, is that we have failed to adjust our sights to the new scale on which we must work, to the new relation between society and the world of scholarship. As a profession we have drifted into a revolutionary situation unexpectedly.[2]

To learn how trustees view their roles in governance, Morton A. Rauh recently queried approximately ten thousand of them and received fifty-two hundred usable replies to a questionnaire.[3] Trustees, he states, see decision making as being from the top down. Rauh's opinion is that their views are mainly either ill-advised or, more probably, at odds with what actually happens in most institutions. He thinks they ought to "forget the now dated and impossible charge of 'governing' " and concentrate on five basic responsibilities: (1) select the president, (2) evaluate the management (especially the president), (3) hold the assets, (4) act as a court of last resort, and (5) maintain a balance between the competing constituencies and relate the institution to the larger society.

Trustees and governing boards can be great sources of strength to an institution, particularly in times of stress and trouble. Ideally, they function as both buffer and conduit between the outside world and the institutions they serve without pay. Theirs is the privilege and the responsibility of representing the interests of the public at large to the academic community, and vice versa. Although the recent Educational Testing Service study of college and university trustees reveals an unflattering statistical portrait, by and large trustee functions are underappreciated. My own observation is that even though these bodies may have the legal prerogative to run our universities, most have the good sense not to attempt it. Students and professors are often prone to forget that some group has to bear direct responsibility for keeping the enterprise solvent and seeing that the chartered purposes are carried forward.

Of all groups concerned in university governance, professors exercise the largest influence on the academic enterprise. Students

2. Kenneth B. Hare in a speech before the University of British Columbia faculty, December 19, 1968. Reproduced in part in *Affairs Universitaires*, February 1969, p. 3.
3. *The Trusteeship of Colleges and Universities* (New York: McGraw-Hill Book Co., 1969).

come and go annually, department chairmanships may rotate, presidents seldom last out a decade, and trustees in many instances serve for limited terms, but tenured members of the faculty usually remain as long as they choose. They have main jurisdiction over what will be taught and how. They pass critical judgments on students and their own colleagues. Until recently, at least, they comprised most of the policy-making committees and other academic bodies that really decided what the university should do. (For some strange reason, student revolutionaries have been slow to realize where most of the real power in academe resides, and in some places they have been blockading the wrong offices!)

Insofar as the lines of authority and processes of governance in some large universities are concerned, however, there is admittedly a good deal of confusion. A researcher at the University of California at Berkeley (which, incidentally, he considers "well-advanced" in governance) has stated that in some areas their faculty senate makes basic policy which the administration then carries out. In other areas, he says, the administration makes basic policy and holds faculty groups responsible for carrying it out; in still other areas, the administration both makes and implements policy.[4]

Decision making and implementation are seldom a simple or unitary process in most institutions, and one reform needed is to make as clear and unmistakable as possible the lines of authority and responsibility. In matters of student affairs, the faculty manifestly cannot intervene sporadically and at the same time refuse to take a major role in day-to-day administration. All parties who wish to participate directly in any area of concern, moreover, must be ready to devote the time, energy, and intelligence the responsibility demands.

In earlier days when the academic community was smaller and less complex, "town meeting" governance, with the president presiding over sessions of the entire faculty, was fairly common. Everybody was eligible to participate and vote. By contrast, at Columbia University, the Faculty's Executive Committee pointed out in its March 20, 1969, report that in the contemporary uni-

---

4. Terry Lunsford, "Authority and Ideology in the Administered University," *American Behavioral Scientist*, May-June 1968, pp. 5–14.

versity such a faculty body can work only if most of its members pay no attention to it, for often there is not even an assembly room large enough to seat them all. Furthermore, experience shows that attendance at meetings is normally only about 15 percent of the membership, with a rise to 25 percent at a time of crisis. The American Council on Education several years ago conducted a study of governance procedures in more than one thousand colleges and universities. The results (unpublished) showed that 104 had faculty senates; 196 had faculty organizations other than a senate; 149 had faculty representation through a council or committee; 441 had faculties meeting under administrative leadership; 14 had faculty representation through a chapter of the American Association of University Professors; and only 77 were without designation of faculty organization or leadership.

Still another Council study, made last year, indicated among other things that in 95 percent of the responding institutions, administrative officials reported some system of student government. Only 16 percent reported that neither faculty nor students had been very influential in setting policies. When the fact of participation was acknowledged, however, the complaints voiced by students often turned to content or extent of participation, and posed questions of whether the power was really structural or merely advisory, and whether, insofar as students were concerned, it should extend beyond rules of social conduct to academic matters.

James P. Dixon, president of Antioch College, is quoted as calling traditional student governments "antediluvian institutions," with tasks that the faculty and administration are not interested in. A California professor has dubbed them "toy governments," "concerned principally with trivia." And a state college dean recently said: "It is now clear that we cannot perpetuate the myth that we have a community of any sort when 90 percent of the membership of that community—students—has nothing official to say about the purpose, direction, or even procedures which govern the so-called community of scholars."

Of student activism it has been noted that recent protests often demand things beyond the power of a college or university to grant—such as changes in American foreign policy. Other demands may concern matters that are under the control of the institution—

admissions policies, social regulations, student aid grants, building locations, course offerings, faculty tenure considerations, and so on, including investment policies. In some instances, the student activists want more student participation in decision making, and in others, they (particularly the Students for a Democratic Society) seek control.

Martin Trow has observed that faculty and student advocates of more participatory democracy are often expressing a faith and ideology rather than describing a reality, because they are inclined to ignore or dismiss "the very large numbers of faculty and students who are reasonably satisfied with the multiversity and who even prefer it to the realities of small participatory educational communities as they exist elsewhere." In his commentary on "Conceptions of the University" Trow says:

> The students and faculty who see in the university an instrument for the radical transformation of man and society are relatively few in number but full of energy and passion, and occasionally well organized. They are strengthened by more widely held feelings of uneasiness and discontent with existing social institutions that arise out of the nation's international and domestic troubles, as well as the way the university performs the variety of functions it has taken on. There is also the difficulty of articulating a philosophy of the multiversity that can command not merely rational assent but also strong loyalties. Add to this the vulnerability of a university to disruption and the threat of disruption by passionate minorities, and we have the essential ingredients of Berkeley's current difficulties. These are likely to persist. It remains to be seen whether they can be contained and harnessed to causes of educational reform, or whether they will continue to be a source of the cycle of confrontation, rule-violation, punishment, and confrontation that only the most committed and nihilistic ideologies can welcome.[5]

Perceived-Preferred Roles

Edward Gross and Paul V. Grambsch's book, *University Goals and Academic Power*,[6] represents a systematic effort to ascertain the nature and scope of differing views about the perceived and preferred roles of various members of the academic community.

5. *American Behavioral Scientist*, May-June 1968, p. 21.
6. Washington: American Council on Education, 1968.

Amid all the current talk about what universities are and what they ought to be, of interest is what a sample of seventy-two hundred presidents, vice-presidents, academic deans, department heads, directors, trustees, and faculty members in sixty-eight universities thought as recently as five years ago. Each respondent to a questionnaire that included a list of forty-seven goals rated these goals on a five-point scale according to how much emphasis he felt each received at his institution and how much it should receive.

The top ten *perceived* goals were ranked: (1) Protect academic freedom, (2) Increase or maintain prestige, (3) Maintain top quality in important programs, (4) Ensure confidence of contributors, (5) Keep up to date, (6) Train students for scholarship and research, (7) Carry on pure research, (8) Maintain top quality in all programs, (9) Ensure favor of validating bodies, and (10) Ensure efficient goal attainment.

The top ten *preferred* goals, on the other hand, were ranked: (1) Protect academic freedom, (2) Train students for scholarship and research, (3) Cultivate students' intellect, (4) Maintain top quality in all programs, (5) Disseminate new ideas, (6) Keep up to date, (7) Maintain top quality in important programs, (8) Develop students' objectivity, (9) Ensure efficient goal attainment, and (10) Protect students' right of inquiry.

Among the forty-seven perceived and preferred goals, it is pertinent to report the following lower rankings in each category: Involve faculty in university government (25 and 19), Run university democratically (29 and 22), Protect students' right of action (41 and 40), Involve students in university government (45 and 46).

Concerning the perceived goals of the university, the respondents also were asked for their opinions on how much influence each of sixteen agencies, groups, or persons had in determining major goals of the institutions as a whole. To give the overall picture in the sixty-eight universities sampled, the survey tabulated the mean scores, along with the standard deviation for each (Table 1).

Gross and Grambsch concluded that, in general, the administration and the faculty share much the same values and work toward essentially the same goals, with no evidence of any deep-seated conflicts. Moreover, no appreciable dissonance was found between perceived and preferred objectives. Institutional size and location

TABLE 1: *Overall Power Structure of American Universities*

Power-holder (Rank Order)	Mean Score	Standard Deviation
President	4.65	.62
Regents	4.37	.82
Vice-presidents	4.12	.82
Deans of professional schools	3.62	.84
Dean of graduate school	3.59	.89
Dean of liberal arts	3.56	.89
Faculty	3.31	.97
Chairman	3.19	.93
Legislators	2.94	1.37
Federal government	2.79	1.06
State government	2.72	1.21
Large private donors	2.69	1.06
Alumni	2.61	.90
Students	2.37	.82
Citizens of state	2.08	1.02
Parents	1.91	.87

were negligible factors in goal perceptions and preferences, but elitist institutions tended to emphasize scholarly qualities, whereas other universities tended to be more service-oriented.

Faculty Views on Governance

A later and enlightening study of who now makes decisions in university matters and what academicians feel about who ought to participate in determining the ends and means of a particular institution is reported in *Faculty Participation in Academic Decision Making.*[7] When the author, Archie Dykes, made the inquiry, he was a Council administrative intern assigned to a large public university in the Midwest. He interviewed in depth a random faculty sample in the College of Liberal Arts and Sciences. His aim was to ascertain the faculty's conception of their "proper" role in decision making. He also wanted to find how they perceived the status quo in campus governance, reasons given for participating, along with views of impediments to the participation process and how the process operates.

The broad areas of inquiry were academic affairs, personnel matters, financial affairs, capital improvements, student affairs, and

7. Washington: American Council on Education, 1968.

public and alumni relations. Each faculty member interviewed was given a range of five choices on every item, with an opportunity to express himself on the varying extent of faculty influence from almost complete faculty control at one extreme to no involvement at the other. In the matter of academic affairs, for example, views were sought on degree requirements, curriculum, student admission requirements, and academic standards. As one might expect, the preponderance of faculty opinion favored faculty control over decisions in the general area of students and learning.

Nearly 70 percent of the faculty thought that their wishes normally should be controlling over such personnel matters as appointments, reappointments, tenure, and dismissals. In financial affairs, only 11 percent of the sample held that faculty influence should be decisive. Concerning capital improvements, 21 percent believed that the faculty should make the decisions, with the majority apparently feeling that they should be involved only to the extent necessary to counteract "misguided administrative emphasis." About a fourth of the respondents held that the faculty should not be bothered with student affairs, and another fourth believed that the faculty should have a strong role. Almost half preferred loose faculty surveillance, with other persons—such as the student life staff—doing the daily work. Public and alumni affairs proved to be the area of least interest insofar as personal decision-making roles were concerned.

Turning now to faculty satisfaction or dissatisfaction with their role in decision making, 51 percent of the respondents believed that the faculty have too little influence on decisions, while 44 percent believed that the faculty's role is not what it should be ideally but is about what one could realistically expect. Only 2 percent believed the degree and kind of faculty involvement to be about right.

A rather high proportion of the faculty—41 percent—felt excluded from important decisions, while 47 percent responded that they did not know whether they were excluded or not. The latter datum may be the more revealing about the changing structure of academic decision making. Bureaucratization in higher education probably means that the visibility of the decision-making processes has been reduced by the shift from direct to representative government. With regard to assessment of its role in decision making, 63 percent said that the faculty were dissatisfied; only 28 percent said that the faculty were satisfied with their role. Although expressing dissatisfaction, they also complained about time-consuming committee work and the burden of keeping informed about institutional affairs.

Despite grumblings, faculty members do participate actively in decision making. Dykes asked the respondents to rank certain factors which motivated their participation. The first-ranked factor was a sense of personal duty as a member of the academic profession, followed closely by "protection of faculty interests." The third-ranked influence was the desire for a voice in decisions affecting the faculty; the fourth was a "feeling of responsibility to the university." The wish to secure peer status ranked last. Academicians perceive few status rewards through participation in institutional affairs, but rather through scholarly accomplishment. A large faculty majority believed that some members participate in decision making far more than others. The most frequently mentioned reason given for those who participate was "special competence"; paradoxically, the second most frequently cited reason was a discreditable motive: they were perceived to be attempting to compensate for incompetence in their own discipline.

To ascertain further who participates and why, Dykes attempted to discover whether opportunities for decision making are equally available to all faculty members. He came up with a strong *no*, with complaints having to do mainly with the junior faculty.

Decision-making deterrents. According to Dykes's survey, research involvement leads the list of factors inhibiting faculty participation in decision making. The second major deterrent was that too much decision making was directed to inconsequential matters and to haggling over details. Concern for teaching was not viewed as a significant impediment.

With regard to the extent to which the faculty feel free to differ with the administration, Dykes determined that a majority felt no particular constraints, although 25 percent believed that they were not free to take exception to the administration. In any case, scholarly reputation and tenure made professors more confident in speaking out. As Dykes remarks, "The individual professor's marketability outside his institution appears to be his main source of security within it."

Other institutional factors also are thought to impede faculty participation in decision making. Respondents ranked the growth and complexity of the university as the chief impediment. Ranking next were two factors—the orientation of faculty to their disciplines rather than to their institution, and the emphasis on research and graduate education to the virtual exclusion of other institutional concerns. Finally, some respondents expressed alarm over the increasing number of administrators, a factor seen as a block to faculty participation.

Organizational arrangements. The faculty ranked the relative effectiveness of organizational arrangements designed to stimulate their participation in decision making as follows: departmental staff meetings, ad hoc faculty committees, standing faculty committees, the faculty senate, and the local chapter of the A.A.U.P. The efficacy of the faculty senate as a deliberative body was frequently questioned by respondents. Dykes determined that only 15 percent of the eligible respondents regularly participated, simply because its proceedings were not a matter of widespread interest. The exclusion of junior faculty also was considered a weakness of the faculty senate.

Because of the importance of the committee system in large universities, Dykes attempted to determine faculty attitudes toward committees. The statement that committee "membership always seems to come from a relatively small group of faculty members" was agreed to by 66 percent of those responding. Many respondents were critical of the methods of choosing committee members and asserted that a small number of faculty were selected repeatedly. On the other hand, 40 percent believed that faculty so chosen are representative, and 54 percent agreed with the statement that committees have considerable influence on institutional decisions. In identifying committee ideologies, 21 percent believed that faculty committees are more conservative than the faculty generally, while 15 percent believed that they are more liberal. Only 17 percent of the respondents thought that committees are closer in their leanings to the administration than to the faculty, while nearly half thought that the campus politicians tend to be on committees.

It is clear from Dykes's data that the department head was the individual faculty member's primary means of access to institutional decision making. Sixty-eight percent of the respondents indicated that they would go to their department head if they wished to influence a decision of a campuswide nature. To influence decisions at the college level, 73 percent said they would go to their department head. These data suggest that few faculty members are willing to go outside the established channels to influence institutional decisions.

In addition to determining the efficacy of official devices for faculty participation, Dykes attempted to assess the informal arrangements. He determined that only at the departmental level are informal associations—such as social gatherings—seen as providing important opportunity for the faculty to influence official decisions.

Emergent generalizations. Based upon the study as a whole, certain tentative conclusions were reached about faculty participation in academic decision making. First, faculty members have ambivalent attitudes about participation in decision making. While respondents believe that the faculty should have a strong role in making institutional decisions, at the same time they generally are unwilling to give the time such a role requires. Second, few faculty respondents recognize that institutional growth causes shifts in the nature of decision making. The necessity for the shift from direct to representational democracy seems to be poorly understood. Moreover, the faculty assume that they have steadily lost power relative to that of the administration, with little historical evidence to support their assumptions. Third, in view of the impossibility of neatly separating decisions into "educational" and "noneducational" categories, effective faculty participation should be manifested in all areas of concern. Decisions about student affairs, for example, which most faculty would gladly pass on to the administration, may radically affect the educational purposes of the institution.

Fourth, a source of much tension between faculty and administrators is a belief on the part of the faculty that the university is a closed system with a finite power potential. In fact, faculty power or administrative power depends on the other, and yet a perception of dichotomy persists. Fifth, there is a serious discrepancy between faculty role perception and actuality. Respondents exhibited a strong indifference to faculty government, while they criticized the administration for failing to communicate. There is a widespread misunderstanding about decision-making processes.

Finally, the Dykes study shows that the faculty holds a simplistic view of the distribution of institutional power. As Dykes puts it, "the faculty members interviewed attributed to the administration vastly more power than it actually possesses." Moreover, the pressures imposed on the administration, both internally and externally, were only dimly recognized. Current perceptions are, in the main, astray of reality; they unduly retard the development of relationships between faculty and administration and, in consequence, restrict effective decision making within institutions.

Also pertinent here are the findings of a Campus Governance Program, under the direction of Morris Keeton, to be published by the American Association for Higher Education. This study hypothesized that the life and work of a college or university expresses itself in four dimensions: intellectual climate, academic program, student life, and working conditions. These, in turn, are "affected by interactions of people with available resources and policies and procedures governing the ways in which they go about their daily work." The investigators found that people on the campuses studied perceive more problems connected with general resources than with any other area.[8]

As one might expect, different academic groups had varying conceptions of problems. A majority of the students, for example, were bothered about student parking and food services, but only a minority of the faculty expressed concern. With regard to provision of secretarial and clerical services for faculty, the situation was reversed. In view of the hue and cry of student militants about institutional efforts to control social and political behavior, it was of interest to me to note that on the campuses studied, under 5 percent of the faculty and administration and only 10–15 percent of the students perceived this area as presenting any important problems.

Let me summarize here some of the main points I have tried to bring out. Institutional autonomy or self-governance, as I mentioned earlier, varies widely among universities, but my judgment

8. *Shared Authority on Campuses* (Washington: The Association, 1971).

is that in recent years the academic enterprise has become subjected to more *outer* direction, with a corresponding loss of *inner* direction. This shift has been produced by a number of causes, and is one manifestation of the growing collectivism of contemporary social life. On the typical college or university campus, widespread confusions and misconceptions prevail about answers to the question, Who now decides what? Incongruences as well as congruences are commonplace in the existing perceptions of university goals and power. Moreover, if a cross section of the liberal arts faculty in one large Midwestern state university is at all representative, important discrepancies are manifest between academicians' perceived and preferred roles in decision making.

The inquiries cited also lead to the conclusion that desires to effect changes are prompted by self-interest as well as by a studied concern with what policies and procedures are best suited to advance institutional purposes. There is, however, a shortcoming in the evidence of what certain members of the academic community like and dislike about existing schemes of governance; that is, only scanty information is available about what the majority of students do and do not want. Objective data are likewise missing about the concerns of the public at large and about the attitudes of those constituencies upon whom the burden of supporting colleges and universities largely falls. As we go about the business of reexamining university governance with a view to improving it, I would urge that the public interest in higher learning not be overlooked. Indeed, in the final analysis it must be made paramount.

Proposed Changes

Although universities of bygone eras were probably never the serene places depicted by nostalgic sentiment, academic enterprise then was without question more orderly than now. Greater consensus prevailed about the ends and means of higher education. Going to college was regarded as a privilege of the few rather than a right of the many. Arrangements for governance were neatly hierarchical and few persons openly rejected the roles assigned to them. The circumstances that changed and are still changing all this are widely familiar.

As McGeorge Bundy recently noted, there is now "a deep

uncertainty about two fundamental elements in the structure of the university—its economics and its politics. We really do not know just how the modern university should be paid for, and we are just beginning to learn how and by whom its powers should be held and exercised."[9] Bundy points out that the distribution of authority and responsibility is being questioned as never before, with, in particular, students attacking traditional forms.

Up to now, I addressed two questions: Who *now* decides what? Which facets of governance are sources of dissatisfaction, and for whom? Here, I direct attention to three other questions: What changes are being proposed, and why? How can their feasibility and desirability be assessed? What are the implications of proposed changes?

Let us look first at the changes in governance proposed by students. Quite clearly, the Students for a Democratic Society want to take over institutions completely and use them as vantage points for launching a social revolution. Last year in the Madison campus newspaper, for example, a student advocated shutting down the present University of Wisconsin and, "with the great problems of the day in mind," constructing a "meaningful university." About the same time a student editor of Harvard's *Crimson* stated that "The typical university is only slightly more democratic than the Army, if less unpleasant." He believed that students should sit on boards of trustees, be able to compel their choice of course offerings, exercise some control over granting credit, and share equally with the faculty in academic policy making.

At this year's January meeting of the Association of American Colleges, the president of the United States National Student Association, Robert S. Powell, addressed those present as "the educational mandarins of 1969." He was emphatic about wanting to push universities toward more democracy and away from the corporate form. Students, he asserted, should not be satisfied with a mere liberalization of rules affecting their conduct, but should have power to make their own rules. Moreover, they should share equally with the faculty and administration in institutional policy making.

Between the advocates of "total take-over" and students who

9. "Faculty Power," *Atlantic*, September 1968, pp. 41–47.

want simply to get their degrees and get out lie many variations of opinion on the same issues and, also, completely disparate objectives. The majority of students, perhaps, favor more pass-fail courses, relaxed dormitory regulations, and an easing of the general competition, but they can hardly be counted as ardent workers for either revolutionary or reformist causes. The organized black students in many respects constitute a distinct category. They often agitate for minimum quotas for their group in the student body, faculty, and staff, or want earmarked financial aids or special courses in African culture and history. Sometimes they seek "autonomous" departments or institutes effectively segregated from the purview of the institution as a whole.

Lest it be thought that student demands for more participation will simply "go away" eventually if administrators and others ignore them, let me cite the opinions of a random sample of one hundred college and university presidents. The American Council on Education queried them during the summer of 1968 to find out what they thought the decade of the 1970s is *likely* to bring in educational developments, and what they thought *should* and *should not happen*. As to the changing roles of students, 88 percent of the administrators expected that college students will, on an even wider scale, use direct-action methods to assert their demands for changed conditions, and 90 percent foresaw students serving as voting members of most important academic committees on the typical campus. About 9 percent of the officials regarded student activism as desirable and only 1 percent as essential. Only a minority, nevertheless, viewed unfavorably the prospective participation of students as voting members of important policy committees.

Although Notre Dame President Theodore M. Hesburgh received wide commendation for his forthright statements about dealing promptly and firmly with disruptive elements, he, too, advocates a greater voice for students in college and university affairs. He has said, "We should involve students in every legitimate way to the extent that they are willing to assume responsibility, as well as to assert their rights."

Turning now to what the faculty wants in academic governance, I recall a 1966 *Joint Statement on Government of Colleges and Universities*, issued by the American Association of University

Professors, the American Council on Education, and the Association of Governing Boards of Universities and Colleges. This "call to mutual understanding" set forth the general rights and responsibilities of the faculty:

The faculty has primary responsibility for such fundamental areas as curriculum, subject matter and methods of instruction, research, faculty status, and those aspects of student life which relate to the educational process. On these matters the power of review or final decision lodged in the governing board or delegated by it to the president should be exercised adversely only in exceptional circumstances, and for reasons communicated to the faculty.

Interestingly, the statement had much more to say about the roles of other groups than about the status of students. Concerning the latter, it merely suggested:

Ways should be found to permit significant student participation within the limits of attainable effectiveness. The obstacles to such participation are large and should not be minimized: inexperience, untested capacity, a transitory status which means that present action does not carry with it subsequent responsibility, and the inescapable fact that the other components of the institution are in a position of judgment over the students.

The A.A.U.P. has recently circulated a questionnaire to determine present practices regarding faculty participation in governance and to compare them with the standards set forth in the 1966 document. The query directs particular attention to decision-making roles concerning faculty status, academic operation, planning and policy, professional duties, organization of faculty agencies, and faculty-board communication. It categorizes the forms of faculty participation as determination, joint action, consultation, discussion, or no participation.

Still another means of expressing faculty demands here and there is unionization. Although collective bargaining has not made much headway in academic circles, there are about one hundred twenty campuses where the teaching staff is unionized. What may be expected under this kind of adversary approach is illustrated by a Proposed Agreement formulated recently by the Higher Education Division of the Michigan Education Association. It specifies that an association representative shall be entitled to appear at all meetings of the Board of Trustees, and stipulates teaching loads and the maximum number of students (twenty-seven) to be permitted in any class. Although the document makes little mention of the intellectual climate in which the faculty wishes to function, it states that each instructor must have a separate, enclosed office with a telephone, closet space, separate desk, and file cabinet, and a "bookshelf of 3 shelves at least 3 feet long."

Few presidents and trustees have publicly expressed themselves regarding what reforms in governance they would like to see effected, but Kenneth B. Hare, a Canadian university president, has complained about ways the rise of faculty power in North America has sapped the power of presidents. One consequence, he said, has been that universities "lack speedy and effective powers of decision-making, of academic foresight, and of rising to sudden crisis." While being "cheered by the death of the old campus despotisms," Hare also felt "chastened by the inescapable need for big institutions . . . to react decisively and quickly to change of circumstances."[10] He added somewhat wearily that, after having worked in several universities—almost wholly professor-governed, wholly lay-governed, and with mixed boards—he had found the facts of academic life to be much the same in all.

Elsewhere I have suggested that understanding and support be developed for something like an administrators' Bill of Rights. To make the lot of trustees and executives more tolerable, while also giving others more participation in university affairs, certain demanding duties might be more widely shared. For example, senate committees could share more of the onus of deciding which individuals and departments will get less-favored treatment in the allocation of scarce resources. Faculty and student committees could be given multimillion dollar fund-raising assignments. Other groups could be charged with specific responsibilities for maintaining campus order. To make certain that they did not move in and out of assignments at will, moreover, their tenure on the campus could be tied to their demonstrated capabilities in handling them.

10. Speech before the University of British Columbia faculty, December 19, 1968.

Feasibility and Desirability of Changes

As we examine the various changes proposed in university governance, we also need to assess their feasibility and desirability. A conservative view of student participation, for example, has been expressed by Professor John R. McDonough of Stanford University. He doubts that increased voice for students in university governance would improve the decision-making process, and even questions the legitimacy of their claims as a "democratic right." As he has noted, "the student's power to decide is essentially the patron's or consumer's traditional power to exert leverage upon any enterprise. . . . This is a remarkably effective power, but it is a vastly different thing from power to manage the enterprise, which is what . . . [some] students are seeking."[11] Students, he concludes, are among those entitled to be heard but not entitled to decide matters vitally affecting the university's welfare.

Another view of enlarged student participation was set forth last year by Louis Joughin, a member of the A.A.U.P.'s executive staff in Washington. He pointed out that few institutions regularly and systematically search out the reactions of students. He believes that students not only should be consulted, but also should be involved in committees, task forces, and other groups at all levels. In his opinion, however, the area of exclusive authority for students in decision making will remain narrow because the complexity of most institutional operations dictates that no single element in the community is adequate to their successful handling. Conceding that students as consumers should be able to indicate their preferences, he holds that the criterion for their actual participation in decisions should be functional utility rather than absolute right. In brief, if they lack the experience for informed judgment, they should not vote, but if they do have it, it "would be folly to reject their help."

A *Joint Statement* from the Committee of Vice Chancellors and Principals and the National Union of Students (England, Wales,

11. "The Role of Students in Governing the University," *AGB Reports*, April 1968.

and Northern Ireland) recently stated, however, that "the problem of how students can make their views effectively felt within the decision-making process in an individual university is not a simple one." Is university governance to be bicameral or unicameral? If the latter, should student representatives outnumber representatives of the faculty and administration? How are the student representatives to be chosen, and for what terms of office? Should the number of students on various policy committees vary or remain constant? As presumed spokesmen for the student body, should student representatives vote as a bloc or as individuals? Where other university groups have statutory responsibility, is the student presence inappropriate? Some of these questions pertain, of course, to the machinery of government, but others bear directly on the university's purposes and its wider accountability to the public.

After the reform of higher education in France this past year, students can now control up to half the seats in the university's governing assembly. This assembly elects the institution's president. Already, many of the students are demanding the right to determine the kinds of examinations required, the right to have a voice in the employment of professors and in research commitments made by the institution. Furthermore, the leftist students are urging a politicalization of the university. It is no surprise then that a distinguished French social scientist, Raymond Aron, fears for the very survival of the traditional liberal university:

> The young and many of my colleagues destroy a precious institution because they weaken its moral foundation. There is no other moral basis for the university except reciprocal tolerance between teachers and the voluntary discipline of students. There will be no more higher education if the students utilize the university as a place for political agitation. That would signify the Latin-Americanization of French universities, the ruin of the universities.

Although student power has emerged only recently in American higher education, faculty power has been increasing rather steadily for several decades. Many universities have come, as Martin Trow has noted, to function under two forms of governance—the complex administrative apparatus and the departmental structures. The rules and regulations formulated and enforced by the former tend to coordinate the whole enterprise and give it coherence, whereas the latter further a diversity that at times produces fragmentation. Moreover, the one centralizes decision making, whereas the other decentralizes it. A main objection to such loose-jointed arrangements is that the roles in decision making are often ambiguous. Jurisdictions may be confused.

In an effort to bring about changes deemed feasible and desirable at Columbia University, the Faculty's Executive Committee has had internally approved a unicameral senate of one hundred members to concern itself with all matters of universitywide interest. It provides seats for forty-five professors, fourteen nontenured faculty, twenty students, seven administrators, and lesser representation for the research staff, the library staff, the affiliated institutions (Barnard, etc.), the administrative staff, and the alumni. Tenured faculty seats are to be apportioned among the different schools by the size of their tenured faculties, with members serving two-year terms, and no representatives being duly elected unless at least a specified percentage of the designated electorate voted. The group is to meet monthly and on call.

Considering alternatives in governance, the Columbia group rejected both the town meeting type of body, with everybody eligible to vote, and the bicameral type, with a separate student government. The size of the senate, it is believed, allows for free debate without elaborate rules of procedure and without a highly organized and controlled system of leadership. The senate would have thirteen standing committees, with memberships of varied size and composition. All sixteen members of the Student Affairs Committee, for example, would be students. The fifteen members of the Faculty Affairs group would be faculty persons—twelve tenured and three nontenured.

University governance, as McGeorge Bundy has pointed out, calls for much hard work, and professors can join in. They can work through committees and can accept administrative assignments or respect others who do so for the right reasons. To effect feasible and desirable changes, they, more than any other group, must lend their best efforts to the processes of government. Neither they nor any other university group can have absolute power, because the concept has no place in the properly functioning university. Where faculty governance has in effect been a gerontoc-

racy, the younger members must be involved to offset their alienation and to incorporate their efforts in the common cause. I agree
with Bundy, however, that day-in-and-day-out business is to be
carried on, decisions are to be made, which the faculty as a corporate body simply cannot handle. "It needs an agent, and that agent
is the administration." Also, the faculty and the administration need
an intermediary with the outside community, and the intermediary
should be the board of trustees.

Academic governance at many of our institutions has become
too cumbersome, time consuming, and generally inefficient to meet
the needs of the modern, complex university. No single model will
suit equally well the requirements and potentials of all universities,
to be sure, but somehow faculties must organize themselves more
effectively to meet their broader obligations. To offset the backlash of public opinion being generated by anarchy on the campus,
professors face no other option than to increase their participation
in a wider range of university affairs. For them more than for any
other members of the academic community, the implication is
ominous that if universities will not govern themselves, they will be
governed by others.

External Constraints

As universities proceed to broaden and modify their bases of
governance, a first step should be a hard look at external policy
constraints. One such constraint stems from the circumstance that
universities are heavily subsidized rather than self-supporting institutions. Those who supply the funds are not likely to turn over to
students and professors their own powers of the purse. Other limiting factors on the autonomy of any institution are inherent in the
environment in which it exists: its competitive position, its size and
character, its fiscal and manpower deficiencies, the outside bodies
and agencies that limit the range and nature of student and faculty
decisions, and so on. (To give one illustration: the American Chemical Society and the Association of American Law Schools are
already considering measures to counteract the growing institutional
practice of pass-fail grading.) In short, it may be a delusion to
believe that self-governance will be furthered by widening the basis
of local participation.

Another fact of life in the reform of campus decision making concerns the scarcity of resources. Important decisions, as Walter F. Metzger has written, are rarely, if ever, "cost-free" and hence "costs of every kind must be assayed." Well-intentioned students and faculty who urge urban universities to spend heavily on community action programs, for example, must recognize that the cost to them may be higher tuition fees and lower salaries. Similarly, student and faculty time are also scarce resources: spending more time on the multitudinous concerns of institutional governance implies less time available for strictly curricular matters. The diffusion of power necessarily carries a diffusion of risk, responsibility, and accountability.

For universities to continue to serve usefully as places where men and women pursue the truth because it makes them free, the collective enterprise of higher learning also must operate under certain axioms of governance. First, no group—trustee or other—can have absolute power. Another axiom is that order must be maintained alongside freedom and justice. Still another is that the university cannot be made into a microcosm of the body politic, a welfare agency, a retreat from reality, or an arena, without thereby ceasing to be a university. Persons who find these axioms unacceptable simply do not belong in any university community. Rejection of essential university purposes and interference with the rights of others to pursue them ought to be sufficient cause for exclusion from participation.

Although I favor new and extended forms of participation in university governance to harness energies now being wasted in unproductive confrontation, we must all recognize that universities serve many constituencies. If we mean what we say about "participatory democracy," it must be acknowledged, for instance, that the alumni also have a stake in the enterprise. Students' parents are definitely interested parties, as are taxpayers, private benefactors, state legislators, members of Congress, and numerous others who are indirectly affected by what happens in and to the nation's center of higher learning. Professional organizations and other service agencies have a very legitimate concern with standards of accomplishment and modes of certification. Much that is taught and learned has a timeless and universal quality, and its substance and

relevance cannot be whimsically determined by any local or parochial group or groups.

Because of these and other circumstances, undue concessions
to any of the university's most immediate constituencies can erode
the quality and significance of academic enterprise. Every element
in the university community certainly has a right to express itself
about the means and ends of higher education, but capricious
wishes should not be permitted to endanger the survival and well-
being of our institutions and our nation.

Implications
of Changes

In assessing the feasibility and desirability of proposed changes
in academic governance, it seems essential to have a sensible division
of labor. As Chancellor John Caldwell stated at a recent convocation
at North Carolina State University at Raleigh, there is, after all,
work to do.[12] And work is not done when the campus is turned
into a perennial debating society where discourse is frequently interrupted by disorder and even violence. The main aim of the process
of campus decision making is not to draw as many persons as possible into every situation where an issue arises but to improve the
quality of academic life and to enhance the present and future usefulness of higher education.

Admittedly, dogmatism and authoritarianism must go, but there
are other shortcomings in existing modes of governance. The typically interminable processes of faculty deliberation must somehow
be accelerated. (I heard just the other day of one faculty committee that debated four hours over the phrasing of a seven-word
sentence!) There must be a more sensible and explicit division of
labor concerning who is expected to do what. Authority and
responsibility must be clearly delineated, centered in specified individuals and groups, and accepted by all who wish to be functioning members of the community. Ways must be devised to test the
efficiency and effectiveness of alternate procedures of governance,
with an eye to outcomes rather than processes, as the ultimate goals.

12. "Appeal for Action, Unity, Sanity: A Convocation Address," *Educational Record*, Spring 1969, pp. 139–40.

Enlightened self-interest, as well as the common good, should inform all participants that a proper division of labor in the academic community enhances both the freedom and the productivity of the total enterprise.

The pluralism and diversity of American higher education already exemplify many ways of dispersing and controlling power, and new ways are being devised. Some large universities are considering dividing themselves into small, relatively autonomous colleges where departments and institutes would involve faculty, students, and administrators in governance. Others are moving toward the unicameral type of senate control, with designated areas of responsibility for various types of members.

Speaking from his experience at Berkeley and elsewhere, Roger Heyns has advocated more power and effective responsibility for administrators at all levels, with new practices for holding them accountable. Instead of diffusing responsibility loosely, he thinks it would be better to identify major decision-making points, and center responsibility, accountability, and authority in specific persons. He would allocate more freedom to administrators, specify what they are expected to do, and then audit their performance.[13]

As we consider the implications of proposed changes, we need to bear in mind two important questions: Where are we going? and, Who is driving? Mistaken ideas can head universities in wrong directions, and inept handling of governance can wreck complex mechanisms.

What can happen to universities when they are dominated by the wrong ideas or fall into the wrong hands, moreover, is not merely a hypothetical matter. We need only to look back to Nazi Germany to see how the young Brownshirts took over the universities to remake society in the name of their own "high principles." Like their later counterparts in this country, they too thought that institutions of higher education should cast aside their political neutrality and become centers of social action. Or currently, Latin America affords numerous instances of universities where the zeal for activism so continuously interferes with serious scholarship that the campus is a main arena of endless dispute and

13. *Danforth News and Notes*, November 1968, p. 8.

conflict. Passive faculty and student majorities on some campuses in the United States should study these examples of control by militant minorities, lest our universities also have their basic purposes undermined.

The dangers of subversion, however, should not cause us to shut our eyes to the need for reform. Whether we like it or not, we are already in the midst of devolution. *Devolution*, according to Webster, is a word with two meanings. In one sense, it signifies transference from one person to another, or a devolving upon a successor; in the other sense, devolution means retrograde development or degeneration. In the reform of our universities, we should not capitulate under duress to ill-conceived demands for change that can lead only to degeneration.

Viewing the actions of the radical nihilists and their destructive consequences, one cannot escape dismay at those faculty members in some of our most distinguished institutions who have become parties to the breakdown of authority. Their encouragement of student irresponsibility by granting wholesale amnesty to serious offenders and their apparent indifference to the pillorying of administrators are flabbergasting. Their silence or vacillation about criminal trespass, property destruction, interference with majority rights to teach and learn, and other forms of campus disruption is truly astonishing. Even more perplexing, in light of the long struggle of faculties to establish and maintain responsibility for the curriculum and for their own status, is their partial relinquishment of this authority to some of the least qualified members of the academic community.

One does not have to be an alarmist to see that such behavior not only weakens the internal structure of the university but also invites outside interference with institutional autonomy. The backlash of public opinion is already manifest. In many state capitals, legislative bills can be counted by the dozens. In the nation's capital, Congress has enacted some measures and is contemplating others. Outside reactions to disorder on the campus are witnessed in a leveling-off of public and private funding of higher education.

With growing numbers of universities confronting internal and external threats to their freedom and autonomy, the problems of academic governance assume an added urgency. A source of current difficulties, as many studies of collegiate governance have noted, is that academic power in most places is diffuse; it can be brought into focus only with difficulty. To avoid augmenting this particular difficulty, beleaguered institutions should consider very thoughtfully the prospect of any further diffusion—particularly any form that would discount knowledge, experience, and skill.

Although I do not agree with those social scientists who are now predicting the end of the liberal university, I am of the opinion that the only options open to some institutions are to bolster existing authority as promptly as possible or lose no time in legitimating a new basis of authority. If the university is to retain its identity, furthermore, the basis of authority must be capable of maintaining both freedom and order. There can be order without freedom, but there can be no freedom without order.

Granted that the generalized deference toward traditional authority vested in hierarchical office or seniority may simply have evaporated, the university still must have some rationale to give it coherence and proper direction. For the rule of reason rather than of force to prevail, the authority must be rational. Moreover, if academic governance is regarded as essentially a mechanism for problem solving, the modes of decision making should be judged by the results they can produce. The sooner these truisms are accepted by all members of the academic community, the better the university will be able to forestall internal chaos and outside domination.

Whatever the responses of institutions to demands for change, those responses must take into account the fact that colleges and universities are created and maintained for the good of the larger society, and not just for the benefit of those directly connected with them. This generalization holds for students and professors no less than for administrators and trustees. The main institutional interest in the long run has to be the public interest, and not that of its most aggressive immediate constituency.

There are also some other conditions to remember. Change must be linked with continuity. Although the university is admittedly an imperfect mechanism, developed over the centuries through trial and error, it has been tested by experience to the point that it is now indispensable to the advancement of higher learning and of civilization. The nation's investment in and dependence on the survival and further improvement of the institution are too great for us to permit it to be destroyed by those whose presence is inimical to its best interests or to allow it to be crippled by those who really do not know what they are undertaking. In brief, to continue the improvement of American higher education, we cannot afford to substitute devolution for evolution.

In conclusion I want to emphasize that nothing in the realm of university governance is sacrosanct. Distributions of campus power and authority are means—not ends—of the educational enterprise. Although existing forms of governance undoubtedly need overhauling in many institutions, the majority of any academic community's members have more important ends in view than maximizing their participation in the management of institutional affairs. As we proceed with the business of reform, I hope that students, faculties, administrators, and trustees can join as partners rather than adversaries in what is, after all, a cooperative undertaking. When they do so, the collective endeavor of higher education can rid itself of whatever impediments may stand in the way of continued progress.

Under a different title and with somewhat varied contexts, the substance of this piece was set forth in commencement addresses I delivered at the University of Arkansas in Fayetteville on May 30, 1970, and at the University of Maryland in College Park a few weeks later. Interestingly, the Fayetteville campus had experienced comparatively little disorder, whereas the College Park campus, like some other major university settings, had recently been the scene of National Guard presence.

Upholding Institutional Integrity

Y OU GRADUATES and your generation have been called the brightest and best educated in history. You have also been called some other things. The purpose of my remarks today, however, is neither to praise your capabilities nor to fault your shortcomings. Instead, I shall address you as beneficiaries of higher education, as alumni in prospect, and as individuals who, alas, will all too soon reach the "untrustworthy" age of thirty. Just now, you are ending one phase of your lives and moving on into further education or into your careers.

While you are still on the campus, I want to talk with you about upholding the integrity of the university in general and of your institution in particular. The basis of my argument is that higher education not only is the sustainer of the best that man has thought and said in the past but also our principal hope for changing society to meet new needs of the present and future. Since the university is the key agency of higher education, we cannot afford to let it be crippled or destroyed.

Students, like the rest of us, are understandably disturbed by our society's apparent inability to find peaceful resolutions of conflict at home and abroad. Campus events of recent weeks have dramatized their deep-seated convictions about the necessity for change. While one may appreciate the feelings that have led to disruption and strife on many campuses, I trust that most of you share my concern about ultimate consequences for the nation's universities. You will agree, I believe, that universities are too significant in our society for us to be silent witnesses of their debasement, dismemberment, or destruction. To be sure, we need continually to reform them. Their curricula need to be revised, their governance modified, and their relevance to the admittedly desperate problems of our society made more direct. But with all of this in mind, is it not better to be guided by reason than by impulse as we go about making changes? And equally important, does it make sense to let nihilists, revolutionaries, and reactionaries nullify honest efforts toward improvement?

The need for more members of the academic community to become vigorous defenders of what a university should symbolize was impressed upon me recently when I spent five interesting if not heartening days on a campus. During that time the student center was the scene of a sit-in, lie-in, and sleep-in. A conference was blockaded. An attempt was made to halt a trustees' meeting and to invade the president's home. Some militants tried to take over the university's telephone switchboard. A coup d'etat occurred in student government. Meanwhile, a building was burned down.

Much of this, of course, is an all too familiar scenario. I was appalled by the intimidating tactics of some of the leaders and the sheeplike behavior of their small band of followers, but my main concern was for the majority of the students and faculty. Were they totally unaware of what was being planned? Why did they play no role at all in trying to forestall the disruption? Why were they letting this noisy minority preempt the center of their campus? Was it complacency or fear that caused them to be passive spectators of this usurpation of their own rights as members of the academic community? I also speculated about what that 136-year-old university would be like if the revolutionaries actually had gained full control and imposed their so-called liberation aims on the entire student body and faculty.

Although I ascribe no superior wisdom in academic affairs simply to those who are less articulate and more numerous, I do think it is high time for the "silent majority" to speak and act more vigorously. I believe also that safeguarding the university against those who would disfigure or destroy it does not imply standing firmly for the status quo. A reasonable position argues that no university is too good for improvement or too bad for redemption.

Most universities are indeed better institutions than their denigrators would have us believe. They are models of economy, for example, as compared with hospitals; of efficiency, compared with courts of law; and of effectiveness, alongside most political agencies. Unlike many other productive enterprises, private as well as public universities do not charge all the traffic will bear for their services. Their campuses, like businesses and industries, are sometimes shut down, but rarely because the faculty and staff are striking for shorter hours and higher pay. Although urban universities are accused of inattention to the problems of their immediate physical environment, I have heard of none charged with polluting it. In brief, a good deal can be said in behalf of the university as a place and as an institution.

The generally favorable attitude of the American people toward higher education, moreover, is witnessed in the fact that they have established more than twenty-six hundred colleges and universities. One gauge of the usefulness of such institutions is their durability. Despite nervous talk about their fragility, they tend to outlast other kinds of organizations. But even our most prestigious and strongest universities, I would submit, are not indestructible. Although no university appears to be in danger of actual destruction, most of us can name some where operations are being seriously interrupted, missions perverted, and viability threatened.

Alumni and the public at large—no less than students, faculty, administrators, and trustees—have a stake in the continuity of our universities. Incalculable amounts of thought and energy, as well as vast sums of money, have been invested in them. In the main, they have served us well. As our society becomes more complex, we shall depend upon them even more in the future than we have in the past to further individual and collective welfare. I would urge you as beneficiaries of higher education to help shield our institutions against mindless efforts to corrupt their real purposes. As alumni, you members of the graduating classes can and should join forces against the anti-intellectuals and others whose intentions are unmistakably contrary to the best interest not only of the university but also of the public.

If we are to rally in common defense of centers of higher learning, however, we need to understand just what it is that we must cherish and protect. Some members of this audience would doubtless draw up a different bill of particulars, but I want to bring your attention to those aspects of the university whose integrity must be upheld.

1. *The campus as a bastion of rationality and civility.* Because some students and others have legitimate grievances against universities, there is a growing tendency among them and their sympathizers to excuse coercion and even violence as a mode of effecting desired changes. In fact, some regard lawlessness and disruption as a "necessary prelude to reform." Even the less belligerent often couch their wants as "nonnegotiable demands." The more belligerent do not hesitate to overrun the rights of other students and the faculty by invading buildings, blockading classrooms and offices, smashing windows, and destroying other property.

In much human behavior, as in physics, there is for every action an equal and opposite reaction. When academic authority breaks down, the civil authorities usually move in. Curfews may be imposed and security officers multiplied. The consequences can indeed be tragic for all concerned. "But even worse than the physical restrictions," as one editorial writer has noted, "is the loss of rationality in what ought to be the proving ground of reason."

Midst such conflicts, altogether too many members of the academic community, I regret to note, lend no hand at all to defend what libertarians like to deride as "campus law and order." By their silence and inaction they thus become passive observers of the degradation of their universities. When the backlash of public opinion makes itself felt in repressive measures and in reduced financial support from governors, legislatures, and others, some academics do indeed cry out, but, ironically, it is then too late to make a convincing claim for self-governance.

To safeguard the campus as a bastion of rationality and civility, most of the members of the academic community must take an active and enlightened interest in the conduct of its affairs and not wait for avoidable crises to occur before turning out for meetings. The university's constituents, and I include alumni among them, should regard one another as sharers rather than opponents in a common undertaking. Since constituent interests are seldom identical, dissent should not be discouraged, but there must be a unified stand against assaults on rationality and civility whenever they occur and under whatever guise.

2. The university as an intellectual institution. Although the prospect that any appreciable number of universities will be physically destroyed or taken over by extremists now seems unlikely, the probability that some of them will be changed beyond recognition as predominantly intellectual institutions is less remote. In the zeal to be relevant and responsive to all expressed needs and demands, and in accord with the popular fetish of change for its own sake, institutions can indeed become nonuniversities. Our main insulation against this latter eventuality, it seems to me, is the faculty's firm retention of its proper authority over the curriculum. Despite their apparent idiosyncrasies at times, they, better than any other group, understand what a university really ought to be.

No educational institution, moreover, even a comprehensive university, should engage in the futile endeavor of trying to serve all masters. If universities allow themselves to be saddled with responsibilities they cannot discharge or if they take on burdens for which they have inadequate resources or which functionally belong to other agencies, they risk damaging the integrity of the academic endeavor and fragmenting their basic purposes.

Their first obligation, in my opinion, is teaching and doing the best possible job for students. In addition to diffusing knowledge, they have a second duty to seek out new knowledge and enlarged understanding through research. A third function is to render appropriate public services, but not at the expense of the other two functions.

Commenting on the current confusion and disarray in the American nation generally and in higher education particularly, Professor Irving Kristol has noted that many academicians disavow having either the duty or the capacity to supervise the sexual habits and elevate the moral character of their students: "But they appear to have concluded simultaneously that they do have the obligation and capacity to solve our urban problems, conduct American foreign policy, reshape the American economy and perfect the American national character. They will abolish violence from American life—but they will stoically tolerate it on the campus rather than take 'repressive' actions."[1]

Although I do not share the author's further view that "university education in the United States today is an utter shambles," I concede that it soon will be if we fail to concentrate our efforts on the university's central mission as an intellectual institution. Other organizations can and do serve as political arenas, welfare agencies, propaganda centers, and what not, but no other organization can take the place of the university if it ceases to be a place where the highest values are those of the mind and spirit.

3. *The university as a nonpartisan enterprise.* Functionally related to what I have said about the university as a bastion of rationality and civility, and as a predominantly intellectual institution, is the necessity for upholding its nonpartisan character. As we are all aware, our institutions are under increasing pressure—and particularly of late from some of their own students and faculty—to abandon this role. Institutions are being urged from within to declare themselves officially on such diverse issues as American foreign policy, the management decisions of business corporations, and what not. These matters concern all of us collectively as well as individually, of course, but in my judgment it is not the business of the university as such to take corporate positions regarding them.

As some of you know, the American Council on Education some months ago named a Special Committee on Campus Tensions. I certainly agree with what the committee's recent report has to say about efforts to politicize the university:

Through educating decision-makers, conducting research, diffusing knowledge, and proposing solutions to social problems, our colleges and

1. "What Business Is a University In?" *New York Times Magazine*, March 22, 1970, p. 30.

universities can have a considerable, if not decisive, influence on the decisions that affect the nation's quality of life. In each of these roles, colleges and universities serve society best by giving prime allegiance to truth. Truth-seeking, in turn, requires conclusions openly arrived at and the receptivity to new ideas. First and foremost, then, our colleges and universities must be centers of free inquiry.

Efforts to politicize [them] risk public reprisals with consequent restrictions on free inquiry. Legislative moves in this direction, at both state and federal levels, are already deeply disturbing. Likewise, demands made on campus through intimidation or violence are inimical to the spirit of free inquiry. The search for truth is the first casualty.[2]

Students, faculty, and other persons associated with universities have, as a matter of course, the rights of all citizens to assert their opinions and to join or form organizations to press forward with their views. As the courts have affirmed, membership in an academic community does not abrogate any individual's rights and privileges as a citizen. Beyond this—and especially in a political system where those who do not make themselves heard tend not to be heeded—I would urge more political involvement on the part of academics as individuals.

To those persons who mistakenly deplore the university's non-partisanship, it should be pointed out that there is now a social commitment to many basic social values. Liberal education, for example, is based on certain values attached to man's cultural heritage. Law schools operate on the premise that order and justice are preferable to anarchy. Colleges of engineering are organized around the idea that some ways of solving practical problems are better than others. Medical schools stem from the presumption that for most people life is worth living and saving. Professors in general are as high-principled a group as can be found in any occupation. The rationale of the university, in brief, is permeated with ethical and other values.

I find unacceptable any claims that teachers and students now have no real intellectual freedom and that existing values must be swept aside for a blind commitment to social change. One professorial militant, in asserting his views about how all members of

2. *Campus Tensions: Analysis and Recommendations* (Washington: American Council on Education, 1970), p. 36.

the "social university" should be so committed, has said: "To give an example, a course in riot control would simply be declared out of place in such a university, while a course in methods of rioting might be perfectly appropriate."[3] To my way of thinking, this anarchistic attitude underlies some of the disorder on and around the nation's campuses.

We need to remind ourselves that individual academic freedom and a high degree of university autonomy are correlative; both are insulations against political and other forms of unwarranted outside interference. If we permit campus minorities to foist their own biases on the university and push it into conflict with the fundamental values of our society, institutional autonomy will soon be taken away by the publics that support and ultimately control higher education. The first members of the academic community to be muzzled by outside forces, furthermore, would be those who now wish to politicize it.

Those dissidents who would remake existing universities to suit their own ends should be aware that in most states it is a relatively simple matter to get a charter for a new institution. Indeed, I would guess that most of the students and others who form the so-called free universities that come and go each year do not even bother with charters. As a believer in the free marketplace of men and ideas, I think it would be interesting to let competition determine the kinds of universities best suited for the future. Meantime, I must express opposition to letting extremists take over established institutions and barter off their nonpartisan birthright for a politicized future of undefined character.

4. *The university as a useful institution.* Last, I want to emphasize that the public supports institutions of higher education for the valued services they render. All advanced nations draw their highly trained manpower largely from universities, and in addition look to them to enrich the quality of life for all citizens. Unfortunately, of late, the notion that the campus is a kind of secular sanctuary where "everybody can do his own thing," and at public

3. Alan Wolfe, "The Myth of the Free Scholar," *University Review*, State University of New York, Autumn 1969, pp. 6–7.

expense, seems to be gaining currency. The idea of academic freedom is being perverted to rationalize bizarre, unproductive, and even antisocial behavior.

Admissions standards are being altered, required courses eliminated, grading standards modified, and intellectual accomplishment denigrated as an academic objective. Some of these changes have resulted from the altogether worthy motive of trying to assist the culturally deprived, and I certainly advocate providing special and compensatory opportunities for them. In my opinion, however, the disadvantaged, no less than the advantaged, are entitled to quality education.

As the distinguished black educator Sir W. Arthur Lewis has pointed out, whether there is a revolution or not, blacks as well as whites must be placed and judged by what they can and do accomplish in the world of work. Accordingly, it is a delusion for the members of any groups to think that by merely "doing their own things" they can usefully prepare themselves for responsible participation in any kind of social system. The kinds of disciplined minds our society needs to solve its most pressing problems, I would add, are not likely to be developed by endless talk, perpetual protest, and interminable confrontation as a style of life. Moreover, my guess is that the public will not long tolerate academic practices that depreciate the value of the university and its graduates to the nation. We must acknowledge that society is entitled to expectations of useful service from university graduates in return for its investment in them and in the institutions where they were presumably educated.

In closing, let me say that my thesis has implied sustenance of what is *right* rather than what is *wrong* with the contemporary university. I have tried to avoid apologizing for the status quo, and certainly count myself among the advocates of some rather drastic reforms. Fortunately, most of our universities are changing, and many are doing so in the absence of any so-called nonnegotiable demands. My plea to you graduates and to all friends of higher education is that we shield our universities against destruction while we work together for their improvement.

Like all other social institutions, the university is imperfect.

To keep abreast of the times, it must accommodate to change; to rise above mediocrity, it must also promote change and anticipate as well as evaluate future options. The university, at its best, however, is an instrument of both stability and change. No matter what modifications may be desirable, the university must be maintained as a bastion of rationality and civility, a place that educates men and women to be problem-solvers rather than problem-makers, a center of free and objective inquiry, and an institution that is valued and respected for its indispensable services to all mankind.

American Council on Education

The American Council on Education, founded in 1918, is a *council* of educational organizations and institutions. Its purpose is to advance education and educational methods through comprehensive voluntary and cooperative action on the part of American educational associations, organizations, and institutions.